REAL, ROBINS & BLUEBIRDS

The Autobiography of 'Goal Scorer' Brian Clark

BRIAN CLARK WITH RICHARD SHEPHERD

Best Wishes

Brian Clark

VERTICAL EDITIONS

First published in the United Kingdom in 2006 by
Vertical Editions, 7 Bell Busk, Skipton,
North Yorkshire BD23 4DT

www.verticaleditions.com

ISBN
1-904091-17-2
978-1-904091-17-2

Cover design and typeset by HBA, York

Printed and bound by the Cromwell Press, Trowbridge

CONTENTS

MEMORIES OF BRIAN

An appreciation from Bristol-based journalist David Foot who has been covering sport in Bristol for almost half a century. David worked on the former Bristol Evening World covering Bristol City matches when he first watched Brian Clark in action. David has since freelanced on various national newspapers and on radio. He has been a regular cricket writer for The Guardian for thirty years, and is the author of twenty-six books including the biography of Gloucestershire and England cricketer Wally Hammond (shortlisted as William Hill sports book of the year). He has also written the history of Somerset County Cricket Club, and collaborated with Viv Richards and umpire David Shepherd on their autobiographies. He still covers Bristol City and has fond memories of Brian.

It was Bristol City's forty-sixth and last League game of the 1964/65 season – and, as it happened, my birthday. Affectionate memories return in misty nostalgia – of the day when the Ashton Gate club won promotion on goal average, when John Atyeo wept at the final whistle in boyhood joy, when he and Brian Clark were the scorers in a 2-0 victory.

That home match against Oldham Athletic was too tense, too strewn with nervous performances to be remotely memorable for its football. But it was the result that mattered, and in truth it was Brian's goal, late in the first half, that eased the frayed nerves. He ended as top scorer that season and would not claim this one against Oldham was his best. Psychologically, though, it was probably the most important.

He was always a player much liked by Bristol City crowds. They warmed to his lack of ostentation, the shy way that he accepted the compliments of his teammates after his goals. He was a modest man, a quiet though amiable pro who had diligently learned the rudiments of his craft, loved the game that brought him a living, and was never a problem to the various managers under whom he played.

On occasion they would perhaps have liked a bit more aggression, but that wasn't really in his nature. They would no doubt have welcomed more pace – he was never the fastest striker on two legs. There was nothing wrong with his stamina or wholehearted approach. Physically, however, he wasn't built for sprinting. We can imagine how much he privately hated those long tortuous runs up Bristol's Bridge Valley Road that a succession of team bosses fiendishly plotted for the playing-staff.

There were plenty of qualities that he possessed to offset any suspect lack of pace. His timing could be exquisite when the centres were coming over. Apart from an innate sense of direction and power when it came to heading, he could belt the ball with both feet, to the consternation of opposing goalkeepers. Brian was in many ways an old-fashioned centre forward. He had the physique, he knew where the goal was, he wasn't wary of burly and indelicate defenders intent on curbing his resourcefulness.

Yes, of course, it must have been in the genes. His father Don, an equally popular figure at Ashton Gate, was a record-breaking Bristol City centre forward. They both had courage, both refused to be inhibited by heavy grounds, and they both knew that their uncomplicated job was to get the ball into the net.

Brian was an unselfish player. He relished the presence of the somewhat more glamorous Atyeo at his side, but the England International in turn benefited from progressing downfield in tandem with Clark. At times it could be Brian's day – as when, I vividly remember, he scored a hat-trick against Bristol Rovers in the Final of the Gloucestershire Senior Cup, a local accolade ever to be cherished. There were the barren weeks, too, when, as all strikers discovered, the goals dried up and form suffered. Then, the temporary loss of confidence was etched on his face.

He was essentially a home-loving boy, not much interested in

the off-field social life of more gregarious colleagues. Some of us thought that he would settle contentedly in Bristol for ever. It must have come as a jolt to him when Bristol City encouraged him to go to Huddersfield, in exchange for an older midfielder. Brian, even when the goals weren't going in, was a valued and unassuming team man. He was happy picking strawberries with his friends for summer pocket-money and buying his first car for just over £27. There was no surging sense of wild professional ambition. It could be argued that this at times worked against him – I don't think so.
David Foot

...and the thoughts of Peter Jackson, now Rugby Correspondent of the Daily Mail, but who was Football Correspondent for the South Wales Echo covering Cardiff City from 1965 to 1974, a period which included Brian Clark's first spell with the club.

During the time in which he covered The Bluebirds, Peter came to know the players and management very well, travelling with the team throughout the Football League and in Europe.

It was quite a year 1968 – students rioting all over Europe, the Russian invasion of Czechoslovakia, the Vietcong launching their Tet offensive, the assassinations of Martin Luther King and Bobby Kennedy.

Sir Matt Busby's Manchester United won the European Cup, David Hemery struck Olympic gold over 400 metres in Mexico City, Red Alligator romped home in the Grand National, Jimmy Scoular threatened to ban me from Ninian Park for the first time, and Clarky joined the City. I can see him now through the mists of time, joining up with his new teammates one wintry morning at Cheltenham station almost forty years ago en route to Derby back in the days when every football team travelled by rail.

A few hours later and, glory be, he had scored in the opening minutes and followed up with a second. Two more from Peter King – so Brian Clough, 'Old Big 'Ead' or young Big 'Ead' as he was back then, would have to wait a little longer to make Derby the best team in the land. Back then, in the days when journalists and players were still friendly enough to travel together, a 4-3 win guaranteed a reasonably pleasant journey home.

Newport, the last stop before Cardiff, was always the most awkward part, looming down the track like Becher's Brook. Newport, you see, was the first station where paper boys ran up and down the platform with the *Football Echo* and Mr Scoular never failed to interrupt his game of cards to get a copy. Weary of trying to defend headlines reflecting how dismally his team had performed, like 'Battered City Grab Lucky Point', I learnt to put some distance between myself and the manager once we had entered the Severn Tunnel. Regrettably, there would be no escape, least of all in the buffet-car. When I had really excelled myself in misrepresenting his team, as he thought, the human volcano would approach wielding the *Football Echo* as a policeman would a truncheon. The players within earshot withdrew a safe distance to avoid being engulfed by the imminent eruption and enjoy the sideshow.

'Ah, Jimmy can I get you a drink?' I'd say trying not to let him see that I was one bit bothered while feeling an overpowering need to rush to the toilet or reach for the emergency cord. If he was really angry the tirade would last all the way to Cardiff and I knew then it would be only a matter of time before I would be adjudged to have outstayed my welcome. The uneasy alliance lasted a little longer, long enough for me to get to know the players as people as well as footballers. Don Murray was a friend of mine back then, and I hope he still is, but occasionally professional demands made criticism inevitable which provoked one nerve-racking occasion when the aforesaid Donald stormed into the *South Wales Echo* newsroom to tell me what he thought of me and what I could do with my job. As soon as he'd said his piece, which was not suitable to be printed here, he turned on his heel and strode back out of the office in no mood to debate the subject.

Thankfully, we can laugh about it now. While another player once pinned me against the wall by my lapels, I am happy to say that I never encountered any such unsporting behaviour from Brian Clark. He was always the model professional, a selfless team-player and top all-round bloke, which really is saying something about someone who used to play for Bristol City!

Sometimes, when I'm in strange far-flung parts of the world on rugby business and thinking of the good old days, I only have to close my eyes and I can see him now, scoring goals on a scale which must have made him the best £10,000 signing Cardiff City ever made. Most of all, I can see him heading the winner against Real Madrid at Ninian Park in the first leg of the Cup-Winners' Cup Quarter-Final, proof of those days when, in our slightly mad way, we thought it The Bluebirds' divine right to be rubbing shoulders with the old kings of Europe.

There were 47,500 at Ninian that night, although if you take into account all those who have since claimed they were there too, the attendance was probably nearer 447,500! Drawing a convenient veil over the return leg in Madrid, that one result has given every Cardiff City fan, of whom I am still one, the inalienable right to put down all those tedious types who support Chelsea or Manchester United because they think it's the done thing. It only takes one short question: 'So when did your lot last beat Real Madrid? Eh?'

Nothing, of course, lasts forever. Mr Scoular, for whom I had nothing but the utmost respect, duly banned me, inevitably so because my job was to try to tell the fans what was really going on as opposed to the club's version. I edited the City programme for several years before they sacked me for something else I wrote in the *Echo*, and by then Brian Clark had been transferred to Bournemouth. Gentleman footballers are few and far between. John Charles was one, Brian Clark is another and I count myself fortunate to have known both. If, by chance, Clarky's book should knock Freddie Flintoff's off the top of the best sellers' list, it will be no more than he deserves.

Peter Jackson

TIME TO REMEMBER

Of the 262 League and Cup goals that I obtained in my nineteen years as a professional player, the one that I scored for my hometown club Bristol City against Oldham in the 2-0 win at Ashton Gate on 24 April 1965 and which gave us a promotion-clinching victory from the old Division Three, will always remain vivid in my memory. And six years later, on 10 March 1971, I was lucky enough to score the only goal of a European Cup-Winners' Cup Quarter-Final home leg for Cardiff City against Real Madrid at Ninian Park, a goal that was the highlight of my career and one which invariably comes up when people talk to me about my time in football. Whenever I am in my home city of Bristol, the Oldham goal is a still a happy memory for supporters of that era, even though it was forty years ago. And in my 'second' home city of Cardiff, it is the Real Madrid goal that fans like to recall. In looking back at one's life, it is nice to be remembered for something that you have done that brought people pleasure. I was 63 in January 2006 and have felt for several years that I would like to put my story on record while I was still able to.

One of the reasons that I wanted to write about my life was because of my father Don Clark, now aged 88, who was an outstanding goalscorer for Bristol City and who, together with my mother Vera now 83, encouraged me to follow a career in football, always bearing in mind that it could be a short career and that I should make sure that I had a good education with qualifications to fall back upon. It didn't quite work out that way, but I hope that I did well enough as a professional player to make them proud of me.

I also wanted to write about my experiences for the sake of my wife Gillian who has been so supportive of me ever since our wedding thirty-nine years ago, our daughters Alison and Jacqueline, granddaughters Emily and Lauren, and my sister Cherry who always followed my career and is still a close follower of the game together with her husband Martin. Also Jacqueline's husband Gary who is an avid Cardiff City supporter and Alison's partner Chris who is a keen football follower.

Another reason for me to do this book was the sad passing of my former Cardiff City teammate Ronnie Bird who died in March 2005. He was just two years older than me and was the first in our squad of the late 1960s and early '70s to pass on. His death affected me, and made me realise that time is passing quickly.

Football broadcaster, author and journalist Richard Shepherd has put my thoughts into words – the idea of writing this book came to fruition as a result of conversations which we have had over recent seasons when I have contributed to 'Cardiff City World' match commentaries with Richard. His involvement in the game as spectator and professional observer over many years has run very much in parallel with my career as a player. He went to Clifton College in Bristol in 1958 when I was captain of the Bristol Schools Under-15 team, and he watched me when I was playing for Bristol City during his five years at Clifton. He then followed my progress with Cardiff City and then Newport County since he covered those two Welsh clubs when he was with BBC Radio Wales. We have known each other since those days and he has been ideally placed to help me to record my life story.

In doing the research for this book, Gill and I went through the various boxes of memorabilia in our loft – it brought back so many memories that I hope that you will enjoy sharing with me. You may think, on reading my story, that I have an amazing memory for dates, games and places. In fact I don't, because with the passing of years everything becomes compressed with time. Of course I remember certain games in detail, but in compiling my story I have used the various reference books, newspaper-cuttings and match-programmes which cover my respective clubs – the John Atyeo biography by Tom Hopegood and John Hudson, the various histories of Bristol City (David Woods), Cardiff City (Graeme

Lloyd and Richard Shepherd), AFC Bournemouth (Leigh Edwards/John Treleven), and Richard Shepherd's records covering Millwall and Newport County. Terry Grandin's *'Red Dragons In Europe'* brought back all the memories of my European encounters with Cardiff City, and I am grateful to all of those journalists and authors for the use of their researches.

I have been connected with football now for over fifty-five years as a player and spectator, and I look back over those years and wonder where the time has gone. I always enjoyed my career while it lasted, the ups and the downs, because I knew from my Dad's experiences that you are a long time retired when it is over. In writing my story, I have more or less come full circle in my football life – some of you may be old enough to remember the names and games which I shall recall, names such as John Atyeo of Bristol City and John Toshack of Cardiff City, also Harry Redknapp with whom I played at AFC Bournemouth, and dear old Harry Cripps at Millwall.

I would like to thank journalists David Foot and Peter Jackson for their kind words about me. Although I rarely see them now, I think of them as close acquaintances from my playing days – David from when I was at Bristol City, and Peter from my first spell with Cardiff City. Who would have thought that Peter would go on to become one of the leading rugby newspaper correspondents in the country! I'm pleased that I did well enough in my playing days for them to remember me.

Brian Clark
August 2006

1

BRISTOL BORN, AND BRISTOL BRED

It was Wednesday, 13 January 1943 in the middle of the Second World War. In the North African city of Casablanca, our Prime Minister Winston Churchill, American President Franklin D Roosevelt and General Charles De Gaulle, leader of the French Government in exile, were meeting to discuss the strategy of the War. Meanwhile in Bristol, an event of perhaps lesser significance to world affairs was taking place, an event that was however, a major one for the Clark family – I came into this world at Southmead Hospital. We lived at number 10 St Aldwyns Close in Monks Park, Horfield, in Bristol, and there was a playing field at the bottom of our road where I was to spend many happy hours kicking a ball about. The boys in our road would play knockabout matches with nearby Grittleton Road or Luckington Road, and when I was in school, my reports often said that 'If Brian paid as much attention to his school work as he does to his football, then he would be top of the class'.

Being born and living north of the River Avon, I was very much in Bristol Rovers territory. If you were south of the river then you were Bristol City. It was not a hard and fast boundary, but that was generally the case. Mum and Dad had been married for a year before I was born, and my sister Cherry came along four years after me. She would also become a keen follower of the game, and now lives with her husband in Torquay where they are season ticket holders at Torquay United. Dad was from Ashley Down in North Bristol, Mum was from Wordsworth Road about a mile away. She was eventually a tailoress and then fashion buyer with

13

Debenhams, the big department store, where she went on to become a departmental manageress.

When I was born, Dad, who had been a very good rugby footballer at North Bristol Central School, was a PT Instructor in the RAF based at Locking near Weston. He had taken up association football after leaving school and had gone on to become a centre forward with Bristol City whom he had joined as a professional in 1936 at the age of 18. He had worked in a stockbroker's office for the previous three years and never really had any intentions of becoming a professional footballer. But he had played for Bristol City's Colts as an amateur, and they had persuaded him to sign professional forms. He made his first team debut in March 1939, but on the outbreak of War the following September, his contract was cancelled along with everyone else's. He lost five years of his competitive career between the ages of 22 and 27 to the War during which he played as a part-time professional with Bristol City in Regional League football. From 1939 until 1943 he worked for the Bristol Aeroplane Company at Filton, employed in the erecting shop on Beaufighters and Blenheims before going into the RAF for whom he played in their representative side both at home and abroad. During his war-time football for Bristol City he played for them in every position except goalkeeper. When the game restarted on a full peace-time basis in 1946/47, he became Bristol City's record League scorer in that season with 36 goals from 37 games, a record which still stands for the club. He also scored another six that season in four Cup matches (five in the FA Cup, one in the Gloucestershire Cup Final against Bristol Rovers), plus another ten in pre-season and post-season friendlies. It was not until later years that I learned what a good player he was, and heard about his goal-scoring record – but from other people, not him, as he was always very modest about his achievements.

At the time that I was born, Bristol had been and still was a target for German bombers. Dad would come home on a weekend pass from the RAF to play for Bristol City against teams such as Cardiff City, Bath City, Swansea Town, Aberaman and Lovell's Athletic.

We were a happy family and put up with the hardships of war-time Bristol. We had no central heating, nor did anyone else – it was coal fires. There was food rationing and we had no car, so to get anywhere you had to walk or catch a bus or tram, though Dad had a motor bike which he would use if he could get petrol for it.

I was two years old when the war ended in May 1945 and I really didn't know much about what was going on in the world – I just knew we had a happy family life. I certainly didn't know that in April 1945 Dad had played in a record-breaking war-time Cup match against Cardiff City at Ninian Park. It was a second-leg match and because they were level on aggregate at the end of ninety minutes, the rules said twenty minutes extra time and then play, if necessary, until there was a deciding goal. The game went on for a total of three hours and twenty-two minutes until Cardiff got the winner. It kicked off at 3.00 pm, and including stoppages, finished at twenty to seven in the evening! Dad often told me about that match – they couldn't get a train back to Bristol that night and had to stay in Cardiff. I still meet older Cardiff City fans who tell me they were at that match. People who lived in Canton and Grangetown actually went home for tea and came back to watch the final stages of the game.

I gradually came to realise that Dad was a footballer mainly because my Grandmother started taking me to Ashton Gate to watch him playing for Bristol City. Dad would get us a couple of complimentary tickets for each home game in what was then Division Three (South). I first started going to Ashton Gate in about 1949 – I loved watching the football, didn't know who City were playing but I could recognise my Dad on the pitch. At home I was always kicking a ball about in the garden and I still have photos of Dad throwing the ball to me when I was very small. He probably wanted to stay inside with my Mum and my sister but I always persuaded him to come out with the ball.

So I became a regular supporter of Bristol City with my Grandmother – my Mum never went because she was not very much interested in football. She obviously wanted to know how my Dad had got on in his matches, the same with me when I started playing competitively in school and later as a professional.

My earliest memories of going to Ashton Gate were of my Grandmother coming to collect me on match days, catching the bus from Horfield to Old Market in the centre of bomb-damaged Bristol, then the bus to Bedminster. It was the time of the big post-war boom in football attendances and Bristol City, like most clubs, had big crowds, often between 25,000 and 30,000 for each home game and Dad's big mate in the team was right half Cliff Morgan. A typical home match day for us would be Dad leaving the house about midday on a Saturday to get to the ground carrying his holdall. I don't know what he had in it – certainly nothing like the toiletries that modern-day players take with them to games.

Kick-off times in those days would vary because there were no floodlights. In August and September it would be 3.00 pm and as the days grew shorter, the starts would be gradually earlier – 2.45 pm, 2.30 pm, 2.15 pm etc, I always loved Saturdays during the season and still do. I remember that in those days of the late 1940s there was no main stand at Ashton Gate – it had been destroyed by bombs during the war, and the current main stand was begun in the early 1950s. Everyone seemed to wear a hat or cap in those days and most of the crowd stood on the terraces with comparatively few having seats. There was always a brass band on the pitch entertaining the crowd before the game and at half-time – usually the Salvation Army or the Fishponds British Legion, most of them in uniform but there always seemed to be one in a brown mackintosh with his band cap on.

When the game was over we would wait outside the players' entrance for Dad – they changed in a temporary outbuilding in those days – and then make our way home on the bus. As we waited for him, the other players would appear and I would get their autographs. They knew who I was and would say 'Your Dad will be out shortly'.

My first school was Upper Horfield Primary where I remained until I was eleven years old. I was always playing football in the playground and often got into trouble when I went home because I had scuffed my school shoes as well as coming home with sore knees after falling on the hard surface. We had a school team run by Gerry Eld – he was the sports master and if I remember correctly, he played for Clifton St Vincent's in the Downs League which was a big competition in those days. It took place on the Downs, where there were numerous pitches not far from the Zoo and Clifton Suspension Bridge. Mr Eld saw how keen I was on football and included me in the school team. He was a big influence on me and I have never forgotten him. We won the Woodcock Shield, which was for local schools sides, and I was in that side at the age of ten in 1953. Although there were players in that team who were good at sport, I was the only one who went on to become a professional footballer, and while at Upper Horfield I played for the Bristol Schools Junior team.

I was at Upper Horfield until I took the eleven-plus examination that determined whether or not you went on to Grammar School. That was in 1954 by which time Dad had been retired from playing for three years as a result of a knee injury, and he was now Assistant Secretary to Syd Hawkins at Bristol City. I can vaguely remember that, following his injury that he sustained at Leyton Orient in February 1948, Dad would be sat in a chair at home with a bag of sand strapped to his ankle as a weight, trying to exercise his knee. But he never fully recovered from the injury and that always made an impression on me, especially when I became a professional. He tried so hard but the knee kept breaking down and he finally finished as a player at the age of thirty-four in 1951/52. He scored 145 goals for Bristol City in wartime and peacetime matches, and if it had not been for the War in which records of goals and games were not official, I'm sure that he would have been one of Bristol City's all-time leading scorers.

Because he worked at the club on the administration side, he continued to get tickets for me and I still went regularly to Ashton Gate. My big hero at that time in the mid-1950s was centre forward John Atyeo who went on to become an England International on six occasions in the 1955/56 and 1956/57 seasons, and my Dad took me to Wembley to see him play in several Internationals, including the friendly game against Brazil in May 1956 when England won 4-2. It would have been five but John missed from the penalty spot in that game. Dad was also able to get FA Cup Final tickets and we went to several Finals in the 1950s including the 'Stanley Matthews' Final of 1953 when Blackpool came from 3-1 down in the last twenty minutes to beat Bolton 4-3. When I was watching big John Atyeo play for Bristol City, I never ever thought that one day I would be playing alongside him in a promotion-winning Robins team. Another player that I remember from those days in the 1950s was right-winger or inside-forward Alec Eisentrager, a former German prisoner of war who had stayed in this country after the war was over and had been good enough to become a League player after being with Trowbridge Town near where he had been in a prison camp. He is now 79 years old and I saw him not so long ago at a Bristol City former players' function at Ashton Gate. I also remember winger Arthur Milton who had come from Arsenal in February 1955 and was also a Gloucestershire County Cricket Club opening batsman. In fact, he played for England in both sports.

I admired them all and just wanted to be a professional footballer playing for Bristol City. I failed my eleven-plus, mainly because I didn't work hard enough for it – I just wanted to be out on a pitch playing football. So I then went to Ashley Down, a secondary modern school just across the road from where my Gran lived. It was in the heart of Bristol Rovers territory and nearly all the boys in the school were Rovers fans. I used to get some terrible friendly 'stick' because they knew who my Dad was, and of my connections with Bristol City. At the time I went to Ashley Down, Rovers were doing well in the old Division Two, having won promotion in 1953 while City were still in Division Three (South). If Rovers had won on a Saturday and City had lost, I knew what to expect on Monday morning. But if City had won and Rovers had lost, I couldn't wait to get there with a big smile on my face – I'd have gone on Sunday morning if there had been school that day!

It was a good year for me at Ashley Down in 1954/55 because Bristol City easily won the Division Three (South) Championship under player/manager Pat Beasley, a former England International who had played for Arsenal, Huddersfield and Fulham before joining Bristol City in 1950. So I was regularly going into school on a Monday morning with a smile on my face, and there was no stopping my heroes John Atyeo and Jimmy Rogers that season –

John was top scorer with 28 League goals, Jimmy had 25 and The Robins won the title by nine points from Leyton Orient. Jimmy eventually moved on to Coventry City in December 1956, but came back in December 1958 when I was on the ground staff. A couple of years later I was in the City side with him and John Atyeo – a dream come true for me when it happened.

It was in the mid-1950s that I had my first links with Cardiff City whom I was to join nearly thirteen years later. I never usually went to watch Bristol City in away games because it was too far to travel, unless it was against Rovers when they were in the same division or against Swindon Town or Newport County, which was not too far to go. I do however, remember being at Birmingham City in February 1951 for Bristol City's FA Cup Fifth Round tie when they lost 2-0 in front of 48,000 – it was a sad day for Dad as it turned out to be his final appearance for the club. So when Bristol City were away, Dad would get tickets for First Division games at Ninian Park as Cardiff City were in the top division at that time. We would travel by train from Filton Junction to Cardiff General and walk along Tudor Street and Ninian Park Road to the ground – a route that I came to know so well in subsequent years and one that I still use occasionally if I am in the Cardiff city centre on match days.

I would watch players such as Welsh International centre forward Trevor Ford who would often try to charge goalkeepers over the line as you were allowed to in those days – years later I used to meet Trevor at sporting functions in South Wales and would recall those times. I remember Welsh International full backs Ron Stitfall and Alf Sherwood who both played for many seasons with The Bluebirds. Alf had often played against Dad during and just after the Second World War, and I have a photograph of Dad being tackled by Alf at Ninian Park in April 1947 when there were 51,000 at the game.

There was little or no football on television in those days apart from the FA Cup Final, the occasional International match and a few highlights on a Saturday night. So the only chance that you had to see top players was in live matches, and at Cardiff I was able to watch teams such as Wolves who were one of the country's leading clubs, Arsenal with all their great names of the 1950s, Manchester United's Busby Babes and many others. It was a real football education for me and made me even keener to make a career in the game. Dad and I were always talking football, and I learned a great deal about the game by watching it with him and listening to what he had to say. By that time I knew what a good player he had been, because so many people had told me about him.

I had now been at Ashley Down Secondary Modern for about a year – they didn't have a school football team because rugby was the main sport played there. I didn't like rugby, though in later years I always enjoyed going to watch it. On games afternoons at Ashley Down, they did play football so I preferred that, much to the frustration of the sports masters who felt that because I was a big lad, I should be using my weight in a scrum. The school rugby team used to play on Saturday mornings but I was never around as I was always off to watch Bristol City or Cardiff City, two clubs who were to form the major part of my professional career as a player. So for about one year at Ashley Down I played little or no organised football on a Saturday.

In 1956, when I was thirteen, I applied to go to Bristol Technical School because I had been told that they were very keen on football and always had good sides, as well as a good tradition in other sports – rugby, cricket and athletics. I had to take an entrance exam, and with the prospect of being able to play in a good team, I worked really hard in preparation for that exam. There were two departments at the Technical School – Building and Engineering. My parents always wanted me to get an engineering-apprenticeship when I left school, so this was an ideal opportunity if I could get entry into the Technical School. The Building Department was at Barton Hill while the Engineering Department was at Bedminster Bridge not far from Ashton Gate. I was aiming for the Engineering Department where most of the boys were Bristol City followers. I did quite well in the examination that took place in January 1956 – I passed the written exam and then had to go for an interview. One of the people on the panel was the chaplain of Bristol City Football Club – the Reverend FC Vyvyan-Jones who was a Director of the club. He had been Rector of St Michael's Church near Bristol Royal Infirmary since 1945, a Labour member of the City Council, and later Lord Mayor. He knew who I was because he knew Dad well from Ashton Gate. My interview went well, we talked about my ambitions and my football. A few days later he contacted Dad to say that I would be entering the Technical School in the Engineering Department. It was to play a major part in my future football career.

I entered the junior class at Bedminster Bridge in February 1956 – one of my fellow pupils was Dave Stone, a half back who went on to play for Bristol Rovers. It was to be a three-year course in the Engineering Department that would take me up to the age of sixteen and I would then become an engineering apprentice with a suitable firm, which is what my Dad wanted for me because of the way that his football career had ended. He felt that it was a precarious profession to follow and that I should have a secure future. I could understand his reasoning, but I still had my mind set on being a professional footballer.

Each day I had to get from home in Horfield to Bedminster Bridge and I usually cycled unless the weather was bad, in which case I went on the bus. It was about three miles from home and the exercise on the bike was useful. On the very first morning that I went to the Technical School I was put into Form 1C. I had a brand new uniform – blazer, tie and school-cap. I hadn't been in the class more than half an hour when another teacher came in and whispered something to our form-master Mr Davies who then said 'Would Brian Clark please leave the room to speak to this teacher'. I was quite worried, wondering what I had done on what was my first morning there. The teacher who wanted a word with me was Bert Francis who was the Sports-Master as well as teaching English. He was also a coach to the junior teams at Bristol Rovers. So there I stood in the corridor with my new blazer and tie, but I needn't have worried. Mr Francis told me that he ran the school football team and it was a good side. They played fixtures against Thornbury Grammar School, Chipping Sodbury Grammar School, Weston Grammar School – all those kind of teams, and he told me that he would be watching me playing on the Wednesday, which was the weekly sports day for the school, with a view to putting me in the school-team. The sports days were held at Shirehampton on playing fields between The Portway and the River Avon at Sea Mills, and we would travel down there on buses. So on that first Wednesday our form played another form and Bert Francis was watching. I played at inside right alongside our centre forward in a fetch-and-carry role as it used to be known. As we came back on the bus, Mr Francis came and sat next to me, and told me that on the following Saturday morning I would be in the school team against Chipping Sodbury Grammar School.

During the three years that I was at the Technical School (1956 to 1959), I developed physically into quite a big lad for my age. My football developed as well and in 1956/57 I got into the Bristol Schools Under-15 side a year before I really expected to be included. It was a big step, and Dad was a bit worried that it was too early for me – I was fourteen, and the others in the team were a year older than me. It was midway through the 1956/57 season and I did quite well for the rest of that season even though I found it a bit hard physically – a difference of a year at that age is quite big. The step up from playing with my school team to the Bristol Schools side was, I should imagine, rather like stepping up at professional level from a League team to International level.

I still went to watch Bristol City whenever my Schools' playing commitments allowed, and I enjoyed watching top professionals in action. In mid-October 1956, there was a midweek England v France Under-23 International at Ashton Gate. It was a 0-0 draw and I remember the game for two reasons – the highly-rated Doncaster Rovers forward Alick Jeffrey broke his leg, an injury which severely affected his career, and the other reason was that after I got home that night, Dad arrived with Fulham's Johnny Haynes who had not been in that England Under-23 squad that night, but had come from London to see the game. He missed the last train home and had nowhere to stay, so Dad brought him back to our house. Johnny was then well on the way to becoming one of England's leading players, and it was a big thrill for me as a thirteen-year-old to have him in our house. It was not until his death following a car accident in October 2005 that my sister reminded me of that night.

Being in the Bristol Schools side obviously meant that we were considered the best schoolboy players in the city. My big problem was not that I doubted my own ability, though I was a bit concerned about my strength, but was because of my family background. A number of people at the Technical School made it clear to me that they felt the only reason I was in the Bristol Schools side was because my Dad was Don Clark, former Bristol City centre forward and Assistant-Secretary at Ashton Gate. It was the start of something that remained with me for the next ten years, through being Captain of the Schools team, then being on the ground staff at Bristol City, becoming a professional and a regular in the team. It didn't stop until I joined Huddersfield Town in October 1966.

When I got into that Schools side, I was fortunate enough to do quite well and I knew in my own mind that I was in the team on merit, though of course no player does well all the time. I remember my debut being away to Aston Schools in Birmingham in the English Schools Trophy competition, the equivalent at schools level of the FA Cup, and I scored in our 4-0 win. In the next round we were 2-1 winners against Taunton Schools at Taunton Town's Hamilton Road ground and I scored both goals. I still have the cuttings from that Taunton game, and of course it mentions 'Brian Clark, son of Don Clark, the Bristol City FC Assistant Secretary and former centre forward'. But my goals meant that I was able to show everyone that I was my own person and could make it through my own ability. Almost every report in the paper about me from then on stated who I was, who my Dad was, and that he had watched the match. Well, if you are a schoolboy player you would expect your father to watch you play – it didn't help if the papers wrote about it every time. At the time Dad said to take no notice of it, that I was in the team on merit and had proved it. He also said that because of who we were, I would have to try even harder on the pitch.

Those inter-town Schools matches were always played on a

Saturday morning with an eleven o'clock kick-off, and we would have a meal afterwards. If it was a home game we would all go to the match in the afternoon, either Rovers at Eastville or City at Ashton Gate. Although I was a City fan, I didn't mind going to watch Rovers. If the Schools team was away on a Saturday, we would rush back in an effort to make the afternoon kick-off at Rovers or City. Because we were a representative schools team, we had to be seen watching both Bristol clubs rather than favouring one of them. Although John Atyeo was my big hero at City, I greatly admired his opposite number at Rovers – Geoff Bradford who gained an England Cap. They were both the idols of the fans at their respective clubs. I also well remember little winger Georgie Petherbridge, inside-forward Alfie Biggs and full backs Harry Bamford and Josser Watling at Rovers, all of them fine players. Sadly Harry died at the peak of his career in November 1958 after being badly injured in a motor-scooter accident on his way to a schools coaching session in Bristol.

At the end of my first term at Bristol Technical School I hadn't done too badly academically even though I was in the bottom stream, so by the summer of 1957 things had gone well for me – I was enjoying life at school and I was an established player in the Bristol Schools Under-15 team which had won the Cabot Cup, an inter-town schools competition for teams from the West Country, South Wales and the Midlands. But the following year (1957/58) was to be even better. At the end of my first season in the team, Ted King, who was manager of the side and a former England Amateur International, told me that I would be captain the following year. I would be 15 in January 1958 but because I was under that age at the start of the season, I was eligible for the whole season.

By that time Dad was no longer working for Bristol City. In February 1957 he had left the club after a twenty-one year connection at Ashton Gate (1936-51 as a player, 1951-57 as Assistant Secretary). He then joined the famous Bristol wine firm of John Harvey and Sons Ltd, where he had been appointed Bond Manager, later becoming Assistant Production Manager in which he supervised the bottling of the wines and spirits, and looked after both the home market and the export trade. So the Clarks were very much involved in the commercial and sporting life of our home city. His new role did not, however, stop the newspaper reports about me continuing to say 'Brian Clark, son of etc.'

The 1957/58 campaign was to be the most memorable season in the history of Bristol Schools football because, for the first time ever, we won the English Schools Trophy. The competition had been going since 1905 and each round was played on a knock-out basis except for the Final which was over two legs. We had a few players who had been given trials for England Schoolboys, and we had a long road to the Final with our home games being played at Ashton Gate. We had a bye in Round One, then in the Second Round we beat Mid-Somerset away 8-0 at Shepton Mallet and I got two. In the Third Round I scored one in our 8-0 away win at Taunton, and I had another two in our Fourth Round 11-0 home win over Forest Of Dean. We were naturally full of confidence and the Fifth Round saw us beat Maidstone 6-1 at home with myself getting two. I didn't score in the next round when we beat East Ham at home 4-1 with the opposition including a young lad called Ronnie Boyce who went on to play for West Ham United and who scored the winning goal in their 1964 FA Cup Final 3-2 victory against Preston. They also had a wing-half named Eddie Presland who also went on to play for West Ham.

In Round Seven I was back on target with a goal in our 4-2 win over Stoke at Stoke City's old Victoria Ground in the snow. They had a goalkeeper called Gordon West and he went on to play for Blackpool and Everton. There was no stopping us now, and in the semi-final at Ashton Gate we comfortably beat Barnsley 4-1 (I didn't score) to give us a two-leg Final against Swansea Schools. It had been a good tournament for me as captain – I'd scored eight goals in our seven matches in which we had a total of forty-six goals!

So we had made history by reaching the Final in which we were to play a side that had a great tradition in the competition. For a twenty-year period after the War, Swansea Schools provided many well-known names for Swansea Town FC as they were then known. They had won the competition in 1939, 1950, 1953 and

1955, and they had been runners-up in 1934, 1935 and 1952. They were undoubtedly one of the best schools teams in the country when we met them in April and May 1958, so we were going to have to play exceptionally well to win the Trophy. That Final was to teach us one of the best lessons that we ever learned in football.

The first leg took place at Ashton Gate on Tuesday 22 April 1958 in front of a 21,595 attendance. It was an evening kick-off and we had been given the day off school. We all met up at a pre-arranged venue for a meal and travelled to the game together. My Dad told me to forget about playing in front of such a big crowd that was expected, and just to concentrate on the match. Mum and Dad came to the game with my sister and it was the biggest occasion of my football life up to that point. We changed in the home dressing room which was to become so much a part of my daily life in the years ahead, and as I led the team out, I looked up into the main stand where my parents and sister were sitting – it was a proud moment for our family.

The game was thirty-five minutes each way and I can still remember our side, which was: goalkeeper Harry Booth who was at Bristol Technical School with me, full backs Colin Smith (Filton Avenue) and Mal Thomas (Carlton Park). Half backs were Dave Stone, another Bristol Technical School colleague who eventually went on to play for Bristol Rovers at first team level, Steve Poole (St George Grammar), Peter Prewett (Lockleaze) who was later on Bristol City's ground staff with me. Forwards were Terry Burt (Hannah Moore) on the right, myself at inside right, centre forward Dave Summers (Hengrove), inside left Adrian Williams (Baptist Mills) who was also later with me on the ground staff at Ashton Gate, and who was an England Schools International. Adrian eventually signed full professional forms for Bristol City and made four first team appearances in 1960/61 before drifting away. Outside left was Jantzen Derrick (Southville) who was also an England Schools International and who went on to play for Bristol City at first team level with me after we were both on the ground staff, which is how you were taken on by a club before the days of apprentice-professionals and now scholarship-trainees. Jantzen was with City as a full professional from 1959/60 until

1970/71 when he was released and joined French team Paris Saint-Germain, having made 260 League appearances for City. I still see Jantzen at least once a year at Bristol City former players' reunions and to me he is still the same as when we first knew each other, even though we are both now in our 60s.

In the Swansea side was Barrie Hole who was to become an outstanding midfield player with Cardiff City, Blackburn Rovers, Aston Villa, Swansea City and Wales. In later years I often played against Barrie for my various clubs and we used to remind each other of that Schools Final.

We won that first leg 5-0 with our best display of the competition – goals from Terry Burt and Adrian Williams to make it 2-0 at half-time, while in the second half Dave Summers scored our third, I netted our fourth, and Adrian Williams made it 5-0 just before time. Both teams attended a dinner after the game at The Berkeley in Clifton at which His Grace The Duke of Beaufort was present. We had a superb meal and everyone made the most of it. The newspapers were full of complimentary reports about our display, and as usual mentioned 'Brian Clark, son of Don Clark etc, etc'. We could have been forgiven for thinking that we had won the Trophy because Swansea officials said that we were the best Schools team that they had ever seen, but as it turned out we were in for a shock at the Vetch Field.

The second leg was played in Swansea on Thursday 1 May 1958 and we were unchanged. In the nine days between the two matches, we were all on cloud nine! When the three of us from the Technical School – Harry Booth, Dave Stone and myself – went in the day after the first leg, the Headmaster called us up in front of the morning assembly and we all had to receive the applause of the whole school, which was a little bit embarrassing for us! But we were soon brought back down to earth by several of the teaching-staff who were rugby-minded, and who told us that we may have done well on the pitch but what a pity that our school work was not up to the same standard.

There were many Football League scouts watching that first-leg match, and the talk was about to which clubs we would all go eventually – Jantzen Derrick was supposed to be going to

Tottenham Hotspur, Brian Clark would be going to Wolves or Birmingham City, and so on throughout the team. It was difficult for us not to get caught up in it all!

We went to Swansea for the return match by train in those days before the Severn Bridges existed. We were booked in to what was then the Mackworth Hotel in the centre of Swansea where we had a pre-match meal – I still look at that hotel whenever I am down there and think back to that night – and we walked into the Vetch Field that evening as if the Final was already won! There were 10,000 there that night and they were fully behind the Swansea lads despite the fact that they started with a 5-0 deficit. They were all over us in the opening stages of the first half, and after twenty-one minutes we were 3-0 down on the night and were now only 5-3 ahead on aggregate – it was not looking good for us! That was how it was at half-time, and when we got into our dressing room, Ted King our manager really laid into us. He sent the travelling reserves out of the room as well as the teachers who had travelled with us, and gave us a right rollicking that I can still vividly remember to this day! He told us that we were a disgrace to our respective schools, to our families and to ourselves. He said that he was ashamed of us and that we were unrecognisable from the team that had won 5-0 at Ashton Gate nine days earlier.

His words clearly had an effect because eight minutes after the re-start, Terry Burt headed a goal for us that sparked our revival. Five minutes later Dave Summers scored another, I then hit a 30-yarder past their keeper and two minutes later Dave scored again, so we now were 4-3 ahead on the night and 9-3 ahead on aggregate. Colin Smith deflected a last-minute shot past his own keeper Harry Booth so it ended 4-4 and we won the Trophy on a 9-4 aggregate after that dramatic second leg.

The Trophy was presented to us on the pitch, and it was a great honour for me to receive it as Captain. After the dressing room celebrations, we returned to the Mackworth Hotel where we were staying overnight and there was a Dinner at the hotel for both teams that evening. My parents were there for the game but then had to get the train back to Bristol otherwise they would have been stuck in Swansea overnight.

At the Dinner we had the Trophy on our table, and there was another great meal followed by speeches and the presentation of the medals. I thought that my Mum was a good cook, but I don't think that even she could have surpassed the two dinners that we had after each leg of that Final. Four nights later, on the Monday evening, we were in action again against Swindon Schools at Ashton Gate in the Final of the Cabot Cup – we had a comfortable 5-1 win against a side that included future Swindon Town players John Trollope, Ernie Hunt, Wilf Shergold and Roger Smart. We were photographed with the English Schools Trophy before the game in which Dave Stone put us ahead after two minutes before Swindon equalised. Jantzen Derrick and Terry Burt put us 3-1 up at half-time, and in the second half Terry and Adrian Williams scored further goals to end Bristol Schools' season with a great double. And with my school Bristol Technical winning the Woodcock Shield, it was a really memorable season for me.

Two days before our Cabot Cup win over Swindon, Dad and I watched Bolton Wanderers beating Manchester United 2-0 in the FA Cup Final on television, and I thought back to that day three months earlier when the Busby Babes had been destroyed in the Munich Air Disaster. Most people can remember where they were when momentous events occurred, and I can clearly remember where I was. It was on Thursday 6 February 1958 and I went to Eastville, Bristol Rovers' ground, for a late-afternoon training session. Bert Francis, our sports master at Bristol Technical, was coach to the junior sides at Rovers, and as a schoolboy I was invited to go there regularly for training on Tuesdays and Thursdays with their amateurs and part-timers. By inviting me to train there, Bert was obviously hoping that I would eventually join Rovers, especially as I lived in nearby Horfield. But he was to be disappointed as my aim was to be a City player.

On that particular Thursday afternoon, I arrived at Eastville to learn of the Munich tragedy – we didn't train, however, but sat in the dressing room listening to the wireless reports about what had happened at Munich. Everyone who played football knew of the Busby Babes, and though we did not know those players personally, it affected us very much. As the football world mourned their loss, the game went on and I remember that nine days later, I was at Ashton Gate for an FA Cup Fifth Round tie when Rovers beat City 4-3 in front of a crowd of just over 39,000 – it was 3-3 towards the end, but then Geoff Bradford, Rovers England International centre forward, scored their winning goal at the Winterstoke Road End, and many City supporters said for years afterwards that he had been offside. Geoff, who eventually ended his career at full back for Rovers, gained just one Cap for England when he played against Denmark in Copenhagen during October 1955, scoring once in England's 5-1 victory, and he was an outstanding player for Rovers over many years.

And so the 1957/58 season finished triumphantly for Bristol Schools football, and we were the heroes of the city. We had a great deal of press coverage and everyone praised us individually wherever we went.

On the Tuesday afternoon following our Monday night Cabot Cup win over Swindon, the team plus the other players that had played a part in our reaching the English Schools Trophy Final – David Powell, Colin Martin, Richard Lovell, Roger Stone – together with our officials, were invited by the Lord Mayor and Lady Mayoress of Bristol to a Civic Reception at the imposing Council House on College Green opposite the Cathedral. It was a late-afternoon occasion and we were let off school early to attend. It was a memorable event and the Lord Mayor – Alderman Percy Raymond – told us at the reception that we were to Bristol what the FA Cup winners Bolton Wanderers were to the town of Bolton.

It had been the first ever Civic Reception to be held in Bristol for a schools football team, and to mark our success, the Lord Mayor asked the Chairman of The Bristol Education Committee to grant all the schoolchildren in the city a whole day's holiday, which took place ten days later – we were certainly popular amongst them for that!

It was difficult for us not to get carried away by all the praise and the press coverage because none of us had experienced anything like that before. But as far as I was concerned, Dad made sure that my feet were firmly on the ground – he had known the ups and downs of the game at various levels. They didn't have to widen the doors at 10 St Aldwyns Close when I came in. My one regret about that time was that I had not been selected for the England Schools side – Adrian Williams and Jantzen Derrick had made it, but I perhaps lacked a yard of pace to be good enough for selection.

That victory in the English Schools Trophy was the peak of success for Bristol Schools in their footballing history – they did go on to reach the Final for a second time in 1963 but on that occasion lost over two legs to Stoke Schools. Looking back at our 1958 side, I was particularly friendly with goalkeeper Harry Booth who was with me at the Technical School. I'm not sure what became of him but I do remember at the time that my eleven-year-old sister Cherry had a big crush on him – Harry was a good looking guy! Then there was Adrian Williams who lived in Muller Road near the gasworks very close to the Rovers ground, and of course Jantzen Derrick who was an outstanding winger. I occasionally still go to Ashton Gate to watch Bristol City play – the club are always happy to welcome me – and I contact Jantzen to meet up with him. My big ambition now is to get that 1958 schools squad together again for the fiftieth anniversary of our success which will be in 2008. I feel that, as Captain, I ought to do it and I will definitely be following it up. We are all in our 60s now and it would be great to be together once again.

It was now the summer of 1958, and I was about to start my last year in school. There was talk at home of me staying on at school until I was seventeen or eighteen but I just didn't want to, as my aim was to be a footballer.

At that time Bristol was well on the way to recovering from wartime damage. There were new buildings springing up in the Centre, Broadmead was becoming a modern area, the big John Lewis Store had just been completed and the whole place was changing dramatically. Bristol was a football boom-area, with City and Rovers well established in the old Second Division and both getting average League attendances of around 23-24,000.

As for the football press, Bristol was well served, with two Saturday evening sports papers – the *Evening Post* produced the '*Green 'Un*' and the *Evening World* produced the '*Pink 'Un*'. I used to get both when we had won, but if we'd lost I wouldn't buy either. That was the case from my Schools football days up to when I eventually left Bristol City for Huddersfield Town in 1966. I well remember those two cartoon-characters in the sports paper who were always discussing the merits of their respective teams – 'Ashton Alf' and 'Eastville Ernie'.

There was no better occasion than when City and Rovers played each other in Division Two – I can still smell the gasworks that was next to Eastville, a ground that sadly no longer exists, I can picture the huge crowds in Stapleton Road trying to get round the corner by His Majesty's Cinema before going over that bridge across the River Frome.

And when they played at Ashton Gate, there would be local league matches taking place in Ashton Park across the road from the ground, and finishing just before kick-off. Hundreds of fans would stop on their way to the ground through the park and watch the games going on.

2

A RED RED ROBIN

As the 1958/59 season grew near, I was no longer eligible for the Bristol Schools Under-15s side, but was still able to play for Bristol Technical School. My football future, however, lay with Bristol City and I was invited to play as a schoolboy for their junior sides. It was Cliff Duffin, assistant to Bristol City's manager Peter Doherty, who was instrumental in me playing for them. In that '58/59 season, I played for their 'A' team in the Bristol Suburban League Third Division – that was City's fifth team. I also played for their fourth team that was 'Bristol City United' in the Bristol and District League. Our big rivals in the Suburban League were teams such as Portway Old Boys, Chew Magna, Stoke Gifford United, Coalpit Heath Miners Welfare etc – they used to kick us all over the place! We were young boys of 15 to 17 years old, they were tough local amateurs who were quite a bit older than us.

Dad, still with John Harvey and Co Ltd, was now West Country scout for Birmingham City whose manager was Pat Beasley who had been in charge at Ashton Gate from 1950 to January 1958, so he knew Dad well. It was thought that I might eventually go to Birmingham City, but that would have been a difficult situation, especially with Dad being so closely connected with Pat, but in any event I wanted to play for Bristol City and going to the Midlands was never considered. Most of my games in '58/59 were for City 'A' and occasionally I would be promoted up to United and the youth side.

The Youth Cup matches were always played at Ashton Gate on a midweek evening, and when I first started playing for the 'A' team, their matches were at Keynsham. But then we moved to Gloucestershire County Cricket Club's County Ground where there were a couple of pitches behind the Pavilion overlooking the old Muller Road Orphanage, and we used to train and play there.

In addition to playing for City's 'A' team and United, I also played for City's Colts as well as the youth team in various youth cup competitions (FA Youth Cup, Gloucestershire Youth Cup). By the end of that season, I had played thirty-eight matches for City in their various junior teams – twenty-six for City 'A', five for City United, one for the Colts, six for the youth side. I also played four matches for the Technical School for whom I had to appear on a couple of occasions in November 1958 instead of for Bristol City. The School had priority on my services, but they didn't have matches every Saturday, so it was only on a few occasions that I had to miss playing for City. That season in total, I appeared in 42 matches and scored 46 goals – in my scrap-book is a short note that I wrote at the time '…not too bad a season'. It was my former Bristol Schools Under-15 team manager Ted King who was in charge of the 'A' team, so he knew what I was capable of, and I really enjoyed that first season in City's junior teams alongside several of our English Schools Trophy-winning side – Harry Booth, Peter Prewett, Adrian Williams and Jantzen Derrick.

I was able to watch first team games whenever possible, and I well remember an FA Cup Fourth Round tie at Ashton Gate in late January 1959 between Bristol City and Blackpool who were then a top-level side in the old First Division. Stanley Matthews played for Blackpool and there were 42,594 packed into the ground. I watched the match from the old ringside seats that were outside the touchline. The game ended 1-1, Bert Tindill giving City a first-half lead, and Stanley Matthews never got a look in because of City's left-back Mike Thresher who had an outstanding game. The bigger the name, the better Mike played, as I was to find out from first-hand experience when I was eventually with him in the first team.

On 13 January 1959 I had my 16th birthday, and my intention was to leave school at the end of the term. My school reports, whilst continuing to say what a nice boy I was, still gave the opinion that I should put as much effort into school work as I did into football. As a teenager I was interested in pop music and of course sport. Girls weren't a particular interest, though in common with my friends, I looked. My friends knew not to come knocking on my door on Friday nights because I always had a match the next day. We would usually go out on Saturday nights for a shandy or a packet of crisps and a visit to the cinema. Often we would go to coffee bars that were all the rage in those days, usually in Park Street just up the road from the Mauritania pub.

My parents still wanted me to become an engineering apprentice, and at the end of that term it was arranged that I would enter the engineering firm of Brecknell, Dolman & Rogers Ltd, which was in Pennywell Road, North Bristol, not far from Rovers' Eastville Stadium. The Managing Director and owner of the firm was Bristol City's 62-year-old Chairman Harry Dolman. He had been a Director of City since 1939, and Chairman since 1949, so he knew Dad well. I knew him in passing up to the time that I joined the firm because I had met him whenever Bristol City and my Dad played in summer cricket matches against local sides, but I was to know him much better after I joined Bristol City, first on the ground staff and then as a professional. Harry was a self-made man who was then well on the way to becoming a millionaire. He was born in the Wiltshire village of Langley Burrell near Chippenham, and after serving in the First World War in the Royal Flying Corps, had joined the Bristol engineering firm of Brecknell, Munroe & Rogers as a young engineer. The firm later almost went under, but Harry borrowed money to buy a major shareholding, and turned the firm's fortunes around. It became one of the biggest engineering concerns in the area, making machinery for various manufacturers including ticket machines for London Underground and butter-packing equipment amongst other things.

I don't know what a typical Football Club Chairman should look like, but if I had to picture one in my mind, it would be Harry Dolman, a distinguished-looking figure who was very much 'Mr Bristol City'. He was a bluff genial man who ran the club and his firm with equal efficiency, was a much-respected figure, and I recall his Rolls Royce with a personalised number-plate HD 11. He was a great benefactor to Bristol City and in May 1960 gifted the club a large number of shares in his company to wipe out the

City's heavy debt that was in the region of £55,000 – a really big sum in those days and a mill-stone around the club's neck. Harry surprised everyone that year by marrying his 24-year-old secretary Marina who was a keen City fan – his second marriage. She survived him after his death at the age of 80 in 1977, and she still sends Dad a Christmas card every year. I always remember her as a very nice lady and still occasionally see her at Bristol City reunion functions. She is now President of the club.

Harry Dolman really wanted me to go straight onto the ground staff after leaving school, but was prepared to go along with Dad's wishes. I still have a letter dated 4 February 1959 that Harry sent to Dad...

'Dear Don,

Brian came to see me yesterday and spent some while going over the Works here and I think he enjoyed his visit. If you wish to apprentice him, I shall be pleased to arrange it. The apprentice period is five years and I normally allow boys who also sign for the City, two mornings a week off for training during the football season. Apprentices also attend school for one whole day every week during the school session, and if they really want to make a success of Engineering they should go to Night School at least once a week. You will therefore realise it becomes very hard work to do both engineering and give the necessary time to football. Brian, I gather, is exceptionally keen on football and is not all that keen to work in a factory. I feel that football offers such wonderful opportunities these days with good wages, excellent benefits and a fine healthy life, and bearing in mind that he has such fine football ability and no doubt a wonderful future, he may find it too much to try to do both and possibly fall between two stools. If he decides to go to Bristol City, which I hope he will, he could get immediately at least £5 a week and when he becomes a professional the wages are much higher than in the Engineering trade. If you decide to let him become a professional footballer and in a few years' time he does not by chance make the grade, I shall always be willing to offer him another chance with my firm. It is now up to you, Don, and I am willing co-operate in any way that I possibly can. My frank opinion is that Brian will play for England. He is a very nice boy and I wish him success in whatever he does. Please let me know what you decide.'

There were various discussions between Mum and Dad and Bristol City's manager Peter Doherty, but in the end it was decided that I would go into Harry Dolman's firm a month after my 16th birthday. And so, on Monday 16 February 1959, after I had left Bristol Technical School, I reported to the Works Manager Mr S L Bush. Normal start-time was 7.30 am but they said I could come on that first day at 9 o'clock. As I left home I was apprehensive about what lay ahead. There was no fuss made of me – I was just a new starter, and I was taken down to a distant part of the Works. I was given a job of filing excess metal from components of butter-packing machinery after they had come off the guillotine. It took me about an hour and a half on that first day to realise that engineering was not for me! I went home at half-past four and my parents wanted to know how I had got on. I told them that I hadn't particularly liked it, but Dad said perhaps I would enjoy it better the next day.

Tuesdays was training night for youngsters at Ashton Gate so, after leaving home at 7.15 am to get to the Works for the 7.30 am start, I then finished at 4.30 pm and had to cycle from Pennywell Road through Old Market down to Bristol City's ground where I then trained for two hours before cycling all the way back home to Horfield, getting back at about 9.30 pm. I did this on Tuesdays and Thursdays for a couple of weeks and it clearly affected my performance on the pitch on the Saturdays. I was getting very depressed about it, and what Harry Dolman had said in that letter to my Dad was starting to ring true. For the Saturday matches in the 'A' team that took place during my stay at Brecknell, Dolman & Rogers, I didn't really feel like playing because I was tired. I was very miserable and my parents realised it. At the end of two weeks with the firm I handed in my notice though I had to work there for another week. On the following Monday I was at Ashton Gate by arrangement to join the ground staff which already included Adrian Williams and Jantzen Derrick from the Trophy-winning

Schools team. No doubt Harry Dolman, when he heard what had happened, had a smile on his face – he had got what he wanted, and so had I.

The end of the '58/59 season came, but it didn't end for me as a ground staff boy. Together with the other lads, there were numerous jobs to be done – painting, cleaning up, working on the pitch with the groundsman. There were one or two privileges because we all had a free pass to the Rex Cinema in Bedminster and we used to go there once a week after we had completed our chores.

One of our coaches was Bill Harvey, who was later a coach at Cardiff City when I joined them in the late 1960s. Bill looked after the training and the welfare of the ground staff boys at Ashton Gate, and that led to one or two dicey moments as far as the lads were concerned. Jantzen Derrick had this card school going underneath the old wooden stand opposite the main stand. Jantzen and a few of the others would go and play cards when they were supposed to be sweeping the terraces. Adrian Williams would be the lookout man in case Bill Harvey or any of the staff appeared, and they would then all scarper! We used to train in the afternoons but we still had to get the jobs done. They got away with it most of the time but I'm sure that Bill knew where they were when he couldn't see them. I always made sure that my chores were done before anything else.

I had not been long on the ground staff before I realised that there were problems in the dressing room amongst the senior professionals. It became known as the 'split-camp' situation and had resulted from the appointment of the former Northern Ireland International Peter Doherty as manager in late January 1958 when he had succeeded Pat Beasley. Doherty had been an outstanding inside-forward with Glentoran, Blackpool and Manchester City before the War, following which he had won the FA Cup with Derby in 1946, later playing for Huddersfield Town and then Doncaster Rovers whom he had joined as player/manager in 1950. When he first arrived at Bristol City to take up his new job in February 1958, he was also Team Manager of Northern Ireland whom he took to the World Cup quarter-finals in Sweden in the summer of 1958. He had brought in several players from Doncaster Rovers and was continuing to bring in new signings to a club that was largely made up of players from Gloucestershire and Somerset, though of course there were a few exceptions – for example, London-born outside right Wally Hinshelwood, a former Chelsea and Fulham player who had been signed from Reading in February 1956. It was a cause of friction that Doherty seemed to feel that a number of his Doncaster players could do a better job at Ashton Gate than those who were already there.

The established players resented Doherty's training methods and there was a clique of about five of them who always made their feelings known. They more or less ran the dressing room, and one of them was John Atyeo, the club's legendary goalscorer and England International who was a very strong character. Skipper Tommy Burden was another of them – he was a Hampshire lad originally from Andover who had joined the club from Leeds United in October 1954 and was then a part-timer living in Glastonbury and working for the shoe manufacturers Clarks of Street.

So it was very much a 'them and us' situation and you could sense the feeling in the dressing room when we had to go in after matches and morning-training to clear up the kit and clean the place. It still didn't stop them 'initiating' the new ground staff boys, and I had to get up on the table and sing a song! They were always taking the 'micky' out of us, especially me as I was the son of Don Clark.

Most of the established players in that dressing room were ones that I had been watching throughout the 1950s – Jimmy Rogers, Tommy Burden, John Atyeo etc. Big John was very much a hero of mine, and an interesting character. He was from the Wiltshire village of Dilton Marsh, ten miles South of Bath, and lived there throughout his career. He had been a pupil at Trowbridge High School where he excelled at football, rugby, cricket and athletics. But football was his main sport and he played two First Division games for League Champions Portsmouth as a 19 year-old amateur in 1950/51, and also played cricket on occasion for Wiltshire in the Minor Counties League before Harry Dolman then signed him as a professional for Bristol City in the summer of 1951. He won England honours at Youth, Under-23, B and Full levels, and played in two promotion teams for Bristol City (1954/55 and 1964/65). His father, a railway signalman, looked after his son's interests, and for the first five years of his stay at Ashton Gate, John was a part-timer qualifying as a quantity surveyor. He then went into the grocery business for a couple of years and did very well while continuing to be a prolific scorer for the club, and in his last couple of seasons of his fifteen-year connection with the club, he qualified as a Maths and PE teacher at Redland Training College. Along the way he played six times for England in '55/56 and '56/57, scoring five goals and helping England qualify for the 1958 World Cup Finals in Sweden. But the England selectors unaccountably dropped him – it was thought that as a part-timer he could not continue to be effective for England. Every Bristol City fan thought they were wrong!

Each week John would bring in eggs and apples from the family smallholding in Dilton Marsh – and we had to pay him for them! In all the years that I knew him, he always wore a fawn coloured raincoat when it was cold or wet. By the time that he finished playing in 1966, he had made 645 League and Cup appearances for the club, and had scored 350 goals. He was over six feet tall, very popular, and whenever I visit Ashton Gate, I look at the new stand named after him and built on the site of the old Park End banking, and think back to the time that we were in the team together.

As for the manager when I first joined the club, Peter Doherty was something of a distant figure to us ground staff boys, though he did come up to the County Ground to watch us training. He sometimes joined in, and he was a brilliant volleyer of the ball even in his late 40s.

In my second season at Ashton Gate (59/60), I continued to play in the junior teams and also represented Gloucestershire County Youth. It was a memorable season for Bristol City in the FA Youth Cup because we reached the semi-final with victories over Hamworthy (14-0), Reading (2-0), Southampton (4-1), West Ham

United (3-3, 3-2), before we went out to Chelsea over two legs (0-3, 0-3). I well remember our Fifth Round replay 3-2 victory over West Ham under the Ashton Gate floodlights in front of a 13,686 crowd in March 1960. We had a good luck telegram from Peter Doherty who had lost his job as manager shortly before, and we defeated a quality West Ham side who were probably better technically than us, but who couldn't match our determination on the night. They contained six players who went on to establish themselves in their first team – Jack Burkett, Geoff Hurst, Dave Bickles, Martin Peters, Ronnie Boyce and Brian Dear. Our goals that night came from Adrian Williams, myself and Terry Bush. Our side was – Harry Booth, Derrick Huxford, Martyn Thomas, John Davis, Mike Quinlan (Capt.), Peter Prewett, Roger 'Lou' Peters, Brian Clark, Terry Bush, Adrian Williams, Jantzen Derrick.

It was a great performance by us, but we were well beaten in the semi-final by Chelsea whose side included the talented Terry Venables, later to become England Manager. Our performance that season went some way to making up for the disappointment of the club's relegation from Division Two after a five-year stay in the Second Division despite sixteen League goals each from John Atyeo and Jimmy Rogers. After the departure of Peter Doherty, the playing side was run by Chairman Harry Dolman, together with Vice-Chairman Bill Kew, fellow-director The Rev Vyvyan-Jones, our trainer Les Bardsley and skipper Tommy Burden. Les was a former Bury player who had been with several other northern clubs, and he concentrated mainly on our fitness rather than any tactical work. He was very much a fitness fanatic, and after he eventually finished with Bristol City in 1977, he started up a physiotherapy practice that was eventually situated on Wells Road in Knowle and is now run by his son. Les is now 80 and I last saw him at a Bristol City reunion in early 2005. I'll always recall his strong Lancashire accent and his bow legs!

His assistant at Ashton Gate was Len 'Lemmo' Southway who was almost a permanent fixture at the club and was in the nicest possible way a 'sponge and bucket' trainer who did general jobs around the dressing room, looking after kit, boots etc. When I turned professional, Lemmo was 67-years-old and was a kind of father figure to the players. He was Bristol-born, with one of the broadest local accents that I have ever heard! A former defender with the club in the 1920s, he had also played for Merthyr and Aberdare when they were in the Football League. He was a really hard man, and I often saw him turn a cold hosepipe on himself after getting out of the bath in the home dressing room.

Lemmo always wore a hat, in training, in cleaning the boots, putting the kit away – he was bald, so perhaps he wore the hat to keep his head warm. In his youth, he had been a keen speedway fan and he had lost part of two fingers on his right hand, presumably through a cycle accident, though the joke amongst the lads was that he did it himself to avoid Army service! Lemmo always sat in the home dugout at first team games if he was not on reserve team duty, and was well respected throughout the club. He had been there for years and everyone knew him, including my Dad when he was a player at Ashton Gate.

If we were winning comfortably, John Atyeo would run close to the dugout knowing that there were five minutes left, and would say 'How long to go, Lemmo?' Lemmo would hold up his right hand to show five minutes, and John would say 'two and a half, Lemmo?' This was because Lemmo only had two and a half fingers, so John would run away laughing his head off, and Lemmo would be shaking his fist at him! But John wouldn't do it if we were losing.

Back to 1959/60, and it was a memorable season for my ex-Bristol Schools and City youth team colleague Jantzen Derrick who had made his first team debut away to Lincoln City in late December 1959 at the age of 16 years 355 days. He was the youngest ever player to appear for the club in League football, and went on to play a total of six Second Division games that season.

As I became more familiar to City fans through the junior and youth sides, the old comparison between Dad and myself continued. People would often say to me *You are a good header of the ball, but not as good as your Dad.* They would have seen Dad play for City, so for them it was natural to compare us and it was something that I had to put up with. As I approached my 17th birthday in January 1960, Peter Doherty told me that I would become a full professional with the club. But because he wanted me to continue playing in the junior teams, I had to wait until early March to sign because the rules stated that professionals could not play in the junior sides. I signed my first professional contract on 2 March 1960 – Dad witnessed my signature in front of Secretary Syd Hawkins who also signed it. I was paid £9 per week up to 7 May plus win and draw bonuses, and then £8 summer wages from 9 May to 30 June. The maximum wage for League players at that time was £20 per week in the season and £18 per week in the summer.

The manager appointed eventually to succeed Peter Doherty was 44-year-old East Londoner Fred Ford, who for the previous five years had been the assistant to Bert Tann at Bristol Rovers. There were suggestions that Bert himself would take over at Ashton Gate, but in the interest of harmony between the two clubs, he decided to stay at Eastville. So Harry Dolman approached Fred, a former Charlton, Millwall and Carlisle United player and then coach, and in mid-July 1960 Fred was named Bristol City manager. He had to overcome some initial hostility from City fans, but he became a popular manager at Ashton Gate, and he was the man who was to give me my League debut, and also the man who sold me to Huddersfield Town.

1960/61 was to be a major season for me – midway through it I made my reserve team debut, and it ended with me making my League debut in the final game of the season. After playing regularly for the Colts in the Western League from the start of the season, I was picked to play for the reserves against Tottenham Hotspur in a Football Combination match at Ashton Gate on 31 December 1960. I had progressed from the fifth team to the fourth team, to the third team, and now to the second team. Also in the side with me, and forming the forward-line, were Roger 'Lou' Peters (16), Terry Bush (17), Adrian Williams (17) and Jantzen Derrick (17) – the whole team was one of the youngest ever fielded by City in the Combination. In one of the local newspaper's preview of the game, the following appeared: *'Brian Clark, son of Don Clark the former centre forward and later assistant secretary, makes his first appearance in the Reserves after some useful displays in the Colts'* – it seemed that Dad and I were to be permanently linked when it came to my City selection and performances.

Adrian Williams scored for us in a 2-1 defeat by a Tottenham side who were 2-0 up until eight minutes from time, and who included Welsh International full back Mel Hopkins and Frankie Saul, later to be my teammate at Millwall in the mid-1970s. But it was quite a good display by us and I did well enough to remain in the Combination side for the rest of that season. All of the forwards who had played in that game against Tottenham went on to become first teamers under Fred Ford. Also in the side against Tottenham was locally-born centre half Alan Williams who would have been an England Under-23 International, but the match for which he was selected against Scotland was postponed because of the weather and he was never given another opportunity. He later played for Oldham, Watford, Newport County and Swansea. Alan, who became a pub landlord near Ashton Gate after his playing days, was quite a character on and off the pitch. He is now a Jehovah's Witness, and when they hold their Conventions at the Millennium Stadium in Cardiff, he always makes a point of looking me up. I respect his beliefs, but when we get together, he is still the same to me as I remember him forty-six years ago. Let's say that he has matured with age!

Playing in the Combination was a big step up for me at first and Dad would come and watch me in action at home games. It had been hard enough in the Western League against sides who often contained ex-Football League professionals. I used to get home and say to Dad how physical it was in the Western League – his reply was that if I found it hard at that level, wait until I got into the Combination team and see how hard that is. He was right, and I then said to him that I couldn't see myself getting into the first team. He would give me constructive criticism, and in the first month of being in the Combination team I played against Tottenham Hotspur (home), Southampton (home), Leicester City (away), Norwich City (home), Charlton Athletic (away), West Ham United (home), and Chelsea (away), and they all had strong sides because in those days League clubs carried large professional staffs before the abolition of the maximum wage in the summer of 1961.

So now I was going to grounds that I had only dreamed of as a kid, and I stayed in the Combination team until early April when I was dropped back into the Western League side. I had gone several reserve games without a goal, but then got one in our 1-1 home draw against Nottingham Forest on 8 April 1961. Two days later I was in our Western League side at Welton Rovers on their sloping pitch – quite a contrast from Combination games.

Over the next couple of weeks I alternated between the Combination and Western League teams, and there had been press speculation that, together with several of the other young professionals, I would be given a first team opportunity.

I played at Bridgewater for the Colts on Wednesday 26 April 1961 in a 3-2 Western League win, and on the Friday during training Fred Ford pulled me and Lou Peters to one side and told us that he was thinking of including the both of us in the first team the following day when we were playing at home to Brentford for our final game of the season in Division Three. He had probably already made his mind up to include us as the club was in a comfortable mid-table position with one League game to go, but he said that he had not yet made a final decision, depending on injuries, though we should prepare ourselves accordingly and he would make a decision about an hour before kick-off. Obviously he did not want to put any unnecessary pressure on the both of us.

Roger Peters was younger than me and was known as 'Lou' because he had a striking resemblance to Lou Costello of the American comedy duo of Abbott and Costello. Roger had turned professional the previous month and was a Cheltenham lad who had made rapid progress that season in the junior teams and reserves. He could play on either wing and was a stocky all-action player.

After training on the Friday, the list went up on the dressing room notice-board with thirteen players named, including Lou and myself – there were no substitutes in those days, so it was the goalkeeper and ten from the remaining twelve.

We both felt that we would play in view of there being little on the game as far as the club's final position was concerned, but we couldn't be one hundred per cent sure until Fred Ford named the side. The senior lads in the dressing room were confident, when they saw the list on Friday, that Lou and I would play and they said some encouraging words to us.

I remember going home to Horfield that afternoon and telling Dad when he came in from work that I could well be in the first team the next day. He was pleased and so were Mum and my sister Cherry.

I couldn't wait for Saturday afternoon – I was at Ashton Gate in good time, made sure that there was a ticket for Dad, and went into the dressing room just before two o'clock. In came Fred Ford, he put up the eleven on the board, and Lou and I were in – it was a dream come true for both of us because we had come through the Colts that season, through the reserves, and now we were in the first team. It was going to be a memorable day for me and Lou, but it really belonged to skipper Tommy Burden who was recalled to the side for the first time since mid-December for what was going to be his final League appearance before he retired at the age of thirty-six, having played nearly 250 first team games for the club since joining from Leeds in November 1954.

I well remember our team that played against Brentford. There was Tony Cook in goal, a smoker who liked to go in the toilet before the match for a few cigarettes to calm his nerves. He used to pace up and down his penalty-area when play was at the other end – he could never keep still. You would never have thought when watching him that he was an experienced keeper who had played almost 300 games for the club up to that time. After his playing days he became a Prison Officer at Horfield Gaol. Alec Briggs and Mike Thresher were the full backs. Alec, at that time a part-timer who worked at Clark's Shoe Factory in Street, could also play at left-back. Tommy Burden was right-half, Jack Connor was centre-half and Gordon Low was left-half, both of them former Huddersfield Town players. Tommy Burden is now in his 80s and I saw him last year at a Bristol City reunion. He remembered me well and asked after Dad who had been Assistant-Secretary when Tommy came to Ashton Gate. The forwards were Lou Peters on the right, myself, John Atyeo, Bobby 'Shadow' Williams, and Jantzen Derrick on the left. Bobby was nicknamed 'Shadow' because of the way that he used to dart through the opposition to create chances. As for Jantzen, he was quite used to senior football because he had been in the first team for most of that season. I played in the team with him over the next five years and I believe that he was talented enough to have played for England. Why didn't he? – Perhaps he didn't quite have the desire to push himself further, added to which he was often hampered by injury which affected his consistency.

No one made a fuss of me in the dressing room before the match. Big John Atyeo just said to treat it as another game – it was anything but that for me because here I was playing alongside one of Bristol City's greatest players and someone whom I had watched and admired over the previous ten years! There were only 8,466 at Ashton Gate that afternoon – I wouldn't have cared if there had only been 500! I was in the first team, and for Lou Peters and myself, that was the most important thing.

As I ran down the tunnel onto the pitch with the team, the Fishponds British Legion Band were playing our signature tune – 'When The Red Red Robin Comes Bob Bob Bobbin' Along'. I'd heard that so many times over the previous years, and now I felt they were playing it for me. It was a wonderful experience for me to go out onto that pitch with the first team. Dad must have felt very proud watching from the stand. Here I was playing for the side that I had supported as a small boy, collected autographs and always wanted to be part of.

The referee for the game was Jack Kelly of Chorley who was to take charge of the FA Cup Final at Wembley between Leicester City and Tottenham Hotspur the following week. Before the kick-off in our match I made a point of shaking his hand and wishing him all the best for the Final.

I would liked to have scored on my debut, but although we were 3-0 winners, it was John Atyeo who netted all three – a penalty after twenty-eight minutes, a second after thirty-eight minutes and a third with thirteen minutes left. At the end of the game Brentford and ourselves lined up at the tunnel to applaud Tommy Burden off the pitch, but it wasn't his autograph that all the young boys wanted at the end of the game, it was referee Jack Kelly's, and as we went down the tunnel, Mr Kelly was still in the middle of the pitch signing dozens of autograph-books. How did I do on my first League appearance? I still have the report of the game written by *Evening Post* football writer Peter Godsiff whom I came to respect over my time with the club. He wrote *'Clark had a successful first outing, displaying some constructive work and not looking out of his class at all'*.

Dad was very pleased after the game, but didn't give me too much praise. He told me that I had got one foot on the first rung of the ladder, that it was a long climb and no doubt I would fall off a few times on the way up.

I drove home after the match. By then I had my own car which I had bought off Jantzen Derrick when I was just 17. It was a 1936 Ford 8 and I paid him £27 and 10 shillings for it. Jantzen had passed his driving test in it, and I did so with it when the time came. It was a good car, it chugged along, had those old-fashioned indicators that swung out from the door frames, and it got me about. I wish I'd kept that car – it would have been worth now a great deal more than I paid for it, but I sold it in that summer of 1961 to another of our young professionals Terry Bush for £32 and ten shillings, so at least I made a profit on it. My contract was improved at the end of the season, so I was able to buy a newer second-hand car and my wages went up for 1961/62 to £11 in the season and £9 in the summer.

There were no big celebrations for me after that game against Brentford – I went out in Bristol that Saturday night for a few coffees with my friends. They knew that I didn't drink very much and didn't want to be seen around pubs in the City Centre. Of course I eagerly looked at the reports in the *Green 'Un* and *Pink 'Un*, and I still have those cuttings to this day.

So the season ended with me having made my first team debut, and we would be off from the end of April to late July when pre-season training began. I went off with my parents to Torquay for a week – we stayed with Sammy Collins, a former playing colleague of Dad at Ashton Gate. Sammy was then playing for Torquay United. I was still living at home with Mum and Dad – in fact I stayed there until I eventually moved to Huddersfield Town in October 1966.

One of Bristol City's season ticket holders was Fred Callow who owned a fruit farm at Axbridge in Somerset where he grew strawberries. I had known him for many years because Dad had often gone strawberry picking on that farm when he was a player, and used to take me with him when I was a small boy. I got on very well with Fred together with his two sons John and David who were about my age, and Fred's daughter Mary. David was a promising young player who was with Winscombe FC as a left back or left winger, and he had trials at Wolves a couple of years later, but never got to be a professional footballer. In that summer of 1961 Fred suggested to me that I come down to the farm instead of hanging around in Bristol all summer, and help with the strawberry harvest. After I returned from Torquay, I drove down regularly to Axbridge to work on the strawberry picking, and Fred paid me £8 a week. So all of a sudden I was a rich boy – the previous season I had been earning £9 per week, now in the summer I was getting £8 from Fred and £9 from the club under my new terms. I was getting £17 per week – I'd never had so much money in my life up to then. It was a healthy summer for me – no need to wear a shirt in the strawberry fields. I worked with Fred's two sons John and David at Windy Ridge Nurseries on the Axbridge to Cheddar road and I have very happy memories of being there over several summers in the following few years. We would finish work at 5 pm and then go over to the open-air swimming pool at Cheddar. The Callows were all very keen Bristol City fans, and David eventually became a Director of the club.

That summer of 1961 flew by, and I reported back for training in mid-July when we were allocated our training kit. Our local rivals Bristol Rovers always used to go to Weston where the players camped out for a week as part of their schedule – we weren't that brave, and I could never imagine John Atyeo living rough under canvas. We did go for training at Brean Down near the seaside town, but only for a day at a time, and occasionally we went there to train on the sands. We sometimes trained in the park across Ashton Road near the Star Inn that was the home of Bristol City's legendary pre-World War One centre half Billy Wedlock. We also did training-runs along the Portway under the Clifton Suspension

Bridge and up Bridge Valley Road to the Downs – that long run up Bridge Valley Road never seemed to end!

The maximum wage of £20 per week for League players had been abolished that summer as a result of the efforts of Jimmy Hill, Chairman of the PFA, but it didn't really make a great deal of difference to me – I was happy with what I was earning, I was a single lad, I was happy at the club and I was happy at home. I don't know what the other players at Ashton Gate would have been earning at that time. Whatever John Atyeo was getting, he fully deserved it – he was an England International, a prolific goalscorer and a major influence on the team.

One of the regular features of pre-season training in my time as a player with Bristol City was an invitation to the players and staff by Chairman Harry Dolman to visit his impressive home at Chew Magna where he had a bowling green – Harry was a very keen bowler, and he also had a tennis court there. So the squad would spend a day at his home playing tennis and bowls, Harry and his wife Marina would lay on a buffet for us, and for professional players like ourselves it was a journey into another world. There were wonderful views across the Chew Valley Lakes, and they were very generous hosts. In all the time that I knew him, I never called Harry Dolman anything other than 'Mr Chairman'.

Pre-season of '61/62 went very well for me and I scored twice in our public practice match at Ashton Gate for the Reds (probable first team) against the Whites (mainly reserves). These types of matches were the forerunners of the modern day pre-season friendlies. Because Fred Ford selected me for the Reds, it was looking likely that I would start the new season in the first team.

That was how it turned out, and I was in the side for the opening three games – a 1-0 defeat at Notts County, a 1-0 home win over Northampton, and 1-0 home defeat by Shrewsbury. In those matches I played in attack with Jimmy Rogers and John Atyeo. Seven years earlier I had been a young spectator at Ashton Gate watching both of them in the 1954/55 Third Division (South) Championship-winning team.

Fred Ford then left me out and Dad's words of the previous

April were true – I had temporarily fallen off the ladder. But I was only 18 and still learning the game. So it was back to the reserves, but not in the Football Combination. The club had resigned at the end of the previous season for financial reasons and the reserves now played in the Western League, winning the title that season. I had a good season in the reserves and finished as top scorer on 29 goals, but what I really wanted was to be doing it in the first team.

Between late August 1961 and mid-April 1962, I played just two more first team matches – a 1-0 defeat at Southend in mid-September, and a 3-2 defeat at Hull City in late February. I well remember that game at Hull because the home fans tried to attack our keeper Tony Cook as he left the pitch at the end of the game. Cooky had been involved in two incidents with opponents in the last quarter of an hour and it was not a pleasant atmosphere. I missed an open goal in the first half and hit the post with a twenty-five yarder in the second half.

It was during that season that two well-known Gloucestershire County cricketers joined Bristol City – goalkeeper Ron Nicholls from Cardiff City, and inside forward Barrie Meyer from Newport County. Ron, who had originally been with Bristol Rovers, was Gloucestershire's opening batsman while Barrie, ex-Bristol Rovers and Plymouth Argyle, was wicket-keeper/batsman and later became a well-respected Test umpire. We also had long-serving Bobby Etheridge who had also kept wicket for Gloucestershire. In those days you could combine football and cricket because of the length of the close season in the summer.

For much of that 1961/62 season I was a bit frustrated at not getting a regular first team place, but I was still young. As the season came to its close the club missed out on promotion from Division Three finishing in sixth place, and Fred Ford put me back in the first team for the final three matches during which I scored twice in our 3-2 home win over Coventry City on 24 April – my first goals at League level.

It was a Tuesday night game, and the return fixture of the match against them at Highfield Road the previous day when I had come back into the team and we had drawn 1-1. What I vividly remember about that match at Ashton Gate was facing Coventry's centre half George Curtis in what was a David and Goliath encounter, and I was David! It was the first time that I had faced George although he had played the previous day at their place, but on that occasion he had been marking our captain John Atyeo. In this return game, however, John told me to play down the middle and he would support me in an inside-forward role. John normally played centre forward, but as he was captain I did what I was told. After a season mainly in the reserves with a few first team appearances, I felt physically stronger than the previous year, and I needed to be to face George Curtis who I can only describe as a 'man-mountain'! He had his shorts pulled up tight around his waist – I looked over at John Atyeo and he was smiling because he knew from the previous day what it would be like for me.

As for the game, which was seen by just 6,437 – our lowest home League crowd since the war – we won 3-2 after taking the lead through 'Shadow' Williams just before half-time, but then Cooky our goalkeeper had a disastrous seven-minute opening spell in the second half and we were 2-1 down. Just after that David Noake whom we had signed from Luton Town early in the season, crossed from the left, I had a shot blocked but then hit the rebound past Coventry's keeper Arthur Lightening. That made it 2-2 and midway through the second half John Atyeo set up a chance for me and I made it 3-2 with my second goal of the game. I very nearly got a hat-trick but I sent one shot just past the post while shortly afterwards Lightening made an unbelievable save to stop me scoring. We won 3-2 and I was more than happy with two goals. I stayed in the side for the final match when we drew 2-2 at home to Crystal Palace though I didn't score, and there were several of us in the line-up that afternoon who had come up through the junior sides – myself, 'Shadow' Williams, Lou Peters, full back Tony Ford whose son Mike was later to play for Cardiff City and Oxford United, and forward Terry Bush who was from Norfolk and was a junior before turning professional in February 1960. Terry played for Bristol City until 1970 before a knee-injury ended his career. Like Dad, he then joined the club staff and became assistant secretary, later becoming a full-time official with the Transport and General Workers' Union.

So we were a developing side of experience and youth with good prospects for the following season. Although John Atyeo was better known as a centre forward, he played most of that season at inside right supporting our former Newcastle United centre forward Alex Tait who had joined us in June 1960 and was a qualified school teacher. But it was John who was again top scorer that season with 26 League goals and 4 Cup goals, one of which was in the Welsh Senior Cup in which Bristol City were invited to compete that season, beating Merthyr 4-2 at home in the 5th Round before losing 2-0 at Ashton Gate to Cardiff City in front of a 13,579 attendance, the Bluebirds then being at top-level status in the original Division One (now The Premiership).

The 61/62 season wasn't quite over as far as I was concerned. Every May, just after the final League game, came the Gloucestershire Senior Cup Final that was always between Bristol City and Bristol Rovers by invitation – they had been playing each other since 1901 in the Final at the end of every season. A year earlier, in May 1961, we had won 3-1 at Eastville, and now came my first opportunity of playing against Rovers in this fixture which took place on Tuesday 1 May 1962, at Ashton Gate.

Although there were no League points at stake, it was very much a prestigious game. Both clubs and their respective supporters were always keen to win the Cup for the sake of local pride. It was particularly important to Rovers on this occasion because they had just been relegated from Division Two and would be our rivals in the Third Division the following season.

Fred Ford made a few changes for the game – Alex Tait came in for John Atyeo while there were several others, but it was more or less a first team fixture for both sides who treated it as such. It was another dream come true for me – playing in a local derby against Rovers at Ashton Gate, and it was a night that I'll never forget because I was lucky enough to get a hat-trick in our 3-1 win after we had been one down at half-time. All my goals were at the Park End – I got my first after fifty-seven minutes from a pull-back by Shadow, a second six minutes later when I headed in a Lou Peters corner, and a third fourteen minutes from time after Jantzen Derrick's corner was headed to me by Rovers' ex-international centre forward Geoff Bradford who was then playing for them at full back.

We each had a winners' medal and I still have mine amongst my football memorabilia. It took me almost all summer to come back down to earth after the way I had finished the '61/62 season. Our neighbourhood in Horfield was a Bristol Rovers area so I didn't make too much of it when I was out and about in North Bristol. Dad was really pleased about my hat-trick because although the newspaper reports were full of the 'Clark father and son' connection, I was beginning to establish myself in my own right. So I was metaphorically leaving Dad in the stand, and getting on with things out there on the pitch.

One thing I remember about that game against Rovers – the summer weather had come early and it was really hot in late April 1962. Several of us went to the open-air pool at Weston-super-Mare on the Sunday after the final League game against Crystal Palace, and I got sunburnt. When I went in for training on the Monday, Fred Ford told me that I would be playing up front with Alex Tait as John Atyeo had a slight strain – I didn't tell Fred that I had sunburn and I spent the next 24 hours with cream all over me trying to cool it down. I was really sore, but I came through the game all right and that hat-trick certainly helped to ease my discomfort!

I was now 19 years old and getting to the stage where I didn't want to go on holiday with Mum and Dad, preferring to be a bit more independent. It was a little quiet on the Callows' strawberry farm, so Fred Callow suggested that John, his elder boy, and myself took an early holiday, and we both went down to North Cornwall for a week. That was in late May 1962, we took a tent and supplies, and decided that if the weather was good we would stay, if not we would come home. We went in my car and the weather was all right so we stayed for the whole week. It turned out to be a decision that would change my life. Looking back over the years, I think that Fred had hopes that his daughter Mary, who was at a teacher training college in Bath, and I would get together. But there was nothing between us though I always remained very good friends with Fred and his wife, both of them sadly no longer with us, and their sons and daughter.

So John Callow and I were camping at Porth near Newquay in Cornwall, and we were kicking a ball about on the beach with several lads that we had met. A few yards away were a couple of girls and we got talking to them. One of them was Gillian Miles – she was 21 and she and her friend were student nurses finishing their training at The South London Hospital at Clapham Common, and in Cornwall on holiday. It was a fateful meeting because five years later Gillian and I were married! Gill was from Hemel Hempstead and it wasn't a big romance at first. She went back to south London and I went back to work on the strawberry beds before reporting back for pre-season training. But we kept in touch by letter and eventually I went up to London to visit her between matches, while she would come down to visit me, staying at our house. Mum and Dad liked her and our relationship developed. Her parents were farming people just outside Hemel Hempstead on the edge of the Chilterns, a beautiful part of the world. She wasn't particularly interested in football, so my job as a professional with Bristol City didn't really have any bearing on our relationship.

The 1962/63 season was to be my best one so far – although I only played in one of the first four Third Division matches, I then got a regular place and missed only one game during the rest of the season which saw me finish as top scorer (23 League goals and 3 in the FA Cup). Shadow Williams was second top with 20 League and Cup goals while John Atyeo had 18 League and Cup goals. It was another dream come true for me – who would have imagined a few years earlier that I would be in the same team as Big John and scoring more goals than him! I felt that I had matured and was becoming stronger. A regular place in the side helped my confidence and the goals started to flow. Pace was not one of my strengths, that was why I didn't get an England Schools Cap. But I had strength on the ball and I was able to make the most of it. Opponents found me difficult to knock off the ball, and I had the ability to be going as strong at the end of the game as I was at the start. Heavy grounds did not bother me, in fact I quite liked them, not that we had many in that 1962/63 season. It was the year of the

Big Freeze that began immediately after Boxing Day. Between 26 December and 2 March we played just three League and FA Cup matches. They were all at Ashton Gate on bone-hard pitches and one of them was an FA Cup Third Round tie in mid-January 1963 against First Division Aston Villa. It was the first time that I had played against top-level opposition, and I played in basketball boots because the pitch was so hard on an icy cold night. I scored to give us a half-time lead, but Villa equalised for a 1-1 draw. Because of the bad winter, we didn't have the replay at Villa Park until 7 March. We went 2-1 up through Bobby Etheridge and Shadow Williams at half-time, but Villa eventually proved to be too strong for us and we lost 3-2.

The big League matches for us that season were the local derbies against Bristol Rovers, the first time that the two clubs had played each other in League matches since 1959/60. We did the double over Rovers that season, winning 2-1 at Eastville in mid-September in front of 20,708, and 4-1 at Ashton Gate in mid-April when 22,739 saw the game. I was lucky enough to score in each of those matches.

That season, I came across two characters who were to play a significant part in my career during the years ahead. In late September 1962 we had won 5-2 at Bradford Park Avenue and before the match our manager Fred Ford had said to our right back Alec Briggs that he would have to keep a close eye on Bradford's left-winger who, said Fred, was so quick that 'he could catch pigeons'. It was Ronnie Bird who was to be my teammate at Cardiff City several years later, and with whom I remained good friends long after our careers ended and until his sad passing in March 2005. The other one was Bradford's player/manager Jimmy Scoular, the former Portsmouth, Newcastle United, and Scotland wing-half. In that match at Bradford, when I scored twice, Jimmy shouted his way through the game, tackled as if it were the FA Cup Final which he had won with Newcastle in 1955, and generally frightened the life out of everyone on the pitch. He was to be my manager a few years later when he resurrected my career at Cardiff City.

Gill and I would see each other about once a month and I well remember one of those occasions. It was towards the end of March 1963 and we were playing at Watford – the nearest League club to Gill's family home. I got tickets for Gill, her father George and her brother Jim – it was the first time that they had ever seen me play. We won 4-1 and I scored a hat-trick. They thought it was brilliant, so did I, and I spent a happy couple of days at their family home.

Fred Ford and the club's medical staff were a little concerned that I was often suffering from colds, and that towards the end of matches my breathing was a little bit heavy. I had broken my nose in a match and this was a result of it. So at the end of the 1962/63 season I entered the Chesterfield Nursing Home in Clifton for an operation on my nose. I was there for six days and the operation proved a success. I have never had any breathing problems since then, but with various knocks over the years my nose has changed shape a few times!

Players in those days were on season-long contracts, and if the club were going to offer you another year, you would get a registered letter telling you that your services had been retained for another season, terms to be negotiated with the Manager. But as far as I was concerned, there were no negotiations – I had the letter telling me that I was being retained, and when I went to see Fred Ford, he told me what I would be getting. I was just pleased to get another year's contract. I couldn't see them releasing me or putting me up for sale as I was top scorer. The wages, and I did get an increase for 1963/64, didn't seem to be the be-all and end-all in those days. Obviously you weren't going to play for them for nothing, but as long as you got what you felt that you deserved, you were happy. I was settled in my lifestyle, I liked living at home, I had a car and a steady girlfriend.

As for Gill, she had finished her three-year training as a nurse, and now looked to find a permanent position at a hospital. Her parents discussed it with her, I also talked to her about it, and she found a post at the Bristol Royal Infirmary – I couldn't have been happier. She shared a flat with three other colleagues in Parry's Lane off the Downs towards Sea Mills, so we were able to see each other regularly, depending on her shifts as she was often on duty during the nights.

That summer I did the usual strawberry duty at Axbridge in addition to my social life before going back to Ashton Gate. We were developing into a useful side, and in that '63/64 season I played in all forty-six League games, our five FA Cup matches and one League Cup game. One of our new signings that summer was left winger Peter Hooper, the former Bristol Rovers player who had come to us from Cardiff City where he had spent the previous season. He had a great left foot, and was deadly with free kicks and penalties. He provided plenty of chances for myself, John Atyeo and Shadow Williams.

It took him some time to be accepted by the fans at Ashton Gate because of his Rovers connections, but he overcame that with his performances. He had a memorable start with us because our opening League match of 1963/64 was against our local rivals Bristol Rovers at Ashton Gate. The last thing that you want on the opening day is a local derby. If you lose it, the season could not begin in a worse way. Fortunately, we won the game 3-0 in front of a 20,897 attendance with John Atyeo putting us ahead before half-time, Jantzen Derrick scoring after the interval, and Peter Hooper then getting one on his Bristol City debut against his former club. I later found out that the Chairman of the England Under-23 selection-committee, Lt Col CF Linnett, had attended the game to look at my performance with a view to my being included in the side that was to play Wales at Ashton Gate the following November. But I was never selected for the squad. As regards our win over Rovers, they certainly gained revenge in mid-December when we went to Eastville and were hammered 4-0! There was no doubting which area of Bristol was celebrating that day. We finished in fifth position that season, five points off the promotion-places that went to Coventry City and Crystal Palace, both on 60 points. Atyeo, Shadow and myself scored 59 League goals between us – John had 21, Shadow had 20 and I had 18. We were a settled side, with eleven players in the squad who each made over thirty League appearances. Our regular keeper now was Mike Gibson who had been signed from Shrewsbury Town in April 1963, and he had taken the place of Tony Cook who had been left out after three games of '63/64 and who did not appear again in the first team. Mike is still connected with the club to this day in a scouting capacity and I sometimes see him at Cardiff City matches at Ninian Park.

We reached the Fourth Round of the FA Cup that year and we went to Sunderland who were on their way to winning promotion from Division Two. We travelled by coach on the Friday – no motorways in those days – and it was bitterly cold in the North East. We stayed at Seaburn on the coast just outside Sunderland and on the Saturday morning we got the coach driver to take us down to Roker Park to get a feel of the place. When we arrived there, the pitch was being cleared of straw that had been keeping the frost off it. It was an impressive ground, they were an impressive team – too good for us and they were 6-1 winners in front of 46,000. Facing us was a giant of a centre-half called Charlie Hurley – he hardly gave us a look-in in front of goal. It was men against boys and they pummelled us into the ground. But it was great to play there, and made you realise how good you have got to be to play at a high level.

That experience against Sunderland was certainly something to discuss in the Robin Café just outside Ashton Gate. That was where we would go after training for a cup of tea and a sandwich, and generally put the football world to rights. If anyone was suspended in those days following a sending-off, which was rare, they would be out of action for a set number of weeks without pay. So on a Friday after we were paid, there would be a bowl in the middle of the table in the Robin Café and the rest of us would put in our contributions from our wages to help out our suspended colleague. If he was popular, there would be quite a sum in the bowl. But if he wasn't so popular, he would have to make do with whatever we felt inclined to give.

Having finished in fifth place in Division Three, we felt that we could improve enough in '64/65 to win promotion. That is what in fact happened, but it was a very close thing. John Atyeo was coming towards the end of his career, and he wanted to go out on a successful note. He had been at the club since 1951, had won promotion in 1955 but had gone down in 1960. We knew that obviously he would take some replacing when he finished, and the aim was to go up before he retired.

One major departure from the club at the end of 1963/64 was our long-serving goalkeeper Tony Cook who had lost his place to Mike Gibson. I was sorry to see Tony go – he was a typical Bristolian who had been at the club since the early 1950s after being signed from Downs League football. He was a real character – a terrible trainer, always at the rear of the group when we were running and always having a cigarette on our return to the ground. I got on well with him, and he would always make a point of shaking my hand after a game if I had scored. After leaving Ashton Gate, Tony saw out his career with Worcester and Cinderford before returning to Downs League football where he had started. When he became a Prison Officer at Horfield Gaol, I used to see him occasionally, as he lived not far from me in North Bristol.

The 1964/65 season began for us with a 5-2 defeat at Scunthorpe where I scored our two goals. Scoring didn't look to be a problem for us – the previous season, when we finished fifth, saw John Atyeo, Shadow Williams and myself scoring regularly. We were still together at the start of the new season, and though that opening-day result was a disappointment, we put it behind us with five wins and a draw from our next six matches. It was a great start to the season for me because by mid-September I had scored twelve goals from eight games in Division Three and was the League's top scorer. It was my best-ever start to a season since getting into the first team four years earlier. I couldn't do anything wrong – everything I hit seemed to go in.

But we could not maintain promotion form and by mid-February we were just an ordinary side in the top half of the table without suggesting that we could mount a serious promotion challenge. Shadow Williams lost his place in mid-October and only played a couple more games before going to Rotherham United in February 1965. It was in that month that our fortunes changed dramatically. On 13 February we beat our local rivals Bristol Rovers 2-1 at Ashton Gate with Terry Bush and myself scoring in front of a 23,052 crowd. Before the game Rovers were in third place, a point behind the two promotion positions that were occupied by the leaders Hull City and second-placed Gillingham.

We were ninth, seven points behind Rovers. That victory was the start of a run that saw us win twelve of our remaining fifteen matches, drawing two and losing just once!

We shot up the table but still had a great deal to do, and promotion was in the balance with three matches left. On Easter Monday 19 April, we set off by coach for an evening game at Shrewsbury Town knowing when we left that, even if we won, we were relying on other results to go our way. Most of our rivals were playing in the afternoon while we were at Ludlow for our pre-match meal. As we looked at the other results, they all went for us – we had to win at Shrewsbury, and then win our last two games, all three of them by a decisive margin. We did that all right – at Shrewsbury I scored in the first half and it was 1-1 at the interval. Then John Atyeo turned it on after half-time and scored four to give us a 5-1 victory. There was a great atmosphere coming back on the coach that night because we knew that if we won our last two matches – at home to Shrewsbury the following night and at home to Oldham on the Saturday – then we would go up.

The following evening we comfortably beat Shrewsbury 3-0 in the return at Ashton Gate with John Atyeo, Terry Bush and myself scoring in front of an excited 16,423 crowd. So it was all down to the final game against Oldham who included two of our former players – Alan Williams and Peter McCall. It turned out to be a very tense first half – we were edgy, the 28,251 crowd were nervous, and it looked like being 0-0 at the interval. But in first-half injury time, a Lou Peters shot looked to be going just wide at the Park End, and I got there just in time to score for my twenty-fourth League goal of the season. The crowd went wild, the tension was broken and we went in at the interval confident that we could now go on to win. Appropriately enough, it was our captain John Atyeo who clinched it for us with a superb shot at the Winterstoke Road End with seven minutes to go. We won 2-0 to go up in second place ahead of Mansfield Town on goal-average and one point behind the champions, Carlisle United. There were amazing scenes at the end – John was mobbed by the crowd and he was in tears, being overcome by the emotion of it all, especially as he had stated that he would be retiring. He remembered how, five years earlier when the club had gone down, Chairman Harry Dolman had given the team bottles of champagne on the day that the club was relegated as if to say 'don't worry, we'll be back'. John had played in the club's promotion of ten years earlier when they had comfortably won the title of the old Division Three (South) in 1954/55, but this particular promotion had meant a lot to him.

As we appeared in the Directors' Box in response to the thousands on the pitch, it was the highlight of my career with Bristol City. I was top scorer in a promotion season and I had come up through the ranks. Even Dad had not played in a Bristol City promotion team so the often-stated comparison between both of us could now be put to one side – he of course was delighted that his old club had gone up with his son as leading scorer.

After we left the ground, we all went home and it had been arranged that we would have a celebration party at the Mile Three Nightclub, which was on the A38 near Bristol Airport – it was a regular calling-in spot for us after good results. We were celebrating there together with a lot of Bristol City supporters in what was a great atmosphere when, all of a sudden, the Mile Three owner stopped the music and produced six bottles of champagne for the players which had been ordered for us by our manager Fred Ford. He and Chairman Harry Dolman were not with us – they had gone to a private celebration dinner with the Board before going on to the annual staff party of Bristol United Press at The Grand Hotel in the City Centre. It was a really good night at the Mile Three Club. Did we worry about drinking and driving in those days? Somehow it didn't seem to be so strict then, but as far as I was concerned, I was always sensible about it.

One absentee from the party was our skipper John Atyeo for whom it had been an emotional day. John was not a night-clubber, although he would have a post-match drink at the club. He was very much a family man, and not long after the win over Oldham and the post-match celebrations, he was in his car and off home to his wife and daughters in Dilton Marsh. He had stated his intention of retiring after a great career, but now that we were in the old Second Division, I wanted him to stay on and so did everyone else connected with Bristol City. So John had second thoughts and I'm sure that he fancied the challenge of one more season, especially at a higher level. He decided that he would give it a go, and everyone was delighted. He was then a part-timer, having nearly finished qualifying as a Mathematics and PE teacher at Redland Training College.

That night at the Mile Three Nightclub was not the end of the celebrations for our successful season. In mid-June 1965 the club held a Promotion Dinner and Dance at the Ashton Court Country Club. I still have amongst my memorabilia the autographed menu card which states that the beef for the Dinner was kindly donated by one of the Directors, Mr Lionel Smart, who was a Somerset farmer. And in mid-August the Supporters Club held a similar function at Bristol's Top Rank Ballroom – that menu card, which I also still have, says that the post-meal cigarettes were donated by W.D. and H.O. Wills, John Player & Sons, and Gallaher Ltd – all well-known Bristol firms. I can't imagine today's players being seen smoking in public like ours did that evening!

There was one major change in the appearance of Ashton Gate in that summer of 1965 – the old floodlights on the numerous forty-foot red poles around the pitch were removed and sold to Burton Albion. They had been installed in 1953 by Harry Dolman's firm to Harry's own design and I well remember having to paint them with the other ground staff lads at the end of a season, using red oxide to prevent rust. They had been innovative when they were first erected, but the problem with them was that you lost sight of the ball when the goalkeeper cleared high into the air. They were replaced with four massive pylons, one at each corner of the ground, and the new lights were a major improvement.

That summer saw me doing the usual strawberry harvesting at Axbridge with the Callows before I went off on a week's holiday to Guernsey. Although our terms at the club were improved, it wasn't great money so the opportunity to earn a few extra bob in an enjoyable way was quite welcome. I was informed in the usual way that I was being retained by the club – a recorded delivery letter saying that my services would be required for a further year, and stating the terms that were being offered. You were just relieved that they wanted you so I was quite happy.

My first season in what was the original Second Division (1965/66) was quite satisfactory from my point of view. I got 15 League goals, John Atyeo was top scorer with 19 in the League. We finished fifth in the Division, three points behind second-placed Southampton who went up with Manchester City. Our home record let us down with 10 draws in the twenty-one League matches at Ashton Gate. It's all 'if and buts', because a few more home wins would have seen us gain a second consecutive promotion – I wonder if John Atyeo would have given it another shot playing at top level. We had a very settled side with five players making forty or more League appearances while another three made over thirty. I was one of three ever-presents along with goalkeeper Mike Gibson and wing half Gordon Low. The bigger games obviously attracted bigger crowds and when we played promotion challengers Wolves at home on 28 December 1965, losing 1-0, there were 36,183 at Ashton Gate when the new floodlights, which had been put up during the previous months, were used for the first time. It was the biggest attendance in front of which I'd played at the ground during my career with the club. With so many people trying to get on to the standing terraces, many fans could not get in. I could see a lot of people on the roof of Southbow House, the block of council flats that had been built behind the side of the ground opposite the main stand. Apparently they had paid the caretaker as much as £1 to get up there – the normal admission price to the ground was five shillings (25p)!

It was in mid-October 1965 that I took part in a memorable occasion at Fratton Park, Portsmouth. Their long-serving former England half back Jimmy Dickinson had a Testimonial Match in which his club Portsmouth played the FA Cup holders West Ham United. As a curtain-raiser to the game, there was a twenty-minute each-way match between a Portsmouth Championship Eleven, consisting of players who had been in Pompey's First Division title-winning sides of 1948/49 and 1949/50, and an Old England International Eleven.

Jimmy Dickinson had sent out invitations to the former England players including John Atyeo who said that he would appear. On the morning of the game, Wednesday, 20 October

1965, I was at home as we had a day off, and I had a telephone call from Fred Ford telling me that John Atyeo wasn't well and couldn't play at Portsmouth that night. Fred had been asked by Portsmouth if he could supply a forward to play, so he asked me. He said that if the other England players turned up I would be with some great names in that pre-match game. I asked who was playing, and he said that Stanley Matthews, Nat Lofthouse and Tom Finney would be in the forward line with me, while Billy Wright would be in defence, and Gil Merrick in goal – all of them legendary names in the game.

I didn't need asking twice, so Fred drove me down to Portsmouth. I was somewhat overawed at the thought of playing with these great names, after all I was only 22, playing in Second Division football, and they had been great England stars at top level in their day. What would I say to Stanley Matthews and Co in the dressing room?

There was a big crowd at Fratton Park for that Testimonial, and I was only glad that I wasn't being marked by Jimmy Scoular, one of Portsmouth's great names of the late 1940s, but for some reason he was not there that night. When I reached the dressing room, Stan Matthews was very welcoming. I was playing inside him, and asked what he wanted me to do. He said that I should win the ball, just pass it to him, he would do the rest, and I should then get into the penalty area as quickly as possible. Nat Lofthouse was a little quiet and didn't say much to me, but Tom Finney was great – he shook me by the hand and thanked me for deputising for John Atyeo. I still have the match brochure signed by the three of them. Fred Ford also played in the game as a defender since our side were one short – he didn't do too badly considering his age.

So our forward line was Matthews, Clark, Lofthouse and Finney – not a bad bunch of names, and I wonder what they would be worth today? As for that pre-testimonial game, there were a few goals and I scored one of them, laid on by Stan Matthews who got round his opposing full back and pulled the ball back from the bye-line for me to score. It was just like he had done in the 1953 FA Cup Final when he laid on the winning goal for Blackpool against Bolton in his side's 4-3 victory against Nat Lofthouse's team. I had seen that match at Wembley with Dad, as well as the Final of the following year when Tom Finney's Preston had lost to West Bromwich Albion. And now here I was on the same pitch and in the same line-up as these star names! It was a great night with a post-match reception after the main game. Fred Ford and I didn't stay too long because we had to get back to Bristol, and on the way home I thought how lucky I had been to have had the experience of playing alongside those famous England Internationals.

The one game that stood out that season, as far as Bristol City were concerned, was our final match on 10 May when we played Ipswich Town at Ashton Gate. John Atyeo had decided that there would be no going back this time on his decision to retire so it was the very last game of his career. Both teams formed an avenue by the players' tunnel to applaud John onto the pitch and of course he received a tremendous ovation from the 13,893 crowd. He duly obliged by scoring twice in our 4-1 win to take his League and Cup total for the club to 350.

I was now twenty-three years old, I had come up through the ranks, been top scorer in our promotion side, and established myself at Second Division level. You could say that I was in a comfort zone – doing well on the pitch, a happy family life at home with my parents, and a steady relationship with Gill who was well settled in Bristol with her nursing career at the Infirmary. I still had yet to reach my peak as a player, and certainly had no thoughts of moving on from Bristol City.

In that May of 1966 came my first experience of an end-of-season tour. We flew from Bristol Airport, then known as Lulsgate, on 21 May to Dublin and spent five days in Ireland, playing matches against Waterford drawing 2-2, and against Drumcondra, winning 6-2. Ireland was a great place and I thought once again how lucky I was to be able to travel at the club's expense.

During that trip to Ireland, we were staying on the coast in a great hotel overlooking a big expanse of beach. There were about eighteen players in the party plus our manager Fred Ford, trainer Les Bardsley and two of our directors – Lionel Smart and Graham Whittock who was a close friend of John Atyeo. We were all walking along the beach soon after we arrived there and the water was freezing cold. John said that he wouldn't like to be in the water, but Graham said that he would go in for a tenner as a bet if we all clubbed together. We all agreed, so he stripped off completely – not a pretty sight – and in he went! John Atyeo and Alec Briggs then grabbed his clothes and we all hurried back to the hotel with Graham yelling at us from the sea. It was a sunny day with a nip in the air, and we all thought it hilarious to see Graham in the water with no way of coming out as he had nothing to put on. We could see him from the hotel bar and eventually Fred Ford decided that he had better take Graham a bath-robe. I suppose Fred felt that, as manager, he had better see that one of his directors was alright. To be fair, Graham was great about it and saw the funny side. He didn't get his tenner, but we all had a good laugh about it and the whole episode showed what good spirit there was in the club – you could not have imagined anything like that happening six years earlier in the Peter Doherty time of the 'split-camp' situation.

It was a good time for English football that summer with England winning the World Cup, and I was lucky enough to see Uruguay play France at the White City Stadium in West London – it was the only game for which I could get a ticket in those 1966 Finals.

There was also another change at Ashton Gate with the old 'cowshed' stand opposite the main stand being demolished for safety reasons. It was over sixty years old and I was sorry to see it go with its memories of ground staff lads' card schools underneath it.

I was worried about the 1966/67 season coming up – John Atyeo was gone, and if any one player epitomised a club, then it was Big John with Bristol City. He had been a major part of the team for fifteen years, a prolific goalscorer and an England International. He had been so loyal to Bristol City when he could easily have gone to play for a top-level club and he was an inspiration to us all. Whenever we played away from home, as we came out of the ground to get on our coach, numerous autograph hunters would gather round him and he would oblige them all. He was well respected by everyone – mind you, he had a temper on him at times! He had said to Chairman Harry Dolman that he would like to become a Director of the club after his playing days, but that never happened. Perhaps Harry did not have enough influence on the Board in the later years of his connections with the club. Although John was offered a place on the Board a number of years later, they wanted him to invest money into the club, but he didn't feel he should be given those conditions.

So John went off to begin a teaching career at Kingdown School in Warminster not far from his Dilton Marsh home, and I rarely saw him after that. He did return to attend his Testimonial against Leeds United in October 1966 and would come back for the occasional former players' reunions. He would watch Swindon Town and later Bristol City, but his life was in teaching, though he still keenly followed Bristol City's progress through the press and media. He went on to become a housemaster at his school and was Head of the Maths and PE Department. In early 1993 I had heard that John had undergone a heart bypass operation, and I was shocked to hear of his death in early June that year at the age of 61. By that time I had been retired as a player some fourteen years and I went to his funeral in Warminster. There were numerous former Bristol City players present from John's many years with the club. His coffin had red and white flowers on it, and while I would not describe myself as a particularly emotional person, when the organist quietly played 'The Red Red Robin' as the cortege left the church, I was overcome, especially with all the memories that came flooding back – I'm sure that it was the same for many of the lads.

3

A NORTHERN EXPERIENCE

I think the management at Bristol City thought that I would be a natural successor to John going into 1966/67. Perhaps they didn't realise what an influence John had been in the dressing room, and I was surprised that they hadn't gone out to sign an established big-name forward. It was clearly the end of an era at Ashton Gate, and the new one started badly. It began with Terry Bush and myself playing up front and we lost the first four games. In fact we lost seven of the first ten, with only one win and two draws. My goals dried up and I scored just once in that spell when we lost 2-1 at Crystal Palace in late August. Confidence all round was at a low ebb, Fred Ford our manager was under pressure, and something had to be done. The atmosphere in the dressing room was a nightmare, nobody could lift it at all. It was as if we had half expected it to happen following John Atyeo's departure.

On 8 October 1966, we beat Norwich City 1-0 at Ashton Gate with a goal from Gerry Sharpe and it turned out to be my final League appearance for Bristol City – Fred Ford dropped me and I could have no complaints, disappointed though I was. You always hope that things are going to improve in your next game, but it wasn't going to happen for me at Ashton Gate – the spark had gone. There had been talk of me going to Swindon Town several weeks earlier, but as they were our West Country rivals Fred didn't want me to go there. Perhaps he thought that if I regained my goal-scoring form, it might to be too near Bristol City's doorstep. But events were going on behind the scenes and Fred Ford wanted to sign midfield player Johnny Quigley from Huddersfield Town. Apparently the Yorkshire club had been in talks with Bristol City for several weeks, and their manager Tom Johnston came to see me score twice in our Football Combination 4-0 reserve win at Brentford in mid-October. A few days later Fred called me into his office and told me that the deal would involve me joining Huddersfield in part exchange. I often wonder why I joined Huddersfield – it all happened so quickly as far as I was concerned. Fred said that he would like me to go and meet Tom Johnston – I went up there by train that night, and he met me at Sheffield Midland Station. He took me to a hotel in Huddersfield and we talked terms. The money was more than I was on at Bristol City, he told me that he was looking for a big striker and that I had played well against them in the two matches the previous season and at the start of this current one, so I duly signed for them.

Dad thought that it was right for my career at that time – I had never left home before and I was now twenty-three. Gill had left the decision up to me after we had discussed it together, and she said that she would get a nursing post in Huddersfield.

I wasn't the only Clark departure from Bristol City because not long afterwards my sister Cherry also went. She had been a keen supporter of the club and went to matches with our cousin Vicky Pleass. They always watched from the terraces and were always after me to arrange for them to meet the players. Cherry married a Bristol boy and moved down to Cornwall before ending up in Torquay. She transferred her allegiance to Torquay United and is still a season ticket holder at Plainmoor with her second husband Martin – I have a standing joke with them that they are the only two season ticket holders there!

Going to Huddersfield was rather like having to do National Service, that spell in the Forces that all young men had to undergo for more than a decade after the Second World War. I had been spoilt at home – I had all my mates, my Mum looked after me, my laundry was always done, my food was always on the table when I came in. So I had never really had to look after myself. But I felt that at this stage in my life, I had to become independent and stand on my own two feet. So that was the reason I decided to leave Bristol City and go North. I went back to Ashton Gate after signing for Huddersfield and collected my boots. No big fuss was made about my going – one moment I was there, and the next I was gone. Of course I was sad to leave because the club had been a major part of my life since I had been a small boy watching Dad play for them.

I drove up to Huddersfield and moved into lodgings with Mr and Mrs Wallace at 123 Bradley Road, just a mile from Huddersfield's Leeds Road ground. Their son Bobby was a Huddersfield player who was later with Halifax, so they understood the needs of a professional player. The Wallaces were lovely people and made me very welcome. Mrs Wallace's cooking was superb, and I can still see her Yorkshire puddings and her stews! I was very homesick at first, but I used to go with the other players to watch other clubs in the area, particularly Leeds United if we were not playing. Leeds were approaching their peak under Don Revie and it was great to watch them. I was also able to watch Rugby League; that was very strong in the area, and I also went on several occasions to Batley Variety Club, a big-name entertainment venue in those days, to see such stars as Tom Jones, Shirley Bassey and Dave Allen. So I gradually settled down in West Yorkshire and as the months went on, it wasn't so bad.

I made my Huddersfield debut on 29 October 1966 in a 4-2 defeat at Rotherham and scored one of our goals. In the Rotherham side was my former Bristol City colleague Shadow Williams. We had a chat after the game and he told me that I had made the right decision in leaving Ashton Gate – I had been there long enough, he said, and needed to move on for the sake of my career. I got on well with the Huddersfield lads and used to play golf regularly with fellow forward Steve Smith after training. My other golfing partners included Trevor Cherry, later to join Leeds, and Bobby Wallace in whose family home I lived. I had been playing golf since I was 17 when I was living in Bristol. There was no football on Sundays in those years so it was a case of finding something to do. Four of us used to go to Bath early on Sunday mornings to play on the public pitch-and-putt course. There was myself, Paul Lydiard, Pete Ostler and Dick Britton who was from Shirehampton and whose family had a sports shop in Sea Mills. I developed such a liking for my golf that Paul Lydiard and I joined Shirehampton Golf Club where Dick was a member. Paul, Pete and Dick were all Bristol City fans and I would always try and get them spare tickets for matches. I quite liked the discipline involved in golf so it became a passion of mine and I am still a keen player, even more so in retirement, having been a member of Whitchurch Golf Club since 1975 when we returned to Cardiff.

Another big mate of mine at Huddersfield Town was winger Brian Hill – many years later when I was on holiday near Bournemouth with Gill, we passed a couple on the front at Sandbanks. I was sure that it was Hilly, I shouted to him and we fell on each other like long-lost brothers.

In those first few months with Huddersfield, there was not much opportunity to get home after a match because we were usually in for training on a Monday morning. In any event it was a long drive back to Bristol in those days before the Motorway system had been completed.

In January 1967, a few months after my move, Gill managed to get a transfer to Huddersfield Royal Infirmary, and we were now both living in digs in an unfamiliar place. In early March I was told that Cardiff City had made a £12,000 offer for me, and it had been accepted. Gill and I thought about the move, but I turned it down as she had not long been in her new job. When we had been in Bristol, we had both lived in a comfort zone with our respective jobs and friends. Even though we had become engaged, there had seemed no urgency about getting married. But now that we had moved away from Bristol, we decided to go ahead and the wedding was set for 10 June 1967.

My first season at Huddersfield went quite well. We finished sixth in Division Two and I scored eight goals in twenty-three League and Cup matches. Two of my goals came in our 3-1 win at Millwall on 18 March 1967 when, on the morning of the game, we went sightseeing in London and went up the Post Office Tower. Prime Minister Harold Wilson came to the game. He was Huddersfield born and a lifelong supporter of the club. He came into the dressing room before the match and shook hands with us all. I remember him saying to me that I didn't sound like a Yorkshireman. I told him that I was from Bristol and he wished me all the best. I'm glad that my goals sent him back to Downing Street in a happy frame of mind.

There was much to look forward to in the summer of 1967 – our marriage and a move into a two bedroom club house at 21, Wheatfield Avenue, Oakes, in Outlane about half a mile from Gill's hospital where she was an operating theatre sister and well settled in her post. The house had been occupied by Chris Balderstone who had left the club to join Carlisle United. Chris was a dual professional at football and cricket (he played for Yorkshire in the County Championship) and he later became a well-known umpire.

Gill and I were duly married in Great Gaddesden near Hemel Hempstead where she originally came from. It was a big occasion and Bobby Wallace came down for the wedding. My Best Man was Neil Trimble, an old friend of mine from Bristol. I had coached his team Bristol Crusaders on a Wednesday night for a number of years before my move North. Also at the wedding were the Callow family from Axbridge where I had happy memories of helping out with the strawberry harvest in the summer months. We had a five-day honeymoon in Cornwall and then it was back to Huddersfield and the club house which we had been furnishing over the previous few months. Mum and Dad were pleased that I'd got married because I'd had to make my own decisions about domestic matters and was now running my own life.

But as often happens, when everything seems to be going right, there is often a spanner in the works! Hudderfield went on a pre-season tour of Holland and Germany in July/August 1967. My pre-season was going well and I felt really good. Our Coach was the former Manchester United full back Ian Greaves with whom I got on really well because he understood what it had been like for me to leave my home-town club and go elsewhere. But then in one of the games, our winger Mike Hellawell crossed a great ball right on to my head. As I rocketed it into the net, the keeper caught me in the left eye with his fingers. It was a serious injury and I lost my sight for two weeks. When I came back from the tour, Gill met me at the ground and was very upset to see how my face was swollen and bruised. It was a worrying time and I went to see an eye specialist in Leeds. He told me that I had badly damaged the retina and that I was lucky not to have lost my sight in that eye permanently. He said that for the next few weeks I was to have no exertion, no training or playing, and that I had to sleep on my own – we'd only been married for two months!

It was early August 1967 and fortunately I made a good recovery as regards my sight, but not as far as my confidence on the pitch was concerned. Towards the end of the month, with my sight fully restored, I was back in training. Tom Johnston picked me for our sixth game of the season when we lost 2-0 at Blackpool and five days later I scored in our 2-2 home draw against Portsmouth. My fitness was not in question, but I was nervous about going in for goal-mouth challenges in the air. I was worried about heading the ball – would it affect my sight if I had a blow to the head? I had a nine match run in the side and scored three goals, but I was not the player that I had been, and following a 1-1 home draw against Preston on 28 October 1967, I was dropped and eventually only played one more first team game when I came on as substitute at Hull on 30 December. My place at centre forward was taken by Frank Worthington, a great character on and off the field, and when I see him occasionally on television, he may be older but he still has that same impish look about him. He could chase a ball on the field, and chase the opposite sex equally well off it when he went out in his Mini Cooper with full back Billy Legg. Frank was one of a number of Huddersfield players that I knew well – there was forward Tony Leighton, midfield player Jimmy Nicholson who had been with Manchester United, there was young defender Trevor Cherry who went on to become a big name with Leeds United.

After the manager dropped me, I carried on in the reserves. I don't think by now that he rated me. He was a strange man was Tom Johnston. He didn't seem to know any of our first names, and most of the work with the squad was done by Ian Greaves. By this time I had some good news on the domestic front – Gill was expecting our first child. It was a major consolation for me because my career was going nowhere and I was becoming more and more disillusioned. I wasn't doing much better in the reserves, though I did enjoy playing at the big grounds in the North as Huddersfield's second team were in the Central League with clubs such as Everton, Liverpool, the two Manchesters etc.

Around Christmas of 1967 I was seriously thinking of giving up professional football, going back to Bristol, getting a job outside the game, and playing amateur football just for enjoyment. Bristol City's Chairman Harry Dolman had said to me years earlier that if ever I wanted a job then I only had to contact him. But I had ideas of working as a sales representative for John Harvey, the Bristol Wine Merchants where Dad had spent ten years. Gill said that if that was what I wanted to do, she would be agreeable. I phoned Dad and told him my thoughts – he told me not to be so stupid!

4

RESCUED BY THE BLUEBIRDS

Whatever was to happen, Gill and I wanted to return to the West Country. Yorkshire people are lovely folk, but I think you have to be born and brought up there to be fully appreciated. I was really happier in my own part of the world and I was keen to get back there. Then something happened two hundred miles south at Ninian Park on Boxing Day 1967 when Cardiff City striker Bobby Brown seriously damaged his knee ligaments in their 3-0 home win over Aston Villa. It was an injury that finished his career, though I knew nothing about it at the time – but it was an injury that was to change my life.

January 1968 was going by, and I continued in Huddersfield's reserves. For weeks I had felt that, however well I played in the reserves, I was not going to get another first team opportunity. I had been on the transfer list at my own request for a couple of months, but nothing seemed to be happening until Saturday, 27 January, I played for the reserves at home to Leeds United in a 2-0 win – I didn't score but had a reasonable game. I don't know whether anyone from another club had been watching me, but on the following Friday, 2 February, we were training on the ash car park opposite the main stand at Leeds Road when Tom Johnston shouted across from the entrance 'Clarky, over here, I want a word with you'. I wondered what I had done wrong, or perhaps I was wanted for first team duty on the next day. But he told me that Jimmy Scoular had been on the phone from Cardiff City and wanted to sign me, and he said that he had agreed to sell me to Cardiff – the fee was £10,000. Tom Johnston knew that I wanted

76

to return south, and I was delighted with what he had told me. Cardiff were a mid-table Second Division side, they were in the Quarter-Finals of the European Cup-Winners' Cup, and Ninian Park was just forty-five miles from Bristol. Tom Johnston told me to go into the office and telephone Jimmy Scoular straight away. I contacted Jimmy immediately and we arranged to meet at seven o'clock that evening at the Severn Bridge Services – it was going to be a busy day for me to get there as arranged because Jimmy wanted to sign me in time to play for Cardiff at Derby the next day.

I collected my boots from the ground and by now the lads had finished training. They wished me all the best and told me to show Tom Johnston that I could still play. I rushed up to the hospital to tell Gill what was happening, and she was delighted. So off I set on the long drive down to Bristol, going over the moors before reaching Manchester – remember that the motorways were not continuous in those days.

I was glad to be leaving Huddersfield but I was sorry to be saying goodbye to a good set of lads. Looking back, my eighteen months in Yorkshire had seen me grow up and develop as a person, and now I was ready to handle whatever lay ahead in my career. So in a way, I was grateful for my time in the north – it was a good experience for me. But that eye injury, which did not affect the rest of my playing career, is something that I have to live with to this day. As the years have gone on, my sight in that eye is slowly deteriorating with age. I have had two operations since, both carried out at the BUPA hospital in Cambridge, but sometimes my vision is a little blurred.

As I drove on that long journey to Bristol in early February 1968, I thought of what lay ahead. Providing everything was in order with Jimmy Scoular that evening, I would be a Cardiff City player in the first team at Derby the next day and back in Football League action. I arrived at my parents' home in late afternoon, had something to eat, then Dad and I drove the short distance to the Severn Bridge Services where the stocky figure of Jimmy Scoular was waiting. He explained why he wanted me, he told me about Bobby Brown's injury and how he was looking for a big striker to replace him. I couldn't wait to sign, we agreed terms and it was a big weight off my mind to have joined Cardiff City. In fact I signed a contract that was blank in the wages section. I told Jimmy to fill it all in after the weekend – I just wanted to be registered in time. Jimmy told me to be on the train from Bristol to Sheffield the following morning and that he and the squad would be joining it at Cheltenham.

I came to know Bobby Brown very well – he was still at the club trying to attempt a come-back which didn't happen. He runs a pub and holiday caravan park in Pembrokshire and we still see each other occasionally. He always reminds me that had it not been for his injury, I would not have come to Cardiff where I still live. He often says that he would like to have played in attack with me, but it was not to be.

So just over twelve hours after I'd signed, I was joining up with the Cardiff players on the train to Derby and it was the first time that I had met John Toshack with whom I was to have a great scoring partnership over the next few seasons. I spent the journey chatting to the lads and getting to know about the club. Two of the team had signed at around the turn of the season – goalkeeper Fred Davies from Wolves in early January and winger Les Lea from Blackpool in mid-December. They told me the three of us would not be eligible for the European Cup-Winners' Cup Quarter-Final matches against Moscow Torpedo as we had not been signed within the required UEFA three-month qualification period.

It was to be the start of a near five-year memorable period of my career. My first impressions of Jimmy Scoular, against whom I had played five years earlier when I was with Bristol City and he was player/manager at Bradford Park Avenue, were of someone who was a pleasant character – away from a football pitch! But when he was on the bench, he would often rant and rave at his players or make the odd sarcastic remark, mainly through frustration. In one game when we were winning comfortably, I tried to make a back-heel pass not far from the dugout. I heard him say: 'If I'd wanted to sign a ✱✱✱✱✱✱ clown, then I'd have gone to Bertram Mills Circus'. I never tried it again!

He still wanted to be out there playing, but he made up for it in training. In his five-a-side matches, you went on until his team won, and if it was way past normal finishing time for training, you still played on! He treated a five-a-sides as if they were Scotland International matches, and every decision against his team was fiercely contested by him. Yet he was very protective of his players – he could criticise them, but nobody else could! We played Brian Clough's Derby County at Ninian Park in mid-November 1968, the season that they won the Second Division. It was a cracking match which we drew 1-1 after I had given us a second-half lead. Before the game Clough had made some controversial remarks about us in the Press to the effect that we couldn't play. In the end we were unlucky not to beat them, and as we went up the tunnel at the final whistle, Jimmy had Cloughie by the collar against the wall saying words to the effect of 'now say we can't play!' On another occasion after a poor home display by us, Gill and I went for a meal at a Cardiff restaurant. The head waiter came over and put a bottle of wine in an ice bucket at our table. I explained that I hadn't ordered it but he said 'That gentleman over there sent it with his compliments' – it was Jimmy who was there with his wife and some friends.

Going back to my first game for Cardiff City at Derby in February 1968, Dad came up to see the game with my Uncle Bill, and my debut could not have gone better. We faced a Derby County side on a mud heap of a Baseball Ground pitch, with Brian Clough in his first season as manager there. They were mid-table like ourselves, but were to go on to achieve great things under Clough and his assistant Peter Taylor, and their side was beginning to take shape. For the record, the two teams on my debut were:

BLUEBIRDS – Fred Davies; Gary Bell, Don Murray, Steve Derrett, Bobby Ferguson; Barrie Jones, Peter King, Malcolm Clarke, Les Lea; Brian Clark, John Toshack. Substitute – Leighton Phillips.

DERBY – Reg Matthews; Peter Daniel, Ron Webster, Roy McFarland, John Richardson; Gordon Hughes, Alan Durban, Arthur Stewart, Alan Hinton; John O'Hare, Kevin Hector.

Four minutes after the start, Barrie Jones floated a cross into the goal mouth and I got up to send a glancing header just inside the post – a goal on my debut, and there was even better to come in an all-action match. We were under pressure for most of the first half, but thirteen minutes before the interval, Peter King put us 2-0 up with one of his specials. Kingy was often to hit shots like that in the seasons that I played with him.

Jimmy Scoular was more than happy at half-time, but he was fuming in the dugout four minutes into the second half because Derby were level at 2-2 with two goals in a three minute spell. We should have regained the lead on the hour when we were awarded a penalty, but Don Murray's spot kick was brilliantly saved by Reg Matthews. With eight minutes left, Kingy scored for us again and we led 3-2. Derby threw everything at us in an effort to save a point, but with four minutes left, John Toshack turned the ball back for me to side-foot an easy goal for my second of the game. Derby's Welsh International and former Cardiff player Alan Durban scored in the last minute – but it was too late and we won 4-3.

I couldn't believe it – months out of first team football, two goals on my debut for my new club in an exciting win and the Toshack-Clark partnership had already begun to take off. My new teammates left the train at Cheltenham to get the Cardiff connection and I carried on to Bristol Temple Meads with instructions from Jimmy Scoular to report at Ninian Park for training the following Tuesday.

Dad met me at the station having driven back from Derby – he didn't give me too much praise but we both knew that everything had gone right, and even though it was only my first game for Cardiff City, it was obvious that it was the right move for me. I stayed with Mum and Dad overnight, and I was in a really happy frame of mind. When I woke up the next day, I was still so excited by everything that had happened that I went for a run in North Bristol that Sunday morning with the game at Derby still going through my mind.

It was to be the first of two spells with the club, and thirty-eight years after I ended my second period with Cardiff City, I still live in the Welsh capital where I have been happily settled with my family.

When I reported for training at Ninian Park on the Tuesday after we had won at Derby, I drove into the forecourt where the players' cars were parked. Everyone had modest vehicles in those days because we had what we could afford. I noticed a white Jaguar there, and thought that someone here is a bit of poser! You didn't see cars like that very often in those days, certainly not in Second Division club car parks! When I went in I found out that it belonged to our captain and former Everton player Brian Harris who was quite a character with his quick and incisive Merseyside wit. He was known as 'Hooky' – I don't know whether that was because of his nose or his bow legs. But that was what he had been called at Everton where he had spent twelve years as a professional, playing in nearly every position for them, and where you had to be strong to survive at a club where they could always afford to sign top quality players at large fees.

You could always rely on Brian during a match – he could read the game superbly, and Don Murray developed tremendously at the heart of our defence with Brian alongside him using his expert positional sense. And there were always occasions to make you laugh. I remember a game at Charlton where their player Harry Gregory said to his teammates in Brian's hearing 'Give me the ball and I'll run the old man!' Brian said to him 'You will, will you? We'll have a 'tenner' on it'. A few minutes later, Gregory went in to challenge Brian for a loose ball – Hooky held off for a fraction of a second, and the length of Gregory's thigh went along Hooky's studs. After five minutes treatment, Gregory was being carried off on a stretcher. Hooky strolled over to him and said 'By the way, that's a 'tenner' you owe me!'

In my first spell at Cardiff City, many supporters were kind enough to say that I was Jimmy Scoular's best signing. Older supporters whom I meet these days still say that. I have to say that I disagree with that opinion – he bought me to score goals and strengthen his attack and that is what I did. But as far as I'm concerned, Jimmy's best signing was Brian Harris, a superb organiser on the pitch, and great to be with on away trips and in the dressing room. Unfortunately for Brian, injuries such as thigh and groin strains were beginning to catch up with him, and over the next few seasons, apart from 1969/70, he missed quite a few matches. At the end of 1970/71, he became player-coach and then manager at Newport County but he could not get them as a club to maintain the high standards which he had always set, and he eventually resigned, returning to the game in the late 1970s as Coach at Cardiff City under manager Richie Morgan, his former teammate. Brian is now seventy, living in Chepstow, and I still see him from time to time when several of us from the late 1960s and early 1970s get together. When he is with us, that old spark returns and he is as humorous as ever.

The next few weeks after I had signed for Cardiff were busy ones off the pitch as Gill and I made arrangements to move into a house that Cardiff City had leased for us in the Whitchurch suburb of the city. Gill, who was by now seven months pregnant, was busy organising our new home, having resigned from her nursing position which she would resume ten years later. I had been given a choice by Jimmy Scoular when I joined the club – I could live in Bristol and travel over every day, or I could live in Cardiff. I decided on Cardiff because I wanted to be part of the community where the club was based, I wanted to be able to read the local paper and know what was going on in the area. In the few weeks after I joined the club I was staying with my parents in Bristol, but then Jimmy told me that a house in Coryton Drive, Whitchurch, was available. It was not far from where we now live, and it belonged to a couple who were working in Dar-es-Salaam on a long contract and would be away for several years. Their estate agent leased it to the club for any player who might need accommodation.

So we moved in, and our next door neighbours were Denis and Vera Munday. We met them the day we moved in, and Denis was delighted to have me as a neighbour as he was a Cardiff City season ticket holder, especially after I had a good start with the Bluebirds. Other neighbours included John Richards, another season ticket holder, and his wife Heather. John, who sadly died several years ago, was a fanatical City fan, and whenever we won on a Saturday, I would find a copy of the *Football Echo* in my letter box when I got home after a game. If we had lost, there would be no paper, and I wouldn't see him for a few days. Colin and Diane Patterson were also near neighbours – Colin wasn't a season-ticket holder but he used to go to matches regularly, so I had my own little 'Supporters Club' in that group of ten houses. We all eventually had children, and remained friendly over the years with our baby-sitting circle. They made us feel very welcome in Cardiff, and we have never forgotten it – in fact we remain friends with everyone to this day. I was glad that I was able to be supportive in return to Colin and Diane many years later when a police helicopter crash-landed on the roof of their house in Whitchurch. They were fortunate not to be injured, though they lost all their possessions.

My home debut at Ninian Park came a week after the Derby game. We played Preston and I scored in our 2-0 win with John Toshack also on target. In fact I had a great start with City, getting six goals in my first six League matches though I didn't score again in my remaining nine appearances that season. Because of my ineligibility for the European games, I sat and watched as Barrie Jones headed the only goal of the match in the home leg quarter-final against Moscow Torpedo on 6 March in front of just over 30,000 at Ninian Park. And I had to stay at home when the squad went off on a marathon trip to far-off Tashkent for the return game thirteen days later. It was played in Asia because Moscow was snowbound at the time and it took the squad several days to reach their destination via the Russian capital. I was told later that Jimmy Scoular, a patriotic Scot, had a major argument with the opposition officials in Tashkent about wanting to have a Welsh flag flown at the stadium. In the end he got his way – you didn't win an argument with Jim as I found out over the years.

It was a great performance by the boys who only lost 1-0 and in those days there was no extra time, no away goals rule, no penalty shoot-outs. So it meant a play-off in Augsburg, West Germany, and off went the squad again in early April without Fred Davies, Les Lea and myself. They did brilliantly to win 1-0 with a goal from Norman Dean who took my place in the team for those European matches, and it was a great night for young Richie Morgan who made his first team debut in place of Don Murray who missed the match through injury. But the real hero of the night was our goalkeeper Bob Wilson (not the Arsenal one) who had an inspired game and stopped everything that came his way. I could only feel a little bit envious on the team's return as they talked in the dressing room before morning training about their European experiences, though in the seasons ahead, I was to have plenty of my own.

Norman Dean had not been a regular that season, and from playing in the Combination with the reserves every week in front of a few hundred people, he was then taking my position for the European games and he reacted to it brilliantly. I was the first to congratulate him when the team returned from Augsburg and Hamburg following his goals – I have to admit that I wish it had been me scoring them.

That quarter-final victory over Moscow Torpedo had European football certainly talking about Cardiff City. Everyone was confident that we could reach the Final even though we had a difficult-looking semi-final against HSV Hamburg over two legs. They were a side that contained several players from West Germany's World Cup Final team against England just under two years earlier.

Once again I was left behind in late April 1968 as the squad went off to West Germany. Les Lea was now eligible and went with them, but Fred Davies and myself were still in the qualification period. Norman Dean again took my place and justified his inclusion by scoring to put us ahead in the first half. They equalised after half-time following tremendous pressure, and the lads did brilliantly to defend well and come away with a 1-1 draw. Could we now reach the Final by beating them in the return at Ninian Park? If we did it, then Fred and I would be eligible for the Final. We spoke together about it and the big question was would he select us if we came through the semi-final especially as we were regulars in our Second Division team.

I sat in the stand and watched on 1 May 1968 when just over 43,000 packed Ninian Park for the return against Hamburg. And who should put us ahead in the first half but none other than Norman Dean, his third goal in three consecutive European matches. Norman, who had been signed from Southampton in March 1967, certainly made his mark in those closing months of 1967/68.

Hamburg equalised through Franz-Josef Hoenig before half-time and took the lead in the second half with a goal from International Uwe Seeler which looped over Bob Wilson's head – a soft goal really, and one which looked like putting us out of the competition. But with not long to go, our skipper Brian Harris headed in an equaliser from a Barrie Jones free kick and it was 2-2. Hundreds of fans raced on to the pitch in celebration and there was a danger of the referee abandoning it. That goal was the only one that Brian Harris scored for the club in just over four and a half years at Ninian Park!

I was watching from the back of the stand and thought that we had got a draw. But with the referee looking at his watch, Hamburg's Hoenig ran from ten yards inside his own half with the ball, everyone seemed to back off him, and he hit a low shot from about twenty yards which spun off Bob Wilson's chest and over the goal line at the Canton End. It was the last but one kick of the game because as we kicked off to restart, the referee blew the final whistle and we were out of Europe. I went down to the dressing room and helped dispense the tea and sympathy. There were an awful lot of tears shed that night and there was silence in that dressing room amongst the players. Jimmy Scoular was disappointed with Bob and said a few unkind words to him. It was a bit unfair really because Bob had performed heroics in the previous European matches. Once Jimmy had left the dressing room, the lads were very supportive to Bob. It was sad because he never again played a first team match for the club, remaining with City for the next two seasons and eventually moving to Exeter City in the summer of 1970 after a loan spell with them from January 1970.

So the European dream was over and we went on to finish in mid-table in Division Two. But we won the Welsh Cup by beating Hereford United over two legs though I did not play in either match. I ended the season with six goals in fifteen League matches – not a great total but I was confident that there was better to come from me. At least I could look forward to European action the following season as we had qualified through our Welsh Cup win, but before that I was to have a trip of a lifetime with Cardiff City.

There were whispers around the club before the end of the 1967/68 season that we were to have a summer tour as a reward for the players' European achievements. Jimmy Scoular loved his trips abroad, especially if football was involved, and shortly before the final League game of the season, he put up a list of eighteen players who would be going on a Southern Hemisphere tour of fourteen matches in New Zealand, Australia and Tasmania. The opening match would be against New Caledonia in the island of Noumea off the north-east Australian coast on 28 May. The tour would continue in New Zealand, we would then move on to Melbourne before going to Tasmania, and we would then return to Australia for several matches before finishing in Perth, Western Australia on 7 July – so it would be a seven week tour with matches every few days.

I had mixed feelings about going on the trip because Gill was due to have our first child in the first week of July and I did not want to be absent for that. But as a professional footballer it was my job to go with the squad, and Gill understood that. We had club suits from a tailor in Canton. They were blue suits made of quite thick material, which seemed odd to us as it was coming up to summer, but of course in Australia it was their mid-winter. We had been invited to go there by the Australian Football Federation who footed the bill for everything. The squad took full advantage of their hospitality, and when several of the lads, including myself, get together these days at various functions, we often wonder if they are still paying for it!

In mid-June we were to play New South Wales in Sydney. It was a big game for Australian football, and the night before the match we were at a reception with our opponents. The waiters were constantly refilling our glasses and time was getting on. Brian Harris and Don Murray told us that Jimmy wanted the squad to go back to our hotel because he had found out that the Australian players had left two hours previously. It looked as if our hosts were making the most of their hospitality to us to ensure that we would not be in a fit state for the game! We drew that match 1-1, and Jimmy felt that they had pulled a fast one on us. So we made sure that for the remaining five games we were in bed at a reasonable time before those matches, all of which we won, including the two 'Test' matches against an Australian Eleven in Melbourne whom we beat 6-0 and in Sydney where we defeated them 3-1. If we had been out on hospitality on any evening, we made sure that we trained hard the next morning.

The lads who liked a drink would play five-a-side with the lads who didn't drink – at least not as much as the others. Brian Harris, Bobby Ferguson, Ronnie Bird and Barrie Jones were in what we called the 'grog' team, I was in the 'non grog' team. Our side would invariably go a few goals up, but as the 'grog' team sweated it out, they would catch up and overtake us.

Towards the end of the tour in mid-June, we played Queensland in Brisbane and won 7-2. The game was played in the afternoon, and there was a reception for both teams that evening. The hospitality was first class, and afterwards we were driven back to our hotel in the centre of Brisbane by several of the home team in four cars. Five of us were in the leading car, and I was in one of the following vehicles. At the drive-in entrance to the hotel was a water feature with a fountain. It looked very attractive, but it wasn't so good when the first car, which was travelling a little too fast, drove straight into it! The car came to rest in the middle of the water feature but fortunately none of our lads nor the driver were hurt. However, the only way they could get out was to step out up to their knees into the water feature and be soaked by the fountain. The rest of us found that hilarious and the consequences were to be seen during the remainder of the tour because the trousers of the thick blue club suits, which they were wearing, shrunk. At the remaining matches, the lads who had been in that car looked very odd because their trousers were almost at half mast!

We travelled in total some 35,000 miles from Cardiff and back again, played fourteen matches of which we won eleven drew two and lost just one. I was top scorer with fourteen goals, Ronnie Bird was behind me with nine. There was talk of an extra match following our final game of the tour – against Western Australia in Perth when we won 6-1. But we had all been living out of a suitcase for seven weeks and we wanted to get home, especially me. We had been flying long distances between matches and it emphasised how big Australia was. Thirty-eight years on, I would like to go back there with Gill, especially to Perth which I liked, and I did in fact go to Australia again several years later when I was with AFC Bournemouth.

That tour of 1968 brought us all close together, especially living, eating and drinking together for nearly two months, and it laid the basis for a great team spirit which saw us mount three successive promotion challenges over the next three years with a very settled squad. I roomed with full back Dave Carver and we still are very friendly all these years later even though he now lives near Great Yarmouth. The players who went on that trip are now long retired, but whenever we meet up, we exchange stories about that memorable tour to Australasia. Ronnie Bird was the life and soul of the party, his big mate was Barrie Jones – they were inseparable and remained close friends until Ronnie's untimely death in March 2005. As well as the players who went on the tour, there was also Jimmy Scoular's right-hand man Lew Clayton, our trainer/physio who was a bluff Yorkshireman who had played for Barnsley, Carlisle, Queens Park Rangers, Bournemouth and Swindon. He was very loyal to Jim and had been with him ever since the manager had originally come to Cardiff City four years earlier. Also on the trip was Club Director Viv Dewey, son of our Chairman Fred Dewey. Viv's wife was originally from Melbourne so it was an ideal opportunity for them to visit relatives. I got on well with Viv who was not much older than our players. Years later, when he had long severed his connections with Cardiff City, Gill and I were walking in West Wales when a car passed us going in the opposite direction. It turned round and came back, and Viv was the driver. We spent a pleasant time catching up on old memories.

But in early July 1968, I was desperate to come home from Australia. I was keeping in touch with Gill by telephone, she assured me that she was all right, and I was relieved that Mum and Dad had come over from Bristol to stay with her at our home. A couple of days after our final game on 7 July, we set off for home on a twenty-one hour flight that couldn't go quickly enough for me. As soon as we landed at Heathrow in mid-afternoon of 10 July, I telephoned home but there was no news of the baby's arrival. A coach was waiting to take us down the M4 to Cardiff and as soon as I got off at Ninian Park, I got a lift home to Whitchurch. It was now coming up to mid-evening and I was jet-lagged. There was an emotional reunion with Gill and my parents who then headed home to Bristol. Dad had to get back to work – the previous year he had left John Harvey and Co. after ten years with them, and had become Transport Manager at the British Aircraft Corporation in Filton where he had worked during the war. His job now was to organise all the travelling arrangements for everyone involved on the Concorde project, including the Chief Test Pilot Brian Trubshaw. And Dad was there in 1969 when Captain Trubshaw piloted Concorde on its British maiden flight.

So Gill and I were left on our own, and at 3.00 am on 11 July, Gill woke me from my deep sleep and said that I had better get her to the maternity hospital without delay! I hadn't driven for seven weeks, but I got the car out straight away. Before going to bed the previous night, I hadn't slept for two-and-a-half days, so when I got into the waiting room at the Glossop Terrace Maternity Unit, Gill went into the Delivery Room and I put four chairs together, borrowed a blanket and pillows from one of the nurses, and was out to the world. A few hours later, I was woken up by the unit sister who congratulated me on being the father of a little girl whom we called Alison Jayne.

When I had gone into that waiting room, I was the only person there. When I was awakened, the room was full of expectant fathers, several of whom were having to stand because I was occupying four chairs and stretched out asleep. They must have thought what sort of person is this, going to sleep while his wife is giving birth? They didn't know that I had just flown 12,000 miles! It was a great home-coming, though, very special and we have never forgotten that time.

Jimmy Scoular gave the tour party ten days off following our return home and I was able to be involved in parenthood and everything that went with it. One thing that I noticed on returning home was my increase in weight. I was usually around 12 stone and 12 pounds. But the hospitality on the tour had been so good that I was now 13 stone and 7 pounds, and quite a few of the other lads also had the same problem. It hadn't affected us during the tour matches because the standard had not been that high, and if we needed to, we could always extend ourselves to make sure that we won.

So our pre-season training began towards the end of July, and our first League match was scheduled for 10 August 1968. In retrospect, the tour was really two weeks too long and while we trained hard in what was left of the pre-season period, it was a lot to do to get fully fit for a hard Second Division season. We did not start too well – in fact we lost our opening three matches, two of them at home. On the opening day, Crystal Palace beat us 4-0 at Ninian Park in front of over 16,000 stunned fans and Jimmy Scoular threatened after the game to fine us and put senior professionals on the transfer list. Our Chairman Fred Dewey publicly stated that too many of us were stale after the arduous summer tour.

I hadn't scored in any of the games, the atmosphere at Ninian Park was not good, and in addition the baby was crying all night! But I couldn't tell Jimmy Scoular that – he certainly would not have been interested in our domestic problems. The Press were having a go at us, and you couldn't blame them with the start that we were having.

In those days the daily and Sunday nationals had staff men based in Cardiff covering South Wales football, while the main coverage came from Peter Jackson on the *South Wales Echo* and Clive Phillips on the *Western Mail*. Both were experienced football reporters and I got on well with them. They used to travel away with us on the team coach or by train, and if their reports criticised the team, Jimmy Scoular would often threaten to leave them behind – he could criticise the team, but nobody else could! Of course, they had a job to do, and though we did not like to read criticism of ourselves, we had to put up with it. I remember on occasion when we came back from the North or from London by train, and the *Football Echo* would be on sale as we stopped at Newport. If there was heavy criticism of us, Jimmy could give Peter Jackson an uncomfortable twelve miles until we got to Cardiff. Fortunately, over most of the four-and-a-half seasons of my first spell with Cardiff City, we didn't lose too often.

After losing those opening three games of '68/69, there was a dramatic change in our fortunes. We went to Bury and drew 3-3, I got my first goal of the season, Barrie Jones and Tosh got the others, and we then went on to win our next four games! There was a significant team alteration for that game at Bury. Gary Bell gained a place at left back after having made comparatively few appearances in his previous two-and-a-half years with the club since coming from West Midlands League football. Gary, who took over from Bobby Ferguson, was to retain the left back position for the remainder of his Cardiff City career before he eventually moved to Newport County in 1974. Gary had originally been a left winger, but didn't quite have the required pace at League level. Switching permanently to left back suited him ideally – he was quick in the tackle, could get forward in support of attacks and he had a great left foot. His crossing was tremendous, and a lot of the goals that Tosh and I scored over the next few seasons resulted from his accurate centres. I still see Gary regularly, in fact I sit next to him at Cardiff City home matches when we both act as commentary-summarisers on the club's internet broadcasts. It is surprising how many of our squad from the late '60s and early '70s have settled in Cardiff.

One consolation from those opening three defeats in August 1968 was that at least we were getting back to full match fitness – better late than never! My first opportunity of European Cup Winners' Cup football came in mid-September 1968 when we played the Portuguese side FC Porto in the First Round with the first leg at Ninian Park. Tosh gave us the lead midway through the first half, heading in a Barrie Jones cross, I then hit the post, and we went 2-0 up six minutes after the interval when Tosh was fouled in their penalty area. Ronnie Bird hit an unstoppable spot kick past their keeper Americo, and we looked well in control. But that only lasted for six minutes because their substitute Pinto scored twice in a three-minute spell. We protested that their winger had run the ball over the bye-line before crossing for Pinto to head the equaliser, but the referee would have none of it. Throughout the game they had tugged our shirts, obstructed us, and the referee had done nothing. He was from Spain, and the club complained to UEFA after the match about the appointment of a referee from the Iberian Peninsula – how could he have been truly impartial? Nevertheless, you cannot afford to give away a two goal lead against European opposition, and it was now going to be hard for us in Portugal.

Ten days after that game came a fixture to which I was particularly looking forward – the Severn Bridge derby against my old club Bristol City at Ashton Gate. I had played against them there for Huddersfield in December 1966 but now I was back to my best form, scoring goals and well settled in the Cardiff line-up. It was a strange feeling as our coach arrived at Ashton Gate – I knew the area and the ground so well from growing up there in football terms. I had a good reception, obviously there was some friendly 'stick' from the home fans, and it was a special day for me. Quite a few of the Bristol City side were former colleagues of mine – Mike Gibson, Alec Briggs, Jack Connor, Gordon Low, Jantzen Derrick – and while it wasn't in my mind to beat them because they were my old club, I just wanted to put on a good display and hope that we were successful. There was a 20,632 crowd there that afternoon including a lot of Cardiff fans, and we came away winning 3-0 win with great goals from Peter King, John Toshack and Barrie Jones. Dad was there to watch of course, and he must have had mixed feelings – obviously he wanted me to do well, but he wanted Bristol City to win. That victory established us in the top half of the table after eleven games and we were now settling down in the Division with the thought that we might be able to make a promotion challenge.

There was just time to spend a few hours with Mum and Dad back in Horfield because I had to be back in Cardiff on the Sunday to prepare for our return European game against FC Porto out in

Portugal. It was the first time that I had travelled with Cardiff City on a European fixture and it turned out to be an unfortunate experience for all of us. Brian Harris had been injured in the Bristol City game so couldn't play, and local boy Steve Derrett took his place.

We flew out on the Monday and when we arrived at our hotel, it was being partially re-constructed. There were builders' materials in the foyer, there was hammering and drilling, in fact it was mayhem. Jimmy Scoular was furious, and in a couple of hours we moved just down the road to a hotel where the Press and a few of our supporters were staying. As for our opponents, they were in a resort twenty miles away. They were a talented side and most of their players were Portuguese Internationals.

Apart from Steve Derrett coming in alongside Don Murray, we also included Graham Coldrick at right back while Ronnie Bird was left out, with Les Lea taking his place on the left. We were one down after eight minutes, Don Murray then had some lively exchanges with their goalscorer Djalma and was lectured by the referee who then went on to make a bewildering decision shortly afterwards when I was blatantly fouled in their penalty area. The referee rightly pointed to the spot, he was then surrounded by protesting Porto players, he consulted his linesman, and then awarded Porto a free kick! Tosh and I had problems because every time we attacked, the linesman put his flag up for offside. A few times we may have been offside but generally we were looking to make sure that we were onside. Jimmy kept having a go at the linesman but he continued to flag us and there was a feeling on the bench that they were out to get us! Jimmy told Graham Coldrick to run the ball up the line and kick the linesman as he went past him. 'Codgie', as Graham was popularly known, was quite used to dealing with the opposition, but he hesitated at having to deal with the match officials! So he didn't kick the linesman and Jimmy became more and more irate. We had a major problem seven minutes before half-time when Codgie was sent off for a foul, and that left us with a mountain to climb. Codgie was a Newport lad who had come up through the ranks at Ninian Park. He would have been a regular in the side but often suffered knee problems that hampered his career, and he was to join Newport County in March 1970.

So we had to battle on at the Estadio das Antas without Codgie in front of a hostile 60,000 crowd and we equalised early in the second half when Tosh headed in a Steve Derrett free kick. With thirteen minutes left, Pinto put his side 2-1 up on the night and 4-3 ahead on aggregate, but we still could have saved the game. Four minutes from time, Tosh was fouled by Pinto in their area, and this time the referee did award us a penalty. Tosh took it himself but their keeper Americo saved his effort and we went out. But despite what happened in the match, we really lost the tie at home by conceding that 2-0 lead.

The crowd were in an ugly mood despite Porto's win and I sensed that there might be trouble at the final whistle. The entrance to the dressing rooms was behind the bye-line down some steps, and I made sure that I was reasonably near to them at the end of the match. When the final whistle went, Portuguese fans came on and tried to attack our lads and management as they left the pitch. The police raced onto the pitch wielding batons and they weren't particular as to whom they hit. I was safely in the dressing room as the other lads came in and our substitute goalkeeper Bob Wilson was bleeding from a head wound. Don Murray had welts across his back from being hit with batons and most of the other players had bumps and bruises. If Tosh had scored that penalty and given us a 2-2 draw, which would have meant a play-off, I doubt whether we would have got out of there at all! As we left the ground, we were all on the floor of the coach with stones being thrown at it. We were glad to get back to the airport for our return flight to Cardiff – it was a frightening experience and those unhappy memories of that occasion still remain with me.

That experience and the result seemed to knock the stuffing out of us because we took only one point from our next four League matches. One of them was a 2-0 defeat at Millwall in mid-October when Brian Harris returned after a three match absence with a thigh strain. But he broke down again in that game against Millwall and this time was out until mid-March. Steve Derrett took his place alongside Don Murray at the back and did very well over the rest of the season, so much so that he won his first Senior Welsh Cap the following March.

It took an inspired tactical switch by Jimmy Scoular to change our fortunes from an ordinary mid-table side to promotion challengers. Following our 2-0 home defeat by Bolton in mid-October, he put Barrie Jones into a midfield role. Barrie had always been an orthodox outside right but tended to be out of the action for periods in a match. He was a very talented player, good on the ball, and switching him to midfield suited him ideally. He was always looking for the ball, using his skill and pace to good effect in order to create opportunities for Tosh and myself, and he could still get into wide positions to put in good crosses. Barrie was never going to win big tackles – he wasn't that strong. We would leave the heavy stuff in midfield to Mel Sutton. He didn't have Barrie's skill but Mel was a strong runner and would never let you down. He had come to Cardiff City from Aston Villa the previous season after being an amateur with them and in this '68/69 season Mel gained a regular place after the first couple of months. He looked an ungainly player, not a great passer of the ball but he could win it for the rest of us. He was always apprehensive of Jimmy Scoular and always seemed to look to the bench before making a move. Mel gave us good service up to the end of 1971/72 when he had a cartilage operation and Jimmy sold him to Wrexham for £15,000. It was one of Jimmy's rare mistakes because Mel did well at The Racecourse for the next eight years and made over 400 League and Cup appearances for them as well as having a spell as manager in the early 1980s. I don't think that Jimmy rated him as a good enough player to be part of a promotion challenging team. We as players rated him and he was a sad loss to us. He is now back in the printing industry where he started before joining Cardiff, and we very rarely see him, if at all. I was quite surprised when he eventually became manager at Wrexham and then Crewe because he was such a quiet lad – I couldn't imagine him being in charge of a playing squad and telling them what to do.

The first time that Barrie appeared in his new midfield role was in our 3-3 draw at Hull City on 26 October 1968 – Tosh got two goals and I got the other in what was a very good result against a side well placed in the top half of the table. It was the start of a great couple of months for both of us, regularly scoring either together or in alternate matches. That draw at Hull was the beginning of an eleven match run that saw us shoot up the table from fourteenth place to second position by the end of December. Three days before that Hull game Barrie Jones had been recalled to the Wales squad for the first time in four years and he came on as substitute at Ninian Park in the 1-0 home defeat against Italy in a World Cup qualifier. We were all delighted for Barrie, and his club and International careers had both been fully revived.

They were good times at Ninian Park, and if we were returning for training in the afternoons, we would go for a lunchtime snack in Canton to the Severn Grill which was opposite where Woolworths now is. We would have a cup of tea and a sandwich, and work out any possible match moves on the table with the salt and pepper pots. It was somewhere to go for an hour after training, because in those days the club did not lay on food for the players in the week as they do today. I have happy memories of those times with the lads in the Severn Grill.

In early December 1968 we gained our best win of the season up to that time with a 5-1 result at struggling Fulham, Tosh and myself amongst the scorers. I always liked London trips – we would meet on the Saturday morning at Cardiff General Station, it was not too long a journey to Paddington where we would have our pre-match meal at The Great Western Royal Hotel with a coach ready to take us to the game. It was always a bit of a rush to get back to Paddington for the 6.00 pm train to Cardiff, but on this occasion after that great win at Fulham we had no problems. We had an enjoyable dinner on the train and there was a feeling amongst us that we would be in the hunt for a promotion spot at the end of the season.

That Saturday when we won at Fulham was the Second Round of the FA Cup, and in those days the Draw for the Third Round onwards was made at Monday lunchtime on BBC Radio Two. We listened in the dressing room after training and were delighted when we came out with a home tie against Arsenal who were challenging for the League Championship. There was also good news around that time concerning our Manager – Jimmy Scoular had been offered the Ipswich Town job but turned it down to stay at Ninian Park. Ipswich then appointed Bobby Robson who, during his thirteen years in charge of them, took the club to one of the best periods in their history.

I was pleased that Jimmy was staying – he had signed me, and you always worry about your future as a player when a new boss comes in. Mind you, Jimmy could be a Jekyll and Hyde character. I well remember half-time in one game when we hadn't been doing very well. He laid into us all in the dressing room, in particular Tosh and myself '…Call yourselves strikers, you couldn't strike a ****** match! You've got a yellow streak down your backs as broad as the M4!'

I was so angry that I wanted to throw my cup of tea at him. Nothing more was said as we went out for the second half, and I was determined to make him eat his words. I'm sure that the same went for the rest of us. We played particularly well in the remainder of the game and we won. On reflection, I suppose that was the reaction that he wanted from us.

The form that we were showing, the anticipation of the FA Cup match against Arsenal and the decision of the Boss to stay with us brought a feeling of confidence and enthusiasm amongst our supporters. On 14 December, a week after that win over Fulham, we played Millwall at Ninian Park. We were fifth in the table, two points behind the leaders Derby County, while Millwall were third just a point behind Derby. It brought a crowd of 22,424 to the ground, the club's biggest League attendance in five seasons.

It had been cold overnight and the pitch had been very hard in the morning. As the temperature rose slightly, most of the pitch softened. But the area within twenty yards of the Grange End bye-line stayed hard because of the huge pitched roof over that end which prevented the sun from getting at it. I remember that both captains, after looking at it before the game, tossed up in the referee's room and just went through the motions on the pitch. We played towards the Canton End in the first half and our keeper Fred Davies wore rubbers in the Grange End goal. Millwall's keeper Bryan King wore ordinary studs at the Canton End, and had no problems. But he did not change to rubbers at half-time and with the temperature dropping on that mid-December afternoon, it was a fateful decision by him.

It was an exciting tense game between two promotion candidates neither of whom could break each other down for most of the game. We had most of the chances but just couldn't find a way through and with eleven minutes left it was still 0-0. We then had a free kick wide out on the right and defender Don Murray took it. He found Tosh on the far post, Tosh headed the ball across goal to me, I headed it back to him and his header found the net to put us 1-0 up. The crowd went wild and we were within sight of a vital win. I'd noticed that Bryan King had been slipping slightly when taking goal kicks or fee kicks at the Grange End. With a couple of minutes to go, he had another free kick on the edge of his six-yard box so I took a gamble and stood on the edge of the Millwall penalty area. As he took the kick, he slipped, and hit the ball straight at me at head height. I headed it back past him and we had won 2-0 to go into third place, one point behind leaders Derby. I doubt whether half of the 22,000 crowd saw it clearly – they were probably on their way out of the ground and would not have thought that anything would come from a free kick a few yards from goal.

Five years later, I was to join Millwall and was introduced to their players at The Den. Bryan King shook my hand, pulled me towards him and said 'If you ever mention that ****** goal you scored against me at Ninian Park, you and I will be enemies!' But he said it with a smile on his face and didn't really mean it – he hadn't forgotten that incident several years on.

There was no stopping us now and four days before Christmas 1968 we were 2-1 winners at Bolton who had long been Cardiff City's bogey side. It was our fifth consecutive League win, and after the match Peter Jackson of the *South Wales Echo* told us that we were the first Cardiff side to win at Bolton since 1952/53, sixteen years earlier.

When I had returned from the Australian tour the previous July, I had looked at our fixtures for the season ahead. Christmas period matches were my first concern, and though we were not playing on Christmas Day, we were to go to Aston Villa on Boxing Day. That wasn't too bad, I thought – training probably on Christmas Day morning, and travelling to Villa the following morning. On the Tuesday, two days before the game at Villa, Jimmy Scoular put up on the notice board a list of the squad to travel, and it said underneath that we would be training on Christmas Day afternoon before travelling to Stratford that evening and staying overnight. When I arrived home after training on Tuesday, I chose my moment carefully to say what our arrangements were – it did not go down too well! The same applied to the other lads who were married with families, and Jimmy Scoular was not too popular with the wives that Christmas! Looking back, I don't think that we needed to travel that afternoon – I feel he didn't trust us to do the right thing at home over food and drink as well as getting to bed in good time. But we were all good professionals and knew what was at stake.

So off we went to Stratford, and when we woke up at our hotel the following morning, there was a covering of snow on the ground. We phoned Villa Park and they said that they were clearing snow off the pitch and it would be all right when we got there. When we arrived at the ground, they'd cleared the snow but the pitch was extremely hard and icy in places. These days it would not have been playable. Villa at that time were going through a revival under Manager Tommy Docherty and were getting huge crowds. Tommy wanted to play the game, Jimmy didn't want to. I didn't hear the conversation between them but I would like to have listened to a 'discussion' between those two volatile Scotsmen. The referee had the final say and the game went ahead in front of a 41,296 attendance that included several thousand City fans. It was a day for brave men on that pitch – I'm afraid that Villa were braver than us and won 2-0 with goals from former Bluebird Barrie Hole and Brian Tiler.

It was a rare set-back for us at that time, and two days later we recovered to beat Hull City 3-0 at home in front of our biggest attendance of the season so far – 24,863. That was our last game of December 1968 and we were now second in the table, one point behind Derby County.

We now had seven days before the visit of Arsenal in the FA Cup and there was great anticipation amongst players and fans. It was an all-ticket game that was to be on *Match of the Day*. Tickets were sold out several days before, and Ninian Park was packed to capacity with a crowd of 55,136. When we came down the tunnel, all you could see on the Popular Bank were the heads of the crowd and people jammed solid against each other. Arsenal were third in the League Championship, were already through to the Final of the League Cup and their team was full of quality players. The teams for that game were:

CITY – Fred Davies, Dave Carver, Gary Bell, Mel Sutton, Don Murray, Steve Derrett, Barrie Jones, Brian Clark, Les Lea, John Toshack, Ronnie Bird. Sub – Peter King.

ARSENAL – Bob Wilson, Peter Storey, Bob McNab, Frank McLintock, Ian Ure, Peter Simpson, John Radford, George Graham, Bobby Gould, David Court, George Armstrong. Sub – Jimmy Robertson.

It was a tight match with very few goal-mouth opportunities and it finished 0-0. In my collection of memorabilia is a photo of Tosh and myself in aerial action being watched by Ian Ure and Peter Simpson who marked us both closely. It wasn't a great game, but it was great to be playing against such quality opposition.

I had never played at Highbury before, so I was very much looking forward to the replay three days later. We travelled to London on the morning of the game and checked into a West End hotel where we had a rest in the afternoon. The Arsenal Stadium was everything that I expected it to be – the famous marble entrance hall with the bronze bust of their legendary manager Herbert Chapman. I felt in awe of the place thinking about the quality of players who had appeared there over the years. There were 52,681 there that night and though we put up a brave display, with no score at half-time, we lost through two second half goals scored by George Armstrong and Bobby Gould who was later to become Wales team manager. It's amazing to think that the two matches against Arsenal attracted nearly 108,000! After the game we had a drink with the Arsenal lads in their players' lounge, and when they told us what crowd bonus they were on compared to ours, we couldn't believe it. They certainly lived in a different world to us.

I often talk about that night at Highbury to former Wales, Arsenal and Cardiff City forward Derek Tapscott who lives near me and who I have come to know well over the years. He spent five years in the 1950s with the North London club and he always tells me what a great club they are. I envy him having played for them.

It was in our next League game after the Arsenal Cup matches that we got into Jimmy Scoular's bad books. We were playing at Blackburn Rovers on the Saturday so we travelled on Friday to stay overnight at Southport. Jimmy always liked staying there whenever we were in Lancashire because Southport usually played their home matches on a Friday night and he could go and watch. We players could also go if we wanted to, but on this occasion Southport were playing Swindon the following day.

After dinner at the hotel that Friday we went for a stroll. As we passed a nearby pub, we saw the Swindon players inside. Why they were there I can't remember, but we went in to have a chat with them and had one or two soft drinks while a couple of others had no more than a half shandy. We had been in there for about forty minutes when their full back John Trollope said to us '…Lads, Jimmy Scoular is looking through the window!'

We panicked, got out through a rear entrance and went on a roundabout route beating a hasty retreat back to our hotel. Jimmy was sitting in the foyer with Lew Clayton but he just looked at us and never said a word. Kingy and Tosh hadn't come into the pub and were in bed as they should have been. Nothing was said about our pub visit the next day at breakfast, at the pre-match meal or in the dressing room at Blackburn before or after the match which we lost 1-0. But after training on the Monday, Lew said in the dressing room that Jimmy wanted to see us all individually in his office. He didn't half give each of us a dressing down – Ronnie

Bird was last in and he had a real go at Ronnie '....You, you little ******, you should have known better than any of them'! Jimmy was referring to the fact that they had been together at Bradford Park Avenue in the early 1960s and Ronnie would have known better than any of us how the Boss felt about discipline. The outcome was that for the next League game a fortnight later at home to Bristol City, Ronnie was the only one dropped!

A particular highlight for me in that 1968/69 season was that match against my old club Bristol City at Ninian Park on 25 January. We were now fourth, one point behind second-placed Charlton while Bristol City were two from bottom. When we had beaten them 3-0 at Ashton Gate earlier in the season, I hadn't scored. But as I drove from Whitchurch to Ninian Park for this return game, I was determined to do well and my mind was fully focused. I got there early to soak up the atmosphere, watched Bristol City arrive and had a quick greeting for my old teammates Mike Gibson, Alec Briggs, Jack Connor, Gordon Parr and Terry Bush. There were 26,235 fans to see us win 3-0. I got two first half goals and Peter King got our third midway through the second half. My second goal right on half-time at the Canton End was a shot from the edge of the penalty area that Mike Gibson tried hard to reach. He caught his hand on one of the hooks holding the net against the post and cut his finger badly. I should really have gone to have a look at him and expressed sympathy, but I was too busy celebrating.

The following week we were at top-of-the-table Derby County at The Baseball Ground where a full house 34,589 saw the game. They were looking favourites to win the Second Division title, and the former Tottenham and Scotland wing half Dave Mackay was proving an inspiration in their bid to go up. It was a great game, we played virtually all the good football, but they beat us 2-0. That defeat left us in fourth place, two points behind the second club Middlesbrough.

A week later we had a great chance of closing the gap. It had been virtually at freezing point throughout the country over the previous seven days, and by the Saturday morning most of the League's fixtures had been postponed. Our home game against bottom-of-the-table Oxford United looked in the balance on the Friday but Jimmy Scoular put out a Press appeal for supporters to come in on the Saturday morning to help with our pitch that was ice-bound and had a thin covering of snow. In the morning Jimmy sent someone into Canton to get as many hard sweeping brushes as possible, and everyone set to work on clearing the pitch, Jimmy in the forefront and having a go at anyone whom he thought was not pulling their weight. The referee was eventually satisfied and the game went ahead as one of only four League matches played that day, two of them in our Division.

Just over a month earlier, Jimmy had not wanted us to play in similar conditions at Aston Villa – now he wanted the game to go ahead while Oxford's manager Arthur Turner was not very happy about it. The *Match of the Day* production team rushed their outside broadcast unit to Ninian Park and they were rewarded with a fine performance from us. We won 5-0, Ronnie Bird scored our first before half-time, and Tosh and I got two each in the second half. Ronnie's goal was one of his specials – we were playing towards the Grange End when Tosh had the ball on our left. He turned and played it inside to Ronnie who went forward and hit a thirty yard effort that flew past Jim Barron in the Oxford goal. Captaining them was Ron Atkinson, known in his playing days as 'The Tank'. It was a game that he always remembered. Straight after the game I phoned Gill's father George to tell him that we were on *Match of the Day* and be sure to watch because Cardiff City were rarely on the programme. I didn't tell him that I got two goals!

That goal from Ronnie Bird was a typical effort from him. He liked to drift inside and get on the ball, though more often than not his shots were wide of the mark. But he got his fair share as a winger and a month later he came on as substitute in a Friday night home game against Norwich when we were 2-1 up and hit an absolute scorcher from a long range to give us a 3-1 win. Whenever he came on as substitute after that, the fans expected him to do it again – but he only did it once more as substitute during the remainder of his career with Cardiff City, though he did get quite a few goals when he was in the starting line-up. As long as Ronnie was involved with the twelve for a game, either from the start or as substitute, you would never hear him complain. In all the time that I played with him, the only occasion that I knew him to be really disappointed was when Jimmy didn't select him for the home game against Real Madrid in the European Cup Winners' Cup two years later because Real were his favourite team, apart from Cardiff City, and he desperately wanted to play against them. Ronnie was a good squad player, always in for a spell, then left out, and usually brought back in again. He knew Jimmy Scoular from their days together at Bradford Park Avenue, and knew better than to question Jimmy's decisions. You never won an argument with Jimmy – he was always right!

I discovered this after I was injured in a mid-February 1969 1-0 midweek home win over Blackpool when a 24,206 attendance saw John Toshack score the only goal of the match. I damaged my ankle ligaments early in the game when their defender Terry Alcock tackled me from behind. It was a free kick to us but I couldn't carry on so I went over to our dugout. We carried on with ten men for the next few minutes because Jimmy didn't want to put our substitute Leighton Phillips on if I was going to be all right. Our club Doctor – Leslie Hamilton who was City's Medical Officer for thirty-five years from 1965 until his untimely passing in 2000 – came down the tunnel to have a look at me, and said that he would give me a pain-killing injection. But I knew that the ankle was damaged and I didn't want to run the risk of aggravating the injury so I refused, and hobbled off to the dressing room to get changed.

I should not have driven the car home that night because my ankle was strapped and I was in pain. But I did, and during the night I was in extreme discomfort with my ankle swollen. Early the following morning, I drove down to the casualty unit at St David's Hospital in Cowbridge Road East. A specialist looked at my ankle and confirmed that I had ligament damage, so they immobilised it and I was put in plaster from ankle to just below the knee. I couldn't drive the car now, and I was on crutches. It was getting on for 9 o'clock in the morning so off I hobbled down Wellington Street, along Leckwith Road and down Sloper Road into the ground. It took me about forty-five minutes!

When I reached the Ninian Park treatment room, Jimmy Scoular and Lew Clayton were in there. Jimmy looked at the plaster and said 'What's that?' I felt like saying 'What do you think it is?' But he wasn't in the mood for back answers. I told him what had happened, and he said 'Take some Aspros'. He then said to come with him in his car and we would go back to St David's to get the plaster taken off. 'How can we treat your ankle', he said, 'if you've got plaster of Paris all over it?' He was right in a way because you couldn't treat it. The hospital had done what they would with anybody who had damaged their ankle ligaments. Within half an hour I was back at St David's casualty unit with Jimmy who ordered the sister in charge to get my plaster off. He had to sign a disclaimer and back we went to Ninian Park for treatment, with me now able to take my car from the hospital. A few hours later Jimmy told Les Lea, who was also having treatment for an ankle problem, and myself to drive down to Barry Island and paddle in the sea. Jimmy said to us 'If it's good enough for ******* racehorses, it's good enough for you.' It was February and it was freezing! Les and I spent an hour walking up and down in the water watched by a Press photographer, Brian Laister – Jimmy had told the Press that we would be going to Barry Island, and I still have the photos that they took that morning. It was very cold, so we had a cup of coffee in a café and went back to the ground. It eventually worked, and though I was out for a few weeks, I only missed one game which was a 3-1 defeat at Crystal Palace on March 1st, since the two matches immediately after the Blackpool match were postponed because of pitch conditions.

For the next few games after that defeat at Palace we kept up our promotion challenge, and when Ronnie Bird scored our winner in a 1-0 mid-March victory at Preston, we were in second place. My goals had now dried up because following the two I scored against Oxford in early February, I netted only once more in the League during the rest of that season. Ronnie was now competing for the left wing spot with Frank Sharp whom Jimmy had signed for £5,000 from Carlisle in late February and who made his debut in that defeat at Crystal Palace. But Frank did not make much of an impact during the remainder of the season.

All of us in the dressing room were pleased for Steve Derrett and John Toshack who made their Senior International debuts when Wales drew 1-1 against Germany in their World Cup Qualifier in Frankfurt towards the end of March. Barrie Jones was also in the side and scored the Welsh goal. But by that time we were starting to slip out of the promotion race and we could win only one of our final seven League matches. We ended in fifth place, nine points off promotion. If it hadn't been for that poor start and disappointing finish, I'm sure that we would have gone up with Derby instead of Crystal Palace. It was a good season for John Toshack – he scored 31 League and Cup goals and was top scorer in Division Two with 22. I scored 19 League and Cup goals so we had 50 between us. But for me it was a little bit disappointing because I felt that I should have had more, perhaps 26 or 27 – if I'd managed to get that total it might have made all the difference. One consolation was that we won the Welsh Cup again, beating Swansea Town, as they were then known, in the Final 3-1 away and 2-0 at home.

The Welsh Cup was always of importance to us because there was a place in the European Cup Winners' Cup if you won it. In getting to the Final that season, we won 3-0 at Aberystwyth, 6-0 at home to Bethesda and 2-0 at Chester in the semi-final. We were expected to win those games but they weren't easy. That game at Aberystwyth certainly wasn't easy. The journey to Aberystwyth from Cardiff is uncomfortable on a coach, the ground was packed to capacity with 5,000 people there all of whom, except our small band of travelling fans, were looking to see the Second Division promotion challengers beaten. The dressing rooms were small and it was certainly not what we were used to. Jimmy Scoular looked at the pitch that was somewhat uneven and he told us that it would be the bravest side that would win. He said that we had to get our tackles in early and show them who was in charge – if we didn't do that, he said, we could forget any thoughts of Europe. It was a game that we did well to win as we were without Don Murray and Brian Harris in defence because of injury. Richie Morgan and Steve Derrett played at the back and did a good job for us.

So we were in Europe once again and it had been an

encouraging season for us, especially for Tosh who had been attracting attention from other clubs with both Fulham and Leicester City making firm enquiries about him. He told us of their interest but we said not to consider them and wait until a big club came in for him. John was an intelligent lad who knew that he could be destined for higher things as his subsequent playing and managerial career proved. I felt that he often played better in home games than away where defenders would give us a hard time, especially at Norwich where Tosh and I always got a kick or two from their big central defenders Duncan Forbes and Dave Stringer. Having to battle it out wasn't part of Tosh's game – he was quite skilful on the ground, not a powerful header of the ball but very good in the air in terms of flicking on the ball or finding someone. He was good to play alongside because he had a good touch.

He improved even more during his time at Liverpool after he left Cardiff City.

If the 1968 close season tour Down Under had been too long and had its effect on our '68/69 start, Jimmy Scoular had learned his lesson. A couple of summers earlier, in 1967, he had gone with our trainer/physio Lew Clayton and skipper Brian Harris with a John Charles International squad to Mauritius. They'd had such a great time that Jimmy decided to go there again – this time with us. The 1969 end of season tour would last twenty-eight days from 9 May until 5 June and would involve two matches against Tanzania in Dar-es-Salaam, two matches against the island of Mauritius and three games against Zambia. During the period between matches we would be staying in luxury hotels, enjoying excursions, water sports and other activities in what promised to be a great trip. The big worry for the married lads in the squad was how to tell the other half that they were going on this tour. The same applied to me and I chose my moment carefully – as with the Australian trip, it did not go down too well! We could not have been with a better club as far as overseas travel was concerned. Although we were in the old Second Division, we had a good reputation because of our regular European involvement, and that led to us being wanted for summer tours to these various places. Travel, accommodation and hospitality was top class, and not even teams in the leading positions of the old First Division would have had it as good as we did with Cardiff City in those days.

The tour went well and we had some great experiences, especially some of the lads! In our second game against Tanzania in mid-May, both teams were presented to local dignitaries before the game. Our opponents were introduced first, and bringing up the rear of the presentation party was someone in a long black coat and hat – our opponents bowed solemnly to him as he shook their hands. We didn't take much notice until the group were introduced to us, and the man in the coat and hat was none other than our skipper Brian Harris who wasn't playing that day. Hooky had borrowed the gear off one of the bandsman! It was hilarious, and it was typical of the whole tour which was much more informal than the one to New Zealand, Tasmania and Australia twelve months earlier. On this African tour our main objective after matches was to get back to the hotel, get in the swimming pool and enjoy a few drinks. There were a few formal occasions, especially in Mauritius when Jimmy Scoular and Brian Harris went to meet the British High Commissioner for a luncheon in the company of the island's President, while a few days later we went to meet the Governor General for cocktails!

In one of those matches against Tanzania, four of their side wore no boots, just strapping around their ankles! They were brave men facing someone like Don Murray. The pitch was rock hard with very little grass and it certainly didn't suit me. Many of the spectators were watching the game perched in palm trees around the pitch! At their first corner, Gary Bell said to Brian Harris: 'Which one do I mark?' Brian replied: 'Pick up the black fellow' – they were all black!

There was only one spot of bother on that tour and it happened later that month in the second of our three matches against Zambia at the Dag Hammarskjoeld Stadium in Ndola. Before the game, which was played in front of a capacity 15,000, we were presented to Dr Kenneth Kaunda who was then President of Zambia. We had drawn the first game against them 1-1, and it was the best of three matches for the Northern Breweries Trophy given by the sponsors of those three Zambian matches. The game developed into a rough house and they had two players sent off. Their skipper Dick Chama went five minutes after the interval after laying out Leighton Phillips, and forward Godfrey Chitalu followed twenty minutes later for kicking Brian Harris. We weren't blameless but it was a case of reacting to their behaviour. At one stage Jimmy Scoular told us to come off the pitch – he was going to have the game abandoned, but wiser counsels prevailed and it was played to a finish, the match ending in a 2-1 victory for us with two goals from Sandy Allan, after they had led 1-0 at the interval. Their goal was a penalty following an alleged foul by Don Murray, one of a number of strange decisions made by the referee Mr Bennett Simfukwe. His performance was a factor in the way the game went and I still have a copy of the *Times of Zambia* newspaper in which local reporter Alfred Mulenga was very critical of both sides.

When we came back to Cardiff, we were all bronzed from the African sun – Ronnie Bird and Peter King were almost black! Once again that kind of trip made for great comradeship amongst us and we were really looking forward to the 1969/70 season with the aim of improving on the previous year's near promotion. I was a bit concerned about whether or not we were equipped to go up. I felt that the Directors weren't ambitious enough to allow Jimmy Scoular to add a bit more quality to the squad. I thought that we needed another experienced striker and midfield player. Why didn't Jimmy insist on what was required? I don't know – maybe he was a little apprehensive of the step up to top level where the gap in standard was so big. But that is only my opinion and maybe there were other reasons that he didn't force the issue. Finance was probably one of them because although we were getting crowds regularly of 20,000 and over, there didn't seem to be a great deal of money about in the club. We were treated well in terms of travel, hotels etc but Fred Dewey and his colleagues ran a very tight ship. Sometimes, however, you have to speculate to accumulate and they didn't seem prepared to do that. It was a pity really, because with the quality of players that we had, it would not have taken a great deal more to make us into really firm promotion candidates who could stay the course when it mattered in the final stages of the race.

There was not a large Board of Directors at Cardiff City – just four including Chairman Fred Dewey, his son Viv, George Edwards who had been a Wales International outside left with the club in his playing days, and local accountant Bob Williams. Fred Dewey had also been a Senior Wales International and an Amateur Cap though he had never turned professional. The club's Secretary was Graham Keenor whose Dad Fred had captained the Bluebirds in the 1927 FA Cup Final victory, and Graham's assistant was Lance Hayward who had given up his playing career with the club in the early '60s to become a permanent member of the administrative staff. Although we as players had regular dealings with Graham and Lance, we had very little to do with the Directors although we saw them regularly and one or more of them would travel with us on away games. European trips would see several of them come with us and we tended to mix a little more with them on those occasions. But they never came in the dressing room and we never went into the Boardroom except just prior to each Christmas when we would be invited up after training for sherry and to be presented with our Christmas turkeys from the club. I was reminded of that in December 2004 when ITV Wales did a documentary about past Christmases in South Wales. They found a piece of film in their archives from December 1969 showing us in the Boardroom receiving our birds. There was Jimmy Scoular and the Directors serving us with not too large glasses of sherry, and it was strange to see everyone as they were thirty-seven years ago. So that was a rare social meeting between the players and the Board – Jimmy tried to keep us at a distance from his Directors, he would deal with any problems that we had, and he would deal with the Board at their regular meetings.

In early August 1969 we acquired a new full-time member of staff in Cardiff-born Harry Parsons. He had been a part-time local scout for Jimmy Scoular over the previous few years while running the Cardiff Central Boys Club team in Grangetown. Harry, a former 'Desert Rat' in the Eighth Army under General

Montgomery in North Africa during the Second World War, knew the local Cardiff football scene very well, and his boys club team had produced players such as Terry Yorath who went to Leeds United and Frankie Prince who became captain of Bristol Rovers.

Jimmy Scoular persuaded Harry to give up his long-time job as a driver for a firm that delivered produce from growers in the South and West to Cardiff Fruit Market. I'd seen Harry around Ninian Park in the few years after I joined the club but I didn't get to know him really well until he joined us on a full-time basis. Harry was a real character and he was the only person that I ever met who could stand up to Jimmy Scoular with whom he had a very good relationship.

Jimmy could be very unpredictable and volatile at times as we discovered one Friday morning when we were playing five-a-side matches in the park opposite the ground. There were about three games going on, and in one of them our Coach Bill Harvey was in goal for Jimmy's side. Bill was also the time keeper for all three games. Bill and I went back a long way because he had been on the coaching staff at Bristol City when I had joined the ground staff at Ashton Gate. He later coached Swindon Town and had spells as manager of Luton and Grimsby. So we picked sides and no-one wanted to be on Jimmy's team because he played five-a-side matches as if they were the FA Cup Final – he wanted to win! Whoever was playing against Jimmy's five used to try that much harder because they knew how much it aggravated him if he lost. Bill Harvey was getting on in years and his legs had gone – he was nearly fifty at that time – so he went in goal between the cones that were being used as goal posts. Jimmy's game was very competitive, as always, and he was losing his rag if moves broke down. His team were leading by one goal and there wasn't long left, but then the opposition equalised. The ball went about twenty-five yards on after going between the posts, so Bill kicked a spare ball into play and went off to get the other one which was by the railings on Sloper Road. As he was coming back with the ball, the opposition scored into an empty goal to take the lead, and with that, Bill looked at his watch and blew for time. Jimmy went absolutely spare because he had lost, and started having a go at Bill who explained that he had gone to get the ball and could not be in two places at the same time. Things got heated and all the players looked on in amazement at such a trivial incident turning into 'World War Three' and being blown up out of all proportion. Jimmy in his temper told Bill Harvey to go back to the ground, pick up his cards and clear off! By the time we had returned to the dressing rooms, Bill had left the club. It was very sad, because Bill, who died in February 2002 at the age of eighty one, was a great guy and a very good coach – but that was Jimmy.

If we got beaten away from home, Jimmy would tend to be in a mood on the way back and didn't like to hear anyone being lighthearted. But Harry would break the ice and keep everyone happy. Harry's role around the dressing rooms covered everything – kit, the boot room, laundry, tea making, travelling with the first team and reserves. He was a father figure to the younger lads, and if you ever felt like getting something off your chest about Jimmy, then Harry would always be sympathetic. Harry was worth his weight in gold to the club over the thirty years that he was associated with Cardiff City until his retirement at the age of 76 in 1996. Whenever Dave Carver, Fred Davies and myself went back for extra training in the afternoons, we'd have a cup of tea with Harry who would always have a good story to tell us. Former players that I would come across would always ask how he was in retirement. Harry died aged 87 in April 2006 having lost none of his sharp wit. I visited him quite often in his retirement, and we always had a good chat about our days at Ninian Park together when his son John was on the playing staff. John was a prolific scorer at schools and then reserve team level, but he could not get a regular first team place in the early 1970s and eventually moved on to AFC Bournemouth and then Newport County. It was a proud moment for Harry and his wife Evelyn when John did make a goal scoring first team League debut for us in February 1971.

We could not have had a better opening day to the new 1969/70 season when we went to Carlisle United and were one up through John Toshack after just twenty-eight seconds! And we went on to win 3-2 with goals from Peter King and myself. Our pre-season had gone well after the African tour which had been short enough

1946 Nearly three years old and I was always out in the garden with Dad and a ball.

Mum, Dad, my sister Cherry and myself on holiday in Torquay in the early 1950s.

Early-May 1958, the Bristol Schools U-15 team that I captained to victory in the English Schools Trophy. Back row (left to right): Ted King (Manager), Adrian Williams, Dave Summers, Harry Booth, Jantzen Derrick, Terry Burt, Peter Prewett, AT Vokes (Chairman, Bristol Schools FA). Front row: Steve Poole, Dave Stone, Brian Clark (Captain), Colin Smith, Mal Thomas.

As a young professional (left), my main influences at Bristol City were Chairman Harry Dolman and Manager Fred Ford (right).

The old 'Cowshed' Stand at Ashton Gate with the ground's original floodlights. The groundstaff lads played cards under the stand and we had to put red oxide on the lighting-poles.

24 April 1965, Bristol City 2 Oldham 0. I score the opening goal in our promotion-clinching victory.

10 May 1966, Bristol City 4 Ipswich Town 1. The final appearance of John Atyeo after his long career. Back row (left to right): Jack Connor, Tony Ford, Gordon Parr, Mike Gibson, Alec Briggs, Gordon Low. Front row: Jantzen Derrick, Gerry Sharpe, Brian Clark, John Atyeo, Terry Bush, Danny Bartley.

June 1967, Gill and I are married at Great Gaddesden near Hemel Hempstead. My sister Cherry is on Gill's left.

30 September 1967, Huddersfield 2 Blackburn 1. I am on the right challenging for the ball.

Early July 1968 in Perth, Western Australia, on Cardiff City's summer tour. Les Lea, myself and Dave Carver getting our eye in for the forthcoming season.

7 December 1968, Fulham 1 Cardiff City 5. I head our equaliser past keeper Ian Seymour.

14 December 1968, Cardiff City 2 Millwall 0. I beat Barry Kitchener to head the ball to John Toshack (right).

Three great characters from my Cardiff City days: Manager Jimmy Scoular (left), Don Murray, and Brian Harris.

Late February 1969 at Barry Island with Les Lea trying to heal our injured ankles in the icy Bristol Channel.

4 January 1969 FA Cup Third Round, Cardiff City 0 Arsenal 0. Don Murray leads us out. I am behind him, followed by Barrie Jones, Dave Carver, Steve Derrett, Gary Bell and Ronnie Bird.

January 1969, Cardiff City v Arsenal. John Toshack and I are watched by Ian Ure (left) and Peter Simpson in front of a 55,136 Ninian Park crowd.

The old Grange End at Ninian Park. On a cold day the pitch was always hard under its shadow.

8 February 1969, Cardiff City 5 Oxford United 0. I score at the Canton End. Ron Atkinson is on my left and Tosh is in the middle.

May 1969 we arrive in Dar-es-Salaam at the start of our African tour. Back row (left to right): Leighton Phillips, Peter King, Fred Davies, Brian Harris, Frank Sharp, Don Murray, Richie Morgan, Jimmy Scoular (Manager), Dave Carver. Front row: Les Lea, Lew Clayton (Trainer/Physio), Gary Bell, Ronnie Bird, Brian Clark, Sandy Allan.

16 August 1969, Cardiff City 0 Blackburn Rovers 0. I battle it out with opponent Dick Mulvaney.

Late July 1970. Jimmy Scoular meets our new signing Ian Gibson from Coventry, one of the best midfielders that I ever played with.

10 March 1971, Cardiff City 1 Real Madrid 0. My goal which gave us a first-leg win over the Spaniards in the Cup Winners' Cup Quarter Final.

Scotch for a Scotsman – Jimmy Scoular was named Second Division Manager of the Month for March 1971. We didn't get a drop!

September 1971 the four of us – Gill, myself, Alison (left) and Jacqueline.

22 January 1972, Portsmouth 2 Cardiff City 0. I help out in defence at Fratton Park. Don Murray is on the left.

11 August 1973, AFC Bournemouth v Portsmouth in a pre-season friendly at Dean Court. A few weeks later I joined Millwall.

1 September 1973, Millwall 1 Aston Villa 1. My debut for the South London club.

In action against Villa's Chris Nicholl that day.

5 April 1975, West Bromwich Albion 2 Millwall 1. Nearing the end of my last season with Millwall as I beat Albion's Dave Rushbury (3).

13 March 1976, Cardiff City 1 Rotherham United 1. I am back with Cardiff City for 1975/76.

19 May 1976. In the dressing room with my Cardiff City colleagues after we had completed a 3-2 second leg home win over Hereford United to take the Welsh Cup on a 6-5 aggregate. It was my final appearance for The Bluebirds.

26 July 1976. New boys at Newport (from left) Ronnie Bird (Trainer/Coach), Mark Williams (ex-Arsenal), Gary Plumley (ex-Leicester), John Emanuel (ex-Bristol City), myself, Ron Walker (ex-Workington), Tony Villars (ex-Cardiff City), Steve Derrett (ex-Rotherham).

21 August 1976, Newport County 0 Stockport County 1. Roddy Jones (left) and I watch the Stockport keeper deny us.

17 May 1977, the Great Escape. Newport County 1 Workington 0. I'm in the net celebrating after Eddie Woods (left of post) scores the goal which took us to League safety.

2 November 2002 at Ninian Park. Old friends together again (from left) myself, Ronnie Bird, Gary Bell, John Toshack, Bobby Woodruff, Steve Derrett.

July 2006, Gill and myself with daughters Alison and Jacqui, son-in-law Gary, and grand daughters Lauren and Emily.

to give us several weeks rest when we got back in early June, and perhaps that had its effect in our first League match compared to what had happened the previous season.

Peter King, who played mainly in a left side midfield role, was to miss only three League games that season in which he scored ten League goals plus another seven in our various Cup matches. I wouldn't rate Kingy a great player, but he would run all day for you and always had a consistent match. He had been at Cardiff since coming from his home town club Worcester City, and gave Cardiff City fourteen years great service before an achilles tendon injury forced his retirement in 1974. Kingy was also a good cricketer and a good runner – long after his playing days, following which he became a Physical Training Instructor in the Prison Service, he was regularly taking part in marathons. Kingy and John Toshack were very good friends, they both roomed together on away trips and spent a lot of time together. Kingy was a very under rated player at Ninian Park, an unsung hero who perhaps never got the recognition that he deserved.

Tosh and I were very lucky to be playing in those days in front of three or four players, including Peter King, Les Lea, Barrie Jones and later Ian Gibson all of whom were capable of performing at a higher level.

Following that August 1969 opening day success at Carlisle, there was a very big mid-week attendance of 27,932 for our first home game of the season against newly-promoted Swindon Town who were also holders of the League Cup after their sensational 3-1 win over Arsenal at Wembley towards the end of the previous season. The Swindon visit meant that I met up with my old Bristol City manager Fred Ford who had recently taken over as their manager. He had left Ashton Gate in 1967 and had since been in charge at Bristol Rovers before going as Coach to Swindon where he then succeeded Danny Williams.

It was in that game against Swindon at Ninian Park, when we drew 2-2, when I played against their very strong central defender Frank Burrows, the first of a few encounters that we were to have in the late 1960s and early '70s. They were hard but fair battles – neither of us was particularly quick, but we were both strong and you had to be at your best to get the better of him. But in that match against Swindon he got the better of me because I didn't manage to score.

We didn't win in three matches including that Swindon game, but then we went to my old club Bristol City on 23 August. We had won there 3-0 the previous season but I hadn't scored on that occasion so I was determined to make up for it this time. We won 2-0 with two second half goals, I got the first and Ronnie Bird made sure with a penalty not long before the end.

That was the first of three consecutive victories which took us into second spot by late August. *Match of the Day* were now keeping an eye on our progress and when we played second-placed Leicester City in mid-September, we were in fourth spot and it looked like whoever won would go to the top of the table. There were almost 27,000 at Ninian Park for a tremendous game that had everything. We were one down at half-time after Dave Carver had put through his own goal, I had one disallowed before the break because the referee said that their keeper Peter Shilton had been obstructed, but eventually John Toshack equalised in the second half. Leicester's goal had numerous near misses and the game ended 1-1. Dave Carver took plenty of friendly 'stick' in the dressing room after that one – his first ever goal, at the wrong end, and in front of millions on *Match of the Day*. Dave was a big strong lad who had come from his home town club Rotherham United nearly four years earlier. Dave always gave you 110% and was totally reliable. He and I were very good friends and we were room mates on away trips. We both liked talking about the game, and after home matches we would get away from the ground quite quickly and go and have a quiet drink together with his next-door neighbour Peter Quick at the Discovery pub in the Cyncoed area of Cardiff. Long after our playing days, Dave and I still remain very friendly though we don't see each other very often. He has certainly had legacies from his playing career – two replacement hips and a replacement knee. He's probably no quicker now than he was as a player! Dave eventually became a pub landlord in Norwich and then near Cambridge, and now describes himself as a 'glass polisher'. When I asked him not so long ago what exactly was a glass polisher, he replied in that dry Yorkshire way of his 'I'm a window cleaner!'

Four days after that Leicester match, we were off to Europe again – this time to Norwegian club Mjondalen where we won our first leg Cup Winners' Cup First Round match 7-1, so the return at Ninian Park was a formality and we again beat them decisively 5-1 with a hat-trick from Sandy Allan. He was a Scots lad that Jimmy had signed from Rhyl in March 1967, but although he was quick, Sandy never really established a regular first team place in his time at Ninian Park.

Our only League defeat in seven games from mid-August to late September came at Sheffield United on 20 September when we lost 1-0 to what everyone in the ground, except the referee and linesman, thought was clearly an offside goal. But it's how you recover from those kind of set-backs that indicate whether or not you have the character to move on from that. We certainly did the following week when a 30,083 Ninian Park crowd saw us play the Second Division leaders Queen's Park Rangers on a hot Saturday afternoon. John Toshack scored his first ever League hat-trick, and Rangers included Rodney Marsh, Terry Venables, and a young substitute in Gerry Francis.

Although Rangers had a number of quality players in their line-up, we fancied our chances against them, and that day we really played well. Rodney Marsh usually had a good game against us, and Jimmy Scoular said to Dave Carver in our dressing room before the game, 'Dave, I don't want to see you today. Neither do I want to see Rodney Marsh, so wherever he goes, I want you to go with him.' So Dave took Jimmy at his word and followed Rodney all over the Ninian Park pitch, not giving him any room to play. Dave did a great job against Rodney that day as he had done on previous occasions against Rangers.

We were now really buzzing, and were confident about going to Blackpool the following week, but that was a day of tragedy for us. We went ahead through Peter King, but then Alan Suddick, their former Newcastle United forward, levelled before the interval with a free kick that he bent round our defensive wall. Kingy regained the lead for us in the second half and we were really playing well. Many of the 18,000 crowd were starting to leave because they could not see Blackpool coming back. But our opponents scored again – all of a sudden they were back in it at 2-2 and with two minutes left they went 3-2 up and we were stunned. We were all so frustrated because the game, that was ours for the taking, was now taken away from us. In the very last minute, Barrie Jones who wasn't noted for his tackling, went into a challenge with their full back Henry Mowbray, and his outstretched leg was caught. I heard the crack of his leg breaking and immediately the referee blew for time. Barrie had sustained a compound fracture, the Blackpool fans rushed onto the pitch to celebrate their win, and we stood around Barrie as the first aid men dealt with him. There was a bit of a free-for-all as the home supporters crowded round, and it took about ten minutes before we could get Barrie off the pitch on a stretcher in order to get him to hospital. It was an injury that was to finish his League career – he never played a first team game for Cardiff City after that despite his efforts at a come-back, though he did go on to play for Yeovil Town in the Southern League.

It was a very sad Cardiff City dressing room at Bloomfield Road after that game, not just because of what had happened, but because we all knew what a loss Barrie would be to us and our hopes of going up. Jimmy went to see him in hospital that night following an operation on his leg, and Barrie was there for a week before returning by ambulance to his home in Bishopston near Swansea.

We were staying in our usual Lancashire headquarters at Southport for several days as we were going to Blackburn Rovers on the following Wednesday. During the time after the Blackpool game, we talked about how to replace Barrie, and our goalkeeper Fred Davies suggested to Jimmy Scoular that it might be worth looking at Crystal Palace's midfield player Bobby Woodruff who had been a teammate of Fred when they were both at Wolves a few seasons earlier. We didn't think anymore about it at the time, but Jimmy got busy and Bobby joined us in mid-November 1969 for a £20,000 fee.

That week in Lancashire proved costly because after the

Blackpool defeat and Barrie's injury, we then lost 1-0 at Blackburn. The absence of Barrie soon began to have its effect because out of the next seven games we won only two, although those two victories were decisive – 4-0 against Aston Villa at home including a pile driver and a penalty from Ronnie Bird, and a 6-0 win against Hull City with two goals apiece from Tosh and myself.

When Bobby Woodruff joined us we were ninth in the table, eight points behind second-placed Blackburn Rovers. Bobby proved to be a great signing – he could play up front or in midfield, was very skilful, had a fierce shot from long range, and of course he had that massive throw-in which was as good as a corner or a free kick if it was in the opposition half of the pitch. It was constant pressure on his back from those long throws that eventually ended his League career after he had moved on to Newport County in 1974. He was and still is a very laid back character, and continues to be a very good golfer. He still lives in Cardiff and we remain good friends to this day.

By the time that Bob made his debut for us on 22 November 1969 against Preston North End at Ninian Park, we were out of Europe – the Turkish side Goztepe Izmir had proved too good for us in the Second Round of the Cup Winners' Cup that month, winning 3-0 in Turkey while we could only scrape a 1-0 home win in the second leg.

It was a difficult trip to Turkey and it took us eleven hours from Cardiff because there was a baggage handlers' strike at Heathrow. There weren't any steaks on the flight, so we had to have curry, salad or bread rolls, and we flew via Paris and Istanbul. We in fact stayed at the same hotel as Goztepe Izmir and were given meal vouchers to the value of £2.10p – this was because of restrictions on Turkish currency exchange.

The game was played on a pitch consisting of grey ash and sand, and we just couldn't cope. We were three down in thirty-two minutes and were well beaten in that first leg. All we had to show from the tie was that narrow 1-0 home win with a 78th minute goal from substitute Ronnie Bird – one of his specials! But I did at least come out of that tie with one souvenir because I still have a Goztepe Izmir shirt that I exchanged for my blue Cardiff City one after the first game.

Against Preston in Bob's first appearance, we won 2-0 with goals from myself and Peter King. Before that match we were ninth in the division, but the victory over Preston was the start of a seven-match winning run that took us into top spot by 10 January 1970. Brian Harris was having a great season – in fact he missed only three League games in 1969/70. In those days, teams wore 1 to 11 on their shirts, and the number that you wore usually indicated in which position you played. Don Murray was always No.5 in the middle of defence, our full backs Dave Carver and Gary Bell wore 2 and 3, and Brian Harris was always No.6 alongside Don. But during this winning seven-match run, Hooky came out wearing No.9 that was usually worn by a striker or attacking midfield player. Hooky would kick off if we lost the toss, and then go back to his regular defensive role. At Leicester where we won 2-1 in mid-December, the report in the local sports paper criticised us for being too defensive as our 'striker' never went over the half-way line – perhaps the reporter didn't notice Tosh and myself up front!

Don and Hooky were a tremendous central defensive pairing. In his earlier days Don had been somewhat impetuous at the back, but playing alongside Hooky with his vast experience meant that Don could attack the ball, and Hooky would be there to sweep up behind and start attacks from the back.

We did have a surprise set back during that run to the top of the table – in the Third Round of the FA Cup we played Fourth Division York City, drawing 1-1 at Bootham Crescent. We drew the replay 1-1 at Ninian Park two days after we had beaten Sheffield United to go into first place. That replay should have been on the Wednesday following our draw at Bootham Crescent, but the weather in South Wales was freezing in the few days after our draw at York. On the scheduled day of the replay, the Ninian Park pitch was very hard and the Grangetown goalmouth was icy. Jimmy Scoular wanted the game to go ahead so he arranged to borrow a flame thrower from the landlady of The Bear Hotel in Cowbridge whom he knew. Jimmy told Harry Parsons to hire a five ton van and take several apprentices with him to get the flame thrower. When they arrived at The Bear Hotel, the landlady picked it up from behind the bar and handed it to Harry – it was just a small ordinary garden flame thrower. Jimmy would not be beaten however, and did his best with it in the goalmouth. But the weather was so cold that it had little effect. As he tried to melt the ice, Dot Lyons from the club's administrative office came down the tunnel and shouted to Jimmy that there was a telephone call for him. As he turned round with the flame thrower in his hand, the creosoted goal net caught fire! Everyone who was watching thought that it was hilarious, but they could not laugh too much as Jimmy did not think it was funny – well, he wouldn't, would he! As it turned out, a local referee was called in who said that the pitch was too dangerous for the game to go ahead, and it was postponed until the following Monday, two days after we beat Sheffield United to go top of the table. So when we went to Birmingham City's St Andrews for the second replay, we were the Second Division leaders. Perhaps we had the feeling that all we had to do was turn up to beat a Fourth Division side, but they beat us 3-1 after extra time – we had been too complacent!

John Toshack's performances were attracting interest from the leading clubs, and when we played my home town club Bristol City on a freezing cold Monday night on 29 December, at Ninian Park, Liverpool's manager Bill Shankly was at the game to see Tosh head a last minute winner for our 1-0 victory, and the indications were that our Welsh International striker would be going higher in the not-too-distant future, less than a year later as it turned out. It was a typical Tosh header – Bobby Woodruff's chip from the right, and Tosh guided his effort over a helpless Mike Gibson. I knew Mike well of course from our time at Ashton Gate – he was a good keeper but on the short side, which I was glad about that night!

Having gone to the top of Division Two and been knocked out of the FA Cup, our League season started to go downhill – we had sixteen matches left of which we won only four, drew seven and lost five. It certainly wasn't promotion form and once again we could not show enough consistency during the last third of the season. We finished seventh with 49 points, two more than the previous season, and we were only four points behind the two promotion positions which went to Champions Huddersfield

Town (60 points) and runners-up Blackpool (53 points). There were only two points for a win in those days, but with a little more consistency we could so easily have gone up.

Our only consolation was that once again we won the Welsh Senior Cup in which I achieved my best-ever goals total in a senior match. It was a Fifth Round home tie against Barmouth and Dyffryn United of the Mid-Wales League in mid-January, and we were 6-1 winners – I scored five times and Tosh got the other. It was one of those nights when everything I hit went in. I would have liked there to have been more than just 4,901 to see me do it! We went on to beat Wrexham 3-0 at home before overcoming Swansea City in a two-leg semi-final. There was an 18,000 crowd at Ninian Park for the first leg when we drew 2-2 while 16,000 were at the Vetch when we won 2-0, and we had a comfortable 5-0 aggregate win over Chester in the two-leg Final. But they were not easy games, and we had to do well to win them in what were tense matches. When you look at the attendances that the League clubs were getting in the Welsh Cup, and the interest that our visits to non-league clubs attracted, the competition was on a high in those days. But since the League clubs have come out of the competition with the European target being denied them through UEFA politics, the Welsh Cup for me has lost a great deal of its prestige. All I can say is that I have happy memories of playing in it, especially being then able to play in European competition.

Once again that season Tosh and I scored 50 goals between us – I had 28 (18 League, 10 Cup) and he had 22 (17 League, 5 Cup). So in two consecutive seasons we had scored exactly 100 goals between us – I had never achieved anything like that with John Atyeo at Bristol City. So it was a very good pairing, we complemented each other well on the pitch, didn't particularly work on any set moves together but we always knew where the other one would be, particularly when either of us got on the end of a cross. We had good respect for each other – I was pleased for him when he scored and he was pleased for me when I scored. I look at videos now of the two of us in scoring action together, and we never went overboard in our celebrations – perhaps it was because we were scoring so often!

5

ANOTHER
NEAR-PROMOTION MISS

There was no summer tour for us in that close season of 1970, so I didn't have the job of telling Gill that I would be off on an all expenses paid trip to some far-off exotic venue with my teammates, and we were able to spend a pleasant summer together as a family.

I was sad to see Les Lea leave the club at the end of the 1969/70 season when he joined Barnsley. Les was a good friend of mine, and a very keen gardener – in fact I sometimes think that he preferred gardening to football! When we were in Australia in 1968, Les really wanted to be at home with his plants and vegetables. There was one occasion in early February 1970 when Les was coming back after injury and played in a reserve match at Bristol Rovers who were then still playing at Eastville which had a greyhound track around the pitch. In the area behind one of the goals were three diamond-shaped rose beds that were the groundsman's pride and joy and which had been there for years. During a break in play for an injury, Les went over to have a close inspection of the flowers – the referee had to shout to him to stop sniffing the roses and get back on the pitch as the game was re starting. But Les was a good midfield player, having originally been a winger at Blackpool, and he had been a consistent member of the squad. I wasn't surprised to hear that after his playing days he joined the Barnsley Parks Department.

Another departure that summer was goalkeeper Fred Davies who went to AFC Bournemouth where I was to join him a few seasons later. He was replaced at Ninian Park by Crystal Palace keeper Frank Parsons who certainly had a bit of style about him –

his wife was an attractive model, and he had a pedigree Afghan hound.

Would it be third time lucky for us in 1970/71? I thought that it could well be when I heard that Cardiff City had paid £35,000 in late July 1970 for Coventry City's Ian Gibson, one of the most talented midfield players that I have had the good fortune to be with in a team. He had helped Coventry to win the Second Division title in 1967 and reach top-level status for the first time in their history. Jimmy Scoular knew him well because they had both been together at Bradford Park Avenue in the early 1960s before Jimmy, as player/manager, had sold him for a large fee to Middlesbrough.

Gibbo was quite a character. He loved betting on dogs and horses, hardly looked like a player in his appearance on the pitch – but he could play! He would take a lot of punishment in games, and would usually be on the treatment table for most of the week, with his pet dog waiting patiently in the corridor. I remember that on one occasion, after Gibbo had been given several reminders from the bookmaking fraternity, he was on the treatment table after training when Jimmy Scoular came in to tell him that two large tough-looking gentlemen were waiting for him outside. He jumped off the table, grabbed his clothes and his dog, ran down the players' tunnel, across the pitch and over the Bob Bank to get out of the ground by the railway line!

Gibbo was an immense influence on the pitch during the time that we were together at Cardiff City – just over two seasons. He could work his way from midfield to the bye-line and then find you with a perfect pass. As good as Barrie Jones had been in midfield, I still think that Gibbo was better, and that's no disrespect to Barrie who was a very talented player.

I looked at the fixtures for the new '70/71 season and saw that we would travel to Leicester City for our opening match. They had finished third the previous season, just missing out on promotion, so it was going to be a difficult start for us at Filbert Street where they then played. It was in fact a great start for us because we were 1-0 winners in front of nearly 28,000, including a lot of Cardiff supporters, and I scored our goal with a diving header past their keeper Peter Shilton four minutes before half-time. In those days there was only one substitute, and to illustrate what a settled side we were, no fewer than nine of the twelve had been in the team for nearly three years. Our line-up at Filbert Street that hot August afternoon in 1970 was: Parsons, Carver, Bell, Sutton, Murray, Harris, Clark, Gibson, Toshack, Woodruff, King. Sub – Bird.

We were beaten only once in our opening nine matches (four wins, four draws) – unfortunately for me, the one defeat was at Ashton Gate where we lost 1-0 to my old club Bristol City who beat us with a last-minute goal after we had been the better side. We should have had a first half penalty when my former teammate Gordon Parr handled the ball as Ian Gibson tried to flick it over his head, but Leeds referee Gordon Kew didn't see it.

One of our four victories in those opening two months was an early September 2-0 home win over Birmingham City who brought on as substitute a young 16-year-old named Trevor Francis to make his League debut.

By the end of September 1970, we were in third place after being top for most of that month. I had scored five goals in those first nine matches, Tosh had netted only three, but we had both also had two each in our 8-0 first leg home win over PO Larnaca of Cyprus in the First Round of the European Cup Winners' Cup. It was all over after that first leg and when we went to Cyprus at the end of September for the return, it was a tame 0-0 draw on a bone hard pitch in stifling afternoon heat – Jimmy Scoular was not very happy about our performance!

In early October we played Middlesbrough at Ninian Park in what was a fateful match for keeper Frank Parsons. A win was likely to put us back on top of the table, but we lost 4-3 after being 3-1 ahead! John Hickton had put them 1-0 up after twenty minutes, I managed to equalise before half-time and we went in level. But in the second half, Bobby Woodruff put us ahead with a great shot, and then Peter King made it 3-1 with an unbelievable volley at the Grange End. Gary Bell then gave away a penalty, referee Ron Challis having none of Don Murray's strong protests – I've got the video of all that and it brings back such memories. But Frank Parsons saved the spot kick and we looked set for victory.

Unfortunately Frank then let two saveable efforts slip through his hands and it was level at 3-3. Four minutes from the end, Don Murray conceded a debatable free kick on the Middlesbrough left, and Hughie McIlmoyle's header gave poor Frank no chance. Jimmy was furious that we had lost the game from such a commanding position, and was scathing in the Press about Frank who was immediately dropped. He didn't play again for the first team that season, and the following year made only two first team appearances before leaving the club at the end '71/72 to join Fulham. Jim Eadie, who had joined us from Scottish junior club Kirkintilloch Rob Roy in the summer of 1969, came into the side for the next match when I scored the winner in a 1-0 victory at Watford, and we were back on track. Jim made the most of his opportunity and found himself playing in European football later that month when we easily beat French side Nantes 5-1 at home in the first leg of the Second Round of the Cup Winners' Cup when even Ian Gibson got in on the scoring act!

The last day of October 1970 saw the visit of Second Division leaders Hull City under their player/manager Terry Neill, the ex-Arsenal and Northern Ireland defender. It was a memorable day for John Toshack who scored a hat-trick in our 5-1 win – one with his left, one with his right, and a header. It was to be his last appearance at Ninian Park as a Cardiff City player because he was being trailed strongly by Liverpool. A few days later we went off to France for our return with Nantes when Tosh and I scored in our 2-1 win to put us through to the Quarter-Finals on 7-2 aggregate. It was John's 100th League and Cup goal for his home town club, having scored on his debut in November 1965 as a 16-year-old, and there was now little doubt that he would not be with us for much longer. Brian Harris only just made the trip – his passport and other personal possessions had been stolen from his car, but he managed to get a replacement passport just in time for the flight.

The following Saturday – 7 November – Neath-born Leighton Phillips, already in the Wales senior squad and rapidly developing into a talented midfield or central defensive player, scored with a tremendous 25 yard drive at Queen's Park Rangers for a 1-0 win that put us third, and that was Tosh's final appearance for us. We survived a penalty in that match when Terry Venables shot wide from the spot. Over that weekend, the club concluded a £110,000 deal with Liverpool for Tosh's transfer and he went up to Merseyside with his wife Sue on the Monday to meet Bill Shankly. But not before Brian Harris had told John to make sure that his wife was wearing something blue. 'They like blue at Liverpool' said Hooky, knowing full well what would happen when the new signing turned up Lime Street Station with his wife wearing the colour associated with Liverpool's deadly rivals Everton for whom Hooky had played for so many years. Sure enough, Shankly was not too happy about it, especially with the large media and fans' presence at Tosh's arrival. John phoned Brian to tell him what had happened – Hooky thought that it was hilarious! I later found out that Bill Shankly had been in touch with Brian about Tosh's progress on and off the pitch. Bill and Hooky knew each other well from the Merseyside football scene even though they were with rival clubs, and Brian felt that Tosh was ready for the step up.

It was disappointing for our fans that he had gone, especially as we were well placed in the Second Division promotion race, in fact it's a talking point to this day as I often find when chatting to fans who were following us in those years. But I have to say that none of us in the dressing room blamed him for taking such an opportunity, and if it had been me, then I'd have done the same thing. I'd love to have played at the highest level but I never got the chance. Tosh certainly made the most of it, winning a number of honours with Liverpool including an FA Cup winners' medal at the end of that season. Would we have gone up if he had stayed? Who can say. Years on, I often wonder what would have happened if he had stayed at Ninian Park until the end of the season. Our careers might have been so different had we made it to top level. But with Tosh gone, were Cardiff City ambitious enough to go out and sign a top class replacement? The next few weeks would provide the answer.

John's departure did not seem to have its effect immediately because the following week we beat Blackburn Rovers 4-1 at Ninian Park. I came back into the starting line-up after being on the bench for the previous five League games and scored twice,

Bobby Woodruff and Kingy netted the others. Bobby had been playing up front with Tosh in the previous few weeks, now I was with him in attack and that win put us back into second place. We played very well that day as if to show that we could cope without John Toshack – it was our fourth consecutive League victory, and we were now unbeaten in seven consecutive Second Division games since the 4-3 home defeat against Middlesbrough. We were averaging just over 22,000 fans at home games so far that season, but against Blackburn it was a little concerning that we had only 18,213. I felt that I knew the reason because a lot of fans had said to me that week when I was out and about that they were disillusioned about the sale of Tosh, especially when we were so well placed in the division. They could understand it if we were struggling near the foot of the table, but we weren't, and they said that the Board had cashed in on their major asset. That was their feeling, and it was understandable. But the records show that, apart from a low 15,619 for a 3-1 win against Sunderland in mid-December, attendances for the rest of that season remained above 20,000 as we maintained our promotion challenge.

6

A REAL GOOD NIGHT

A few days after the Blackburn game, the draw for the Quarter-Finals of the European Cup Winners' Cup was made in Paris by the French singer Mireille Matthieu. When we had beaten Nantes in the previous round, skipper Don Murray and Jimmy Scoular had gone on record as saying that they were hoping for the legendary Real Madrid in the quarter-final, but you rarely get who you hope for, or do you? After training on the day of the Draw, I was driving through Cardiff's Queen Street, which you could in those days, and I caught sight of a newspaper placard '…Plum European Draw For City!' I stopped to buy the *South Wales Echo* and the front page headlines said that we had drawn Real Madrid – a dream come true, and I couldn't believe it.

We had in fact been drawn away in the first leg due to be played on 10 March 1971, but because Real's local rivals Atletico Madrid were drawn at home in the European Champions Cup and playing on the same night, UEFA ruled that our first match against Real would be at Ninian Park. That suited me because I always felt that it was an advantage to play the home leg first in those European games. With Tosh gone, I felt that if I could maintain my form and avoid injury, then I would be certain to play against them – but you can never be too sure. In my mind were thoughts of Di Stefano, Puskas, Gento, Kopa, four of their great names from the time when they were regular winners of the European Champions Cup every season from 1954/55 to 1959/60. Those players had now long gone, but it was still Real Madrid and they were still a great side. This to me was what European football was all about, and I thought how lucky I was to be part of Cardiff City's squad for what would surely be two of the most memorable games in the club's history.

The talk in the dressing room before training the following

morning was all about the tie, and Ronnie Bird was particularly excited about it – Real had been his favourite team as a boy, and Francisco Gento – their great left winger of the 1950s and early 1960s – was Ronnie's idol. But Ronnie had hardly been in our line-up that season – just three substitute League and Cup appearances, so he would probably have to displace Peter King in the side to have a chance of playing against them.

But now the absence of John Toshack was showing on the pitch because, over the next five matches, we lost three, drew one, won only once, and scored just five goals. The three defeats were all away from home against sides well below us in the table. We lost 1-2 at bottom club Charlton, 0-1 at Oxford United, and 1-2 at Millwall. With two points for a win in those days, those seven points lost were to prove very costly at the end of the season. In that Oxford match, 17-year-old Merthyr-born Derek 'Danny' Showers, then a current Wales Youth International who went on to play at Under-23 and Senior level for Wales, made his first team debut alongside me in attack. His nickname 'Danny' was because he resembled the American comedy star Danny Kaye, but although Derek was always a regular scorer for our reserve team in the Football Combination, he never managed to do it at first team level. He made 100 League and Cup appearances for the club but only scored 13 goals, and he eventually joined AFC Bournemouth in July 1977.

One of the problems for us at that time was with Bobby Woodruff playing up front with me, whenever there was a throw-in, Bobby would take it. So I was then the only recognised target man in the box. We were not playing well and I couldn't put my finger on it. Was it Tosh's departure? Was it thoughts of the Real Madrid games? Perhaps it was a combination of both.

There was talk of us signing Sheffield Wednesday striker Alan Warboys but nothing seemed to be happening, until a £42,000 deal to sign Alan was completed on Christmas Eve. He made his debut for us on Boxing Day against Swindon at Ninian Park when 24,813 saw us draw 1-1 to go fifth in the table.

I had played against Alan the previous August when we had won 2-1 at Hillsborough and he had been a right handful for Don Murray and Brian Harris on that occasion. Alan was a big strong lad who liked to batter his way through defences, completely different to John Toshack. I got on well with Alan who was a very likeable Yorkshireman, but we didn't compliment each other's styles on the pitch. Whereas Tosh had a good touch, which became even better during his time at Liverpool, Alan liked to knock people about and was more of an individualist. It worked for him because he scored 13 goals in his 18 League appearances for Cardiff City that season. But he was not going to be eligible for the Real Madrid matches as he had not been signed within the required registration period for the quarter-final games, so at least I knew that I would play against them a few months later.

Alan was also ineligible for our FA Cup Third Round 1-0 home win over Brighton, not having been signed in time, so I kept my place. But then Jimmy decided to play Alan and Bobby Woodruff up front so I was on the bench for a few matches. We played Alan's former club Sheffield Wednesday at Ninian Park in early January and he had a great game, scoring twice in our 4-0 win to put us fourth in the table, and then followed that up with another two seven days later when we were 3-1 winners against Portsmouth at Fratton Park. Jimmy Scoular was delighted at that result – he had been an outstanding wing half for Pompey for eight years after the Second World War and was one of the stars of their League Championship sides of 1948/49 and 1949/50. He always had a great welcome from his old club whenever we played there.

Our Ninian Park pitch was, however, beginning to deteriorate despite the hard working efforts of groundsman Keith Oliver and his staff. When we played Brentford in the Fourth Round of the FA Cup during mid-January, the pitch was a mud heap. They were sixth from bottom of Division Four, and the mud proved a great leveller. You couldn't play a back pass to the keeper in those conditions – we did, and were punished for it! They deservedly beat us 2-0 in one of the shocks of the round. Alan suffered a thigh injury in that match so I came on as substitute, but although I could cope with those kind of conditions, I could not do anything to change the game for us. Alan was something of hypochondriac. He always had to have a couple of tablets before a game as he had a headache, he would invariably want a pain killing injection in his leg – Doc Hamilton always put water in the syringe! But it meant that Alan would go out and give his usual performance.

Although Alan was then in and out through that thigh injury over the next couple of months, his arrival saw a change in our fortunes, and we were now in a ten-match unbeaten League run, including a sequence of four consecutive victories in January/February that was to take us to the top of the table. One of those four wins was at mid-table Sunderland on 13 February when we beat them 4-0 at Roker Park, and nobody did that in those days – Jimmy loved that one because Sunderland had always been deadly rivals of his when he had been at Newcastle United after leaving Portsmouth. Harry Parsons was also delighted that day because his son John came on as substitute for Alan Warboys, and scored. John had scored on his League debut a week earlier as substitute in the 1-0 home win over Oxford United and netted four goals in four consecutive League and Welsh Cup matches – perhaps here was the new 'Toshack' or 'Clark'. But John was on the small side, and with Warboys and myself both well-built forwards, Jimmy perhaps felt that John wasn't suited to the rough and tumble of life in attack at the top end of Division Two. Nevertheless Harry was very proud that his son was in the squad, and would certainly not have tried to influence Jimmy in his team selections.

The Real Madrid home game was now not far off, and four days before the match we met Carlisle United at Ninian Park in a game that would see the winners go top of the table. Jimmy had said to us that he would give a fiver to anyone who scored a hat-trick because we had only obtained one that season when John Toshack had netted three against Hull City on his final home appearance in November. Jimmy put me on the bench for that game against Carlisle – he didn't want to run the risk of me getting injured before the Real Madrid match four days later, especially with Alan being ineligible. It was Alan Warboys' day against Carlisle – we won 4-0 and he scored a hat-trick at the Canton End within ten minutes of the start, to the delight of the 22,371 who saw it. When he netted his third, he ran over to Jimmy in the dugout with his hand outstretched for his fiver. I was sat next to Jimmy and I can still remember what he said – I won't repeat it here, but it was to the effect of saying to Alan to get back onto that pitch and get another three! Alan scored again before half-time and went off with a recurrence of his thigh injury twenty minutes from time, which gave me the chance to have a brief run-out in the last quarter of a game which was well won by that time. Nevertheless I was relieved to get off the pitch having avoided injury.

So now we were top of Division Two and about to take on the mighty Real Madrid a few days later. I've read in recent years articles in which it's claimed that Real were not a great side. But when they came to us, they were in third place in the Spanish League, well in the running for title and had beaten fellow contenders Barcelona and local rivals Atletico Madrid in the previous few weeks. They were full of quality and included their two current Spanish internationals Pirri and Amancio who had played in the 2-1 win over Italy in Sardinia the previous month. Their last European Champions Cup success had been in 1966 when they had been 2-1 winners in the Final against Partisan Belgrade, and six of that Real team were still in their line-up – Sanchis, Pirri, Zoco, Amancio, Grosso and Velazquez. So it was an outstanding side that would be playing against us.

How well I remember those few days leading up to Wednesday, 10 March 1971 – they were hectic. We had a day off on the Sunday, but from then on it was busy. There were constant media interviews during and after training, thousands of fans were in and out of the ground getting tickets, and there was a tremendous excited atmosphere about the place. We trained on the Monday and Tuesday, while on the Wednesday morning I went for my usual walk over the golf course in Whitchurch. Everybody that I came across wished me all the best and said that they would be there. In fact many people that I came across outside the club over those few days said that they were going, even though they weren't regular fans. The club stated that it was a sell-out at 47,500 for safety reasons at an evening match, but I'm still convinced to this day that there were around 50,000 at Ninian Park, with a number of people 'pinching in' at various access points, especially at the back of the 'Bob Bank'.

There was, however, controversy before the game as far as our team selection was concerned. 17 year-old Bridgend-born Nigel Rees had made his debut at outside left in early January and had done well enough to keep his place. Nigel, who had been a Wales Secondary Schools Rugby Union International before joining

Cardiff City as an apprentice, had then been selected by the FA of Wales for a Welsh Youth International against Scotland at Wrexham to be played on the same night as the Real Madrid match, and the FAW were insisting that Nigel should play for them or be disciplined. He was in an impossible position because he wanted to play in both games, but couldn't. Fortunately, it was all sorted amicably and the FAW agreed to release him to play for us – the correct decision in my view because it was a fantastic opportunity for Nigel to be able to play against Real, and he could always appear again for Wales Youth. Meanwhile Ronnie Bird, who was still out of first team contention, was hoping that Nigel would have to play for Wales, because then Ronnie would have been in line for Real.

The fact that Ronnie could not, in the end, play against the Spaniards, though he was on the bench, was one of the biggest disappointments of Ronnie's career. It was the only time that I had ever seen him really down, but in the dressing room before the game he was his usual self, wishing everyone all the best and in particular Nigel Rees – I've never forgotten that.

On the day of the game, I got to Ninian Park by 4.30 pm as did all of us because we had been told that if we left it any later then we were likely to be caught in heavy traffic. I went upstairs to what is now the John Charles Suite but was then the Grandstand Club, had a cup of tea and read the evening paper. Dad was coming to the game – he came to most of our home matches because it was an easy journey across the Severn Bridge from Horfield in North Bristol. I was excited but not nervous, and thought how lucky I was to be playing in this match. I watched from the window as Real arrived – I wonder what they thought of the visitors' dressing room at Ninian Park compared to their own facilities. It was apparently very cold in our away dressing room that night because, unknown to me, Jimmy and Harry Parsons had been up to their tricks and had turned the heating off!

The only disappointment for me on the night was that Real Madrid played in all red and not their famous all white. I still don't know to this day why they did that, but it was a minor disappointment on that never-to-be-forgotten night. It is history now that we won that first leg tie 1-0 with my goal at the Canton

End in the 32nd minute. It was the culmination of a great move started by Gary Bell who put Bobby Woodruff in possession on our left. Bobby skilfully beat an opponent and sent Nigel Rees away on the Grandstand touchline. Nigel looked to have been blocked by two defenders but the ball broke nicely for him and he was clear on the left. He knocked it forward, got to the bye-line and found me with a perfect cross – I was unmarked about twelve yards out and it was a perfect header into the net, easy in fact though I say it myself. So easy that I dreamt over the following few nights that I'd missed it!

We should in fact have won by more than one goal on the night, we had the opportunities, and in the end Real were quite happy to keep it at 1-0. We made sure that they didn't have any really dangerous chances to threaten our keeper Jim Eadie and they hardly ever looked like scoring. What a night that was – I still have the video of the highlights of the game, and friends often ask me if they can see it. What a noise the crowd made because when I scored, BBC Wales TV commentator Idwal Robling says on the video that he can hardly hear himself talk! I also have a recording of the radio commentary of the goal and I must have watched that goal countless times – it's bought me a few drinks over the years. People still tell me that they were there on that night, and I have to say that when I finished my playing career and became a sales representative for industrial safety wear, that goal certainly helped because a lot of my prospective clients remembered it, were prepared to see me and wanted to talk about that night before we got down to business.

Was it the greatest goal that I ever scored? All I can say is that the goal that I scored in Bristol City's promotion match against Oldham in April 1965 was more important, and we got another in that game through John Atyeo. But the one against Real Madrid was the 'glory goal' because of the opposition and was in front of nearly 50,000 people against one of the best known sides in Europe.

It was unbelievable in the dressing room at the final whistle – champagne, camera crews, photographers. No thoughts of the second leg at that stage, we had beaten them on the night and that was all that mattered at the time. I've never seen Jimmy Scoular so excited. As for the rest of that night, I phoned Gill to say I wouldn't be back for some time and I didn't go home until the early hours –

we ended up at the Electricity Club in Pontcanna near Llandaff Fields and didn't want the night to end.

For young Nigel Rees who had provided the cross for my goal, it was probably the most memorable night of his career and he justified the decision that had been taken to pull him out of the Wales squad. Ronnie Bird on the bench was naturally delighted that we had won, but he couldn't show his disappointment at not having played because Nigel had made the goal. Up to the time of his death in March 2005, Ronnie would often recall that night commenting that Jimmy had made the right decision because of the way it turned out. Nigel meanwhile played very few first team games during the remainder of that season, had a few appearances over the next two years but then left the club to join Bridgend Town in the Welsh League. We had a number of young Welsh players in those days whom you thought would go on to greater things but didn't. Nigel was one of those who had the ability but did not make the most of it. He is now 53 and I still see him occasionally at Cardiff City's home matches. He half admits that he did not make the most of his chance at professional level.

It was back to reality the following Saturday when we went to Blackburn Rovers, a 1-1 draw that I remember well, not so much for the fact that they were tough opposition that day or because I scored, but because when we ran onto the pitch we had a tremendous reception from the Ewood Park crowd and the Blackburn players as the public address announcer referred to our great win over Real Madrid.

The Blackburn result dropped us to second place, but a week later, Alan Warboys scored against Queen's Park Rangers for a 1-0 win at Ninian Park to keep our promotion challenge going and put us back into top spot. We trained on the following Monday morning and in the afternoon left Cardiff Airport on a charter flight for Madrid to play the second leg against Real two days later. There was now even more interest in the tie from the national newspapers – could the Second Division leaders hold out in the second leg and provide one of the major shocks in European football history?

We stayed in a central Madrid hotel and trained at the Bernabeu Stadium on the Tuesday morning. There were several thousand Real fans there to watch us, and it was an unbelievable experience for me to go into that stadium. It was like a Roman amphitheatre and they showed us around their trophy room. It is not just a football club, they have a netball team and play many other sports there. This was big time stuff for us coming out of the Second Division of the Football League, and I thought to myself that it would be like this if we were in what was then the League's First Division at top level playing clubs such as Manchester United and Arsenal – we needed to win promotion.

While it was a big game to us, it perhaps wasn't to their fans and there were only 65,000 at the match, whereas they regularly attracted over 100,000! We were unchanged from the first leg after Nigel Rees had been given a penicillin injection the night before the game because of a throat infection, and we were confident that we could hold them. It was in fact 0-0 at half-time and as we came off the pitch, their fans started throwing seat cushions at their players – they came down like frisbees! – which was an indication that we were doing well against them. Peter King had forced a great save from their keeper in the first half, Nigel Rees missed a good chance with a header straight after the interval – if that had gone in we would probably have beaten them. But that was a turning point because they then scored twice in a two-minute spell (50 and 52). The equaliser came when our keeper Jim Eadie and Don Murray both went for a cross and Jim could only punch the ball to Velasquez who hit a fifteen-yard volley into our net. The second came when Pirri's pass was flicked in by Manuel Fleitas. European competition rules had now been changed, and away goals counted in the event of a tie on aggregate, so we needed one goal to go through. They marked me very tightly, having learned from the first game, we battled hard, but I never had a clear cut chance. Brian Harris came on as substitute, they tried time wasting tactics, their fans kept hold of the ball when it went into the crowd, but the referee – Karol Suska from Czechoslovakia – gave us nothing. He didn't add on any time for their time wasting tactics, did nothing about the throwing of beer cans onto the pitch by the crowd or the broken bottle that hit Gary Bell, and gave them thirty-five free kicks to our six!

It finished 2-0 so we were out of Europe on a 2-1 aggregate, but it had been a memorable experience and one that I was glad to have had. I still have several souvenirs from that tie – the home video and match programme, a silver watch inscribed with a Real Madrid emblem that each of us received from the President of Real Madrid. I also have a white Real shirt, having swapped my blue City shirt with their defender Benito after the away match. I often look at that white shirt and it brings back so many memories of those two games against Real who went on to defeat PSV Eindhoven in the semi-final, but lost to Chelsea in the Final which went to a replay. We had lost to them, but no one could take away from us that 1-0 win at Ninian Park still remembered by so many people.

Our line-up in both matches was: Eadie, Carver, Bell, Sutton, Murray, Phillips, King, Gibson, Clark, Woodruff, Rees.

We used no substitutes in the first leg, while in the second leg, Brian Harris came on for Nigel Rees in the second half.

Many fans that watched that Ninian Park game as youngsters are now parents who come to home matches with their children. On my regular visits for home matches, I am often stopped on my way into the ground by fathers who want to have a chat and who say to their young sons '…This gentleman scored the goal when Cardiff City beat Real Madrid here 1-0 many years ago in front of 50,000!' You can see the little boys react with a look that says – how come Cardiff City were playing Real Madrid? How were there ever 50,000 at Ninian Park? How did Cardiff City manage to beat the great Real Madrid 1-0? And how can this elderly man be the one who scored the goal? I sometimes wonder myself! But I enjoy the memories and talking about it, and it remains a great moment in my life. On 10 March 2006, the thirty-fifth anniversary of the home leg victory, the 11 that played were all together for probably the last time when we organised a charity dinner at a Cardiff hotel in memory of Ronnie Bird. It was a great night with many memories being shared.

After Real it was then back to the bread-and-butter of Second Division football, and after our return from Spain we went as League leaders the following Saturday to play Birmingham City at St Andrews where there was an attendance of 49,025 which included several thousand Bluebirds fans. Birmingham's 16 year-old forward Trevor Francis, who had made his debut against us back in early September, was becoming a star name with them, and had scored all four in their 4-0 home win over Bolton the previous month. Trevor, who was a West Country boy from Plymouth, went on to become a great player and was the first one million pound transfer when Brian Clough took him to Nottingham Forest in February 1979. Trevor scored in the first half against us, Phil Summerill added another after half-time, and we lost 2-0 to drop into third place – it was our only defeat in a run of fifteen League matches from mid-December to mid-April. Although I didn't enjoy the result, I always enjoyed playing at Birmingham City – there was always a great atmosphere at St Andrews.

Following the Birmingham defeat we had 1-0 home wins over my old club Bristol city and against Bolton, draws at Swindon (2-2) and at Middlesbrough (1-1) and we had been in second spot since the start of April. I and the lads were pleased for Jimmy Scoular who was named Division Two 'Manager of the Month' for March, the first time that he had received such an award. It had been a good March for us, twice going top of Division Two, and those two memorable matches against Real Madrid. Jimmy was given a giant gallon bottle of Bell's Scotch whiskey – I can't remember him sharing any of it with us!

The feeling now amongst the fans was that we had a great chance of making Division One – attendances were regularly above 20,000 and the people who had stopped going for a few games following John Toshack's departure had come back as we maintained our promotion challenge.

But in mid-April 1971 came a fateful home encounter with Watford. We were second, three points behind Leicester City (remember, two points for a win at that time), we were ahead of third placed Sheffield United on goal average, and we had a game in hand on all our rivals with five matches left. In addition, we still had to go Sheffield United later that month. So it was all in our hands, and one of our best League attendances of the season – 26,536 – turned up to see us play a Watford side who were fourth from bottom and too near the relegation zone for their own comfort. They had scored only 34 goals in 38 League games, had won only three times away from home, and we were clear favourites to beat them, having lost only once at home so far that season.

We were all over them for the first hour – Alan Warboys and I both hit the woodwork in the first half, their keeper Mike Walker, who went on to manage Colchester, Norwich and Everton, pulled off several great saves, and we just couldn't score. At half-time I remember our right back Dave Carver, always a worrier, saying to me: 'Brian, please get a goal – I'm afraid that if we don't score, then they will'. Dave was right because on the hour, Watford went ahead with a goal that I still can't believe to this day even when I see it on video. The ball was played into our box, it bounced off Dave, then a close range effort rebounded off Jim Eadie, and their left wing Charlie Woods saw the ball run into our net off his shin! After that we lost our way, just couldn't find a way through their defence, and when we did, Mike Walker was in no mood to be beaten. They were 1-0 winners, a result that more or less ensured their Second Division safety.

Sheffield United defeated Birmingham City 3-0 at home that day to go into second place at our expense. It wasn't the end of our promotion hopes, but it was a body blow and meant that we now had to get at least three wins from our final four matches, avoid defeat at Sheffield United – and only one of those four games was at Ninian Park. I was desperately disappointed that we had lost to Watford, so were the other lads. Watford were a side against whom I had done well in previous matches – I'd scored in our 1-0 win at Vicarage Road earlier that season, I'd scored in the two matches against them the previous season. But what was sad for me was that a lot of supporters suggested to me afterwards that we hadn't wanted to win, that we didn't want to get into the First Division. Nothing could have been further from the truth. And if I could have swapped the Real Madrid goal for one against Watford on that occasion to give us the lead, I would willingly have done so. I'm certain to this day that if we had beaten them, then we would have gone on to gain promotion. It was a very quiet and disappointed dressing room after that defeat, and I wish that somehow those supporters, who were suggesting that we didn't want it, could have been in there to see the reaction amongst the lads.

The pressure was now really on for the next two games – away to Norwich on the following Saturday and then away to Sheffield

United three nights later. Norwich had two long-serving defenders in Duncan Forbes and Dave Stringer who always gave us a tough time, especially Tosh and myself – in fact they used to kick lumps out of us! But on this occasion Alan Warboys and myself got the better of them, and we both scored in the first half to send us in at the interval 2-0 up. Norwich got one back in the second half, but we held on for a 2-1 victory and that meant that if we could win at Bramall Lane on the Tuesday night, then we would be a point ahead of Sheffield United, a game in hand, and two matches left to their one.

Nearly 1,000 Bluebirds fans made the long journey to South Yorkshire that night and there was a huge crowd of 42,963 at Bramall Lane that was then still a three-sided ground which they shared with Yorkshire County Cricket Club. We flew up to Leeds-Bradford Airport and had a coach to Sheffield. They beat us 5-1 on a night when decisions went for them and all their chances went in. We weren't as bad as the score line suggests, but thirty-five years on, the record book says that we lost 5-1! They had gone 2-0 up, but Steve Derrett, playing at the back alongside Don Murray, had put us back in it with a deflected effort and we went in at the break 2-1 down. Their goals came from centre forward Billy Dearden(2), John Flynn, Tony Currie and Cardiff-born Wales International Gil Reece. I came to know Gil well after he came back to South Wales, playing for Cardiff City and Swansea City before eventually retiring to concentrate on his plumbing and decorating business. Gil, who died a few years ago, and his wife Carol owned a hotel in Clare Road and on the wall of their lounge were photos of three of the goals against us that night. In later years Gil often reminded me of that match.

We were now three points behind them with two games left, and all they had to do was to win their final match that was at the Lane – against that same Watford who had dealt such a blow to our hopes.

We knew that whatever we did in our final matches against Orient (home) and Luton (away), Sheffield United were certain to win their match and go up with Leicester City. We flew back that same night, and Dave Carver and I went for a walk to get it out of our system – we felt that all the hard work had been for nothing, wins at Queen's Park Rangers, Sunderland, Norwich to name but a few, and for the third year in succession we had missed the boat again.

Sheffield United duly beat Watford 3-0 – Gil Reece got two of them – and it was no consolation that I scored in our 1-0 home win over Orient that day. It was our lowest home League crowd of the season – 15,750 – and it was a complete anti-climax. The final game didn't matter, and we lost 3-0 at Luton to finish in third place (only two went up in those days) three points behind Sheffield United. If only we had taken a few more points from those games in November/December following Tosh's departure, if only we had gained draws against Watford and Sheffield United or even had won one of those games – it was all ifs and buts.

Thirty-five years on, I feel that the Board should have been looking to spend most of that £110,000 that they received for John Toshack to allow Jimmy Scoular to bring in two or three quality players in midfield and up front, perhaps players who had done it at top level and were keen to get back there. Players coming in at a critical stage of the season would have lifted the squad and made people feel that they were not guaranteed their places. Although we had brought in Ian Gibson at the start and Alan Warboys in late December, as a replacement for Tosh, we just weren't strong enough as a squad. We as players had to take some of the blame – when you are just three points off the target after looking so good for a long time you have to take major responsibility. But I do feel that the Board, under Fred Dewey who ran a very tight ship, might have been more ambitious and gone all out for it – speculate to accumulate? I know that Peter Jackson, then leading Football Correspondent of the *South Wales Echo* and now Chief Rugby Union writer for the *Daily Mail*, still feels the same way all these years later.

It was small consolation that we won the Welsh Senior Cup for the fifth consecutive year to get into Europe once again. It was really promotion that we'd wanted – players such as Don Murray, Leighton Phillips and Gary Bell were desperate to play at a higher level. I was desperate to play in what was then Division One, and one of the big regrets of my career is that I didn't achieve it. Another regret is that I never represented England at any level from Schoolboy to Senior.

The end of that 1970/71 season saw the departure of Ronnie Bird after nearly five and a half seasons at Ninian Park. His final appearance was in the second leg of the Welsh Cup Final against

Wrexham at Ninian Park on 12 May when we won 3-1, Ronnie netting one of our goals to complete an aggregate 4-1 win over them. Jimmy had told him that he would give him another year's contract, but that he planned to sign a left winger and that if Ronnie stayed, he would be second choice. So Ronnie joined Crewe for a season before returning to South Wales to run a hairdressing salon and then go into coaching and non-league management. Our paths were to cross again in future years.

I was sorry to see him go – his outgoing personality always brightened our dressing room and we missed him. But he had been with Jimmy Scoular for a long time including their spell together at Bradford Park Avenue and sometimes you need a change, though in view of the way things turned out at Ninian Park and at Crewe, he might have been better off staying for that extra year.

Also leaving us the end of 1970/71 was Brian Harris who joined Newport County as their player/coach. He was also a loss to the dressing room – a good player, a good story teller and very quick witted. Brian had spent nearly five years at Ninian Park after coming from Everton and he had been a major influence at the club, both on and off the pitch. Brian's departure left me with the feeling that things were starting to change at Ninian Park.

One of the successes of that season was little Ian Gibson who was brilliant, especially at home on a pitch that wasn't the best – devoid of grass over most of its surface from November onwards. He never did much training, was on the treatment table for most of the week, would get off the table on Friday mornings and run two laps round the pitch, and then come in to say that he was fit for the next day's match! That was Ian Gibson.

One major consolation for me in that 1970/71 season was that Gill and I discovered around Christmas that we were expecting our second child, and in July 1971 we had another daughter – Jacqueline Mary. Why was it, I wonder, that footballers always seemed to produce daughters? Perhaps it was all the hard training!

7

ON THE SLIDE

The previous three seasons had proved that, as a squad, we were not quite good enough for promotion. We had been, however, one of the better Second Division sides and I enjoyed playing in the team and especially in Europe. In that summer of 1971 there was no close season tour, nor had there been one in 1970. So Gill, Alison and I were able to have a family holiday in Cornwall before the birth of our new baby. Gill's family had been tenants of a farm in the Chilterns near Hemel Hemstead. When the tenancy ended, they bought a farm in South Cornwall between St Blazey and Lostwithiel on the coast. It was an ideal spot for us and we had a month down there each summer over the next few years with Gill's parents who were lovely people. We spent some happy times at Par Beach and at Fowey, with trips to the North Cornwall coast and Newquay where Gill and I had first met.

When I got back for pre-season training, I found that Jimmy had signed Southampton right back Ken Jones, a very good snooker player. Dave Carver wasn't too happy about that, having been ever present over the previous two seasons. But Ken was to make only ten League and Cup appearances that season, and Dave was once again the regular choice over most of it. On the first day of pre-season training in July 1971 we were working across Sloper Road opposite the ground in the park. I saw Jimmy Scoular cross the road from the main gates, and he came up to me, saying – 'Telephone call from your wife... congratulations, you've got a new baby daughter'. He let me off training immediately so that I could get to the maternity unit, and I thought that perhaps he was human, after all!

In early August 1971 Jimmy signed the 21 year-old Newcastle

United left wing Alan Foggon who had played in their two-leg European Fairs Cup Final win of 1968/69 over Ujpest Dozsa, scoring in the away leg. Alan came with a good reputation – he had made over fifty appearances for Newcastle, having joined them originally as an apprentice, and he was a former 440-yard England Schoolboy Champion sprinter.

I felt that Alan was likely to be a player who could create opportunities for Warboys and myself as Ian Gibson had done following his arrival a year earlier.

Foggon signed a few hours before we played a pre-season home match against the German side FC Schalke 04 that we won 5-3 on a Wednesday evening, and when he came in the next day, he got stripped off for training and he looked overweight. Jimmy asked him if he was always that size and Alan replied that he was a few pounds over but that he'd lose it before the start of the season. Jimmy said that he would definitely have to, and so Alan had to train in a plastic oversuit to sweat it out. Foggon soon settled into the dressing room and got on well with Ian Gibson, Bobby Woodruff and Alan Warboys – they all liked a little 'flutter' in the betting shop! But Foggon never really settled in Cardiff – he made only twelve League appearances that season and was in the team only occasionally after early October. He couldn't repeat his Newcastle form with us, he looked sluggish at times, and he eventually returned back to the North-East in October 1972 to join Middlesbrough. It was the move that he needed because he then became a major player in Jack Charlton's outstanding Middlesbrough team that ran away with the Second Division title. I had a similar problem when I joined Huddersfield from Bristol City in 1966. Sometimes Southern people don't settle in the North and vice versa. Alan was a case in point.

Alan made his competitive debut for Cardiff City on the opening day of 1971/72 against Burnley at Ninian Park. It was a hot day and there was an encouraging attendance of 23,026 who perhaps had the feeling that the club had now made a major signing and were determined to get promotion this time around. And by half-time they felt even better because I had scored twice at the Canton End to send us in at half-time with a 2-0 lead. We were playing well, and you really didn't want the first half to end. Perhaps we came out for the second half thinking that we had already won the match and that they wouldn't find a way back. We stopped doing the things that we had been good at in the first forty-five minutes, and before we knew it Frank Casper had pulled one back for them and then Martin Dobson equalised. We drew 2-2 and the fans were not at all happy that we had let a win slip away.

I was interviewed by one of the national newspapermen afterwards about the way the game had gone. I said in all innocence that if you are 2-0 up, then you don't expect your defence to let in two and perhaps our defence had let us down. I certainly wasn't blaming anyone in particular. In the Monday paper it said 'Clark Blames Defence For City Not Winning'.

They weren't very happy with me in the dressing room when we came in for training, in particular skipper Don Murray and Leighton Phillips who had been our central defenders, and I had to explain to Don what exactly I'd said and to apologise for the way in which it had come out in the paper. Jimmy Scoular called me into his office and told me that I should have had more sense in my reply to the Press and that I should be fully aware in future of what I was saying to them. It was the first time that I had come across this problem with the Press, but Jimmy was right and it taught me a lesson.

That second half against Burnley was a foretaste of what the season held for us because we struggled from start to finish, apart from a few bright spells. We were regularly in or just above the two relegation positions, finishing nineteenth out of twenty-two, and avoiding the drop by just one point! Ironically, it was my best League season for the club in terms of goals – I was ever present in Second Division matches and netted twenty-one times plus another six in various Cup matches. We won only once in our first nine games when we beat Sheffield Wednesday 3-2 at home with, of course, Alan Warboys doing well against his old club – he scored twice.

Two matches into the season Jimmy signed midfield player Roger Hoy from Luton for £25,000. He had started with Tottenham before going to Crystal Palace, and he had a good reputation. But he did not have a happy time with us – in his opening game we lost 4-1 at Orient, and he played in only eight League and League Cup matches up to early October when he suffered a knee problem in our 2-1 home defeat against Millwall. It turned out to be more serious than at first thought and he didn't appear again that season. He had nine League games the following year and in January 1974 joined Bath City after the club had cancelled his contract on medical grounds. He then successfully sued Cardiff City for wrongful dismissal. The whole thing was typical of the way that things were going wrong for the club.

In that match against Millwall when Roger was injured, we had a new goalkeeper. Bill Irwin was signed from Northern Ireland club Bangor for £10,000 and was first choice for the rest of the season. Bill was a likeable Irishman who gave the club good service up to 1978 when he left for the USA to join Washington Diplomats. He still lives in the USA and I saw him in the 2004/05 season when he came to Ninian Park to see a match whilst on a rare visit to this country. Bill came into our line-up in that 1971/72 season at the expense of Jim Eadie who, in February 1973, joined Bristol Rovers where he ended his League career, and Jim still lives in Bristol.

Four days after our home win over Sheffield Wednesday, we were in East Germany to play Dynamo Berlin in our Cup Winners' Cup First Round first leg match. We crossed the Berlin Wall in darkness, changing coaches in no-man's-land – we were seeing the effects of the Cold War at first hand, and it was to be the last time in my career that I travelled abroad for a European match. This was the seventh time that I had journeyed into Europe with Cardiff City – Portugal, Norway, Turkey, Cyprus, France, Spain and now East Germany. They were all interesting experiences and although we had the occasional unfortunate moment along the way, I am glad that I had the opportunity of going to those places as well as taking part in those memorable overseas close season tours of 1968 and 1969.

Dynamo Berlin were a police-sponsored side taking part in European competition for the first time and they were in fact losing Cup Finalists in their own domestic competition at the end of the previous season. When we played them in that first leg, we were just two points off the bottom of Division Two in which we had the worst defensive record! But after Ian Gibson had given us the lead

with twelve minutes left, we looked like coming home with a win
– however, they equalised with the last kick of the game in the
second minute of injury time! The return took place at Ninian Park
in late September, and I gave us a 58th minute lead from Ian
Gibson's pass before they equalised four minutes later, just after
Kingy should have had a clear penalty. He was fouled but the
referee, who was forty-five yards away, waved play on! Seconds
later Jim Eadie fumbled a cross-shot, and the ball ran loose for
them to score. It finished 1-1 after ninety minutes but we could so
easily have won – a Peter King shot had hit the post but Gibbo put
the rebound over the bar with the keeper on the ground. In extra
time my header came off the woodwork, and they cleared one off
the line. And so, for the first time in the club's European Cup
Winners' Cup involvement that began in 1964, there were going to
be penalties to decide it. They were all taken at the Grange End –
Ian Gibson scored for us, they equalised. Then it was skipper Don
Murray's turn, but unfortunately he put his effort over the bar.
Kingy, Gary Bell and Bobby Woodruff all scored, the East
Germans were successful with all their remaining efforts, and they
went through 5-4 on penalties. It turned out to be a disappointing
end in what was to be my last ever European game. No one
blamed Don – it could have happened to any of us, but it was
typical of our season that year because very little went right.
Dynamo Berlin went on to reach the semi-finals where they played
Moscow Dynamo. This time it was the Germans' turn to know
what it had been like for us – they lost on penalties!

In our League Cup fixtures that had also taken place that
month, it was also disappointing. We faced West Ham United at
Upton Park and drew 1-1. Billy Bonds gave them a first half lead
when he out-jumped Gary Bell to score with a header, but Alan
Foggon equalised to give us a replay at Ninian Park. There were
30,109 for the second match for much of which we looked like
winning. I scored after fourteen minutes when Ian Gibson's corner
was headed on by Alan Warboys, and we held the lead until ten
minutes from time when Geoff Hurst equalised, before scoring
the winner shortly afterwards. So we lost 2-1 but it was
tremendous to play against Geoff and Bobby Moore who, despite

his lack of pace, read the game so well. He was a better version of Brian Harris, and Brian was a very good player who many people thought might have played for England in that position if Moore hadn't been the man in possession. They were similar types of players, not particularly quick, but could deal with situations well and never looked to be in trouble. Also in that West Ham side was a fast winger called Harry Redknapp who was to be my teammate when Ian Gibson and I moved to AFC Bournemouth the following season.

As the season reached its half way point in mid-December, we went to mid-table Luton Town in twenty-first place after one win in six games, and we badly needed a good result. When we were getting changed before the game, there was knock on the door, and in came one of the Luton directors Mr J E Bartholomew to welcome us to Kenilworth Road. We recognised him immediately because it was none other than Eric Morecambe (his stage name) of the legendary comedy duo Morecambe and Wise. Luton were Eric's local club as he lived in nearby Harpenden, and he very much enjoyed his football. Jimmy wasn't too happy at Eric coming in because he felt that he had lost his pre-match authority in the dressing room for a brief spell, but he couldn't really say anything except force a smile as Eric spoke to us. Eric was as funny in our dressing room as he was on television in his shows – his glasses were to one of side of his nose, and the lads were in stitches. We were hoping that he would pat Jim on his cheeks and lift him up by his jacket collar as he would on TV with Ernie Wise, but he didn't. It didn't affect our performance on the pitch – we came away with a valuable point from a 2-2 draw after twice being behind. Leighton Phillips scored for us in the first half, and I netted our equaliser ten minutes from the end.

In contrast to our disappointing League form – only late in the season did we win two consecutive Second Division games – we had a good FA Cup run, reaching the Fifth Round. We won 3-1 at Sheffield United in Round Three, having lost there 5-1 in that vital League game the previous April. We were level at 1-1 with five minutes left after Don Murray had given us the lead after nineteen minutes. But with a replay looking likely, Dave Carver and Bobby Woodruff scored two late goals to take us through. How we would gladly have exchanged those two results!

In the Fourth Round we played Sunderland at Ninian Park in front of 27,000, drawing 1-1 after Peter King had given us a first half lead. It was a Wednesday night game, having been postponed from the previous Saturday because of pitch conditions, and we already knew that if we won, then we would play Don Revie's Leeds United in the next round. The replay took place at Roker Park on the following Monday afternoon – there was a power strike at the time so they couldn't use the floodlights, but they still had a 39,348 crowd.

So after our Saturday 2-2 Second Division draw at Charlton, we went home briefly and travelled to the North-East on the Sunday afternoon. Once again it was 1-1 draw, I netted our goal after twenty-five minutes. We were two minutes away from a place in Round Five when little Bobby Kerr equalised, and the game went to extra time without any further score. The second replay was to be held at Manchester City's Maine Road ground two days later on the Wednesday afternoon, so we stayed in the North and immediately after the match at Roker Park set off for Manchester. What was originally a two-day trip turned into four days – we didn't have enough clean shirts and underwear so we had to go into the City Centre and buy a few necessaries!

Not many fans up there were interested in the game – so the 8,868 who turned up were mainly Sunderland fans with a few hundred of our own supporters. This time we came out on top 3-1, but it was close. I gave us the lead after twenty-one minutes, Mick McGiven equalised for them five minutes later, and it looked like going into extra time again. But with five minutes to go, Bobby Woodruff put us ahead and Billy Kellock settled it in injury time. Billy was an 18 year-old Glasgow boy who had been a Scotland Schoolboy International before joining us as an apprentice a few years earlier. He turned professional in early February of that season and made his League debut against Charlton just before we had met Sunderland in the first replay. He had a great start and went on to make several appearances in midfield during the rest of that season. I knew what it was like for him because I had made my own debut at that age when I was with Bristol City.

So now it was to be Leeds United at Ninian Park in Round Five and, despite our being one from bottom of Division Two at the time, there was tremendous interest in the tie. It was an all-ticket game that attracted a 49,180 attendance to Ninian Park – the last-ever occasion that a crowd of over 40,000 was at the ground for a Cardiff City match, the capacity having been reduced for safety reasons over the years to the current 21,000.

At the time, Gill and I were living in Heol Briwnant, Rhiwbina, occupying a club house which Steve Derrett had left at the start of that season when he had joined Carlisle United. We had to move there from the Coryton area because the people who owned the house that the club had originally leased for us when I came from Huddersfield, were returning to Cardiff and wanted to re-occupy it. There were several players and ex-players living near us in Rhiwbina, including the late great John Charles. The former Wales International, who remains a legend in Italian football, was then player/manager at Merthyr Tydfil and had played for both Leeds and Cardiff City. I knew him reasonably well from the three or four months that we had been in the area.

On the Wednesday night before the Leeds game, there was a mighty bang on the front door, and the house shook! I opened the door carefully, and filling the door frame was the massive figure of John Charles. 'Hello, Brian' he said in that familiar deep voice, 'Can I have a word?' I invited him in, he sat down, I asked Gill to get him some tea and as I looked at him I thought that this was the greatest centre half or centre forward that British football had ever produced, and here he was sitting on our sofa in our house asking me for a favour. He had friends coming down from Leeds for the match and was there any chance that I could get him some tickets? I thought how sad that a person of his reputation and stature had to ask for tickets for a game such as that, instead of being invited as an honoured guest and being given a few. I managed to get him some tickets the next day, for which he was very grateful while I was happy to have helped him out. I thought at the time how great it would have been for me to have played alongside him during our respective careers, and I remembered a well recounted occasion when the former England captain and centre half Billy Wright had said that John was the greatest centre forward against whom he had ever played, while in that same week the former England centre forward Nat Lofthouse had said that John was the greatest centre half that he had ever faced.

Leeds arrived chasing a League and FA Cup double – they were second in Division One behind Brian Clough's Derby County and were an outstanding team full of quality players, all of whom were Internationals. For the record, the two teams were:

CARDIFF CITY – Bill Irwin, Dave Carver, Gary Bell, Billy Kellock, Don Murray, Leighton Phillips, Ian Gibson, Brian Clark, Peter King, Bobby Woodruff, Alan Foggon (sub. Alan Warboys)

LEEDS UNITED – Gary Sprake (Wales), Paul Madeley (England), Terry Cooper (England), Billy Bremner (Scotland), Jack Charlton (England), Norman Hunter (England), Peter Lorimer (Scotland), Allan Clarke (England), Mick Jones (England), Johnny Giles (Republic of Ireland), Eddie Gray Scotland). Non-playing substitute – Paul Reaney (England).

Leeds had flown to Cardiff on the Friday morning, and I remember that while we were training around the pitch that day, the Leeds manager Don Revie and his assistant Les Cocker came down the tunnel to have a look at the surface – they were not very pleased at what they saw because there was hardly any grass on it!

Ian Gibson was certainly looking forward to the game – he knew Billy Bremner very well because they had both been Scottish Schoolboy Internationals together, as well as later playing in the Scotland Under-23 side.

I had seen most of that Leeds side in action when I had been at Huddersfield and used to go across to Elland Road in midweek to watch some of their matches when we were not in action. It was going to be great to play against them away from the pressures of the Second Division where we were struggling.

They were just too good for us that day and won 2-0, goals in each half from Johnny Giles, and they went on to win the FA Cup, though they didn't get the 'Double', finishing a point behind the

Champions Derby County. The biggest problem that I had on the day was chasing their left back Terry Cooper who liked to get forward whenever he could, and someone had to pick him up.

That was the end of the excitement for us that season – it was clear that we were no longer capable of mounting a promotion challenge as we had done in the previous three seasons, and we ended 1971/72 with four consecutive defeats, sliding into nineteenth place. It was fortunate that we had beaten Orient and Carlisle in successive mid-April home matches otherwise we could have gone down! Our final League game was at Queen's Park Rangers when our keeper Frank Parsons, who was making only his second appearance of the season, had to go off with a damaged finger. Ian Gibson, who was on the bench, came on to play in goal but couldn't prevent us losing 3-0.

Despite our poor placing that season, Ian had a tremendous season, especially on a difficult Ninian Park pitch that really needed potatoes planted in it! That's no disrespect to groundsman Keith Oliver and his assistant who had a near impossible task in trying to produce a decent surface that year despite a major close season pitch operation in the summer of 1971. Ian literally ran his socks off, and though it was Alan Warboys and myself who scored 34 of our 56 League goals, most of the hard work in creating them was done by Gibbo who missed only one League match that season.

Jimmy Scoular knew that that there would have to be major changes – we had blown up three years in a row when, with all our European experience, we should have made it. But now we were on the slide.

We again reached the Final of the Welsh Cup – hard battles against Swansea City (2-0 away), Llanelli (1-0 away), Rhyl (2-1 away). But our regular representation in Europe as Welsh representatives came to an end in May 1972 when Wrexham beat us in the Final (2-1 at The Racecourse, 1-1 at Ninian Park). It was in keeping with the way that the season had gone for us, and Wrexham were to be the dominant Welsh club of the mid-1970s before Swansea City took on that role in the late 70s.

But my Cardiff City career was shortly to come to an end, at least my first spell with the club. We began the '72/73 season with a new name in the side – defender Albert Larmour whom Jimmy had signed for £10,000 from Linfield, and he played in our opening five Second Division and League Cup matches. It was a reasonable start to 1972/73 – we opened with a 2-1 home win over Luton Town in front of an encouraging 16,364 attendance, and after three League and Cup matches Gary Bell was top scorer with three penalties – which wasn't bad for a full back! But any hopes that an opening day win was the start of a successful season were soon dispelled because we lost seven and won only two of our first nine Second Division games as well as going out of the League Cup in a two-leg First Round to Bristol Rovers who were in the Third Division, one section below us. In that tie I met up again with Sandy Allan who had gone to Rovers in March 1970. So by mid-September 1972 we were bottom of the Division and I had scored just two goals – one against Rovers and another against Millwall in a 1-0 home win of late August. I didn't know it at the time, but those goals were to be my last with Cardiff City for the next three years. Shortly after that Millwall game, Alan Warboys was transferred to Sheffield United where he only stayed for six months before going to Bristol Rovers in March 1973, and he was to have a tremendous goal-scoring partnership there with Bruce Bannister – the two of them were known as 'Smash 'n Grab'.

So things were dramatically changing at Ninian Park and the club was going downhill fast! For me it was very much like the situation at Bristol City in the early part of 1966/67 before my move to Huddersfield. I was struggling, the whole team were struggling, and the effects of those three near promotion seasons had really caught up with us. Ian Gibson and I were gutted that we hadn't gone up, we weren't performing as well as we had done even though the effort was still there. But the spark had gone and our attendances were well down on the previous year when, even though we'd had a bad season, we averaged over 15,000 for each League game.

7

OFF TO THE SOUTH COAST

We had played AFC Bournemouth in a pre-season match just over a year earlier, beating them at Dean Court in late July 1971 when I'd had a good game and scored twice in our 4-3 win. After the match their manager John Bond had come up to me and complimented me on my performance. Maybe he had kept in touch with my progress from then on through his goalkeeper Fred Davies who, of course, I knew very well from his time with me at Ninian Park. A few days after our 3-0 defeat at Queen's Park Rangers on 30 September 1972, a result which left us firmly at the bottom of the table with five points from eleven games (two wins, a draw and eight defeats!), Jimmy Scoular called me into his office and said that he'd had an offer from Third Division AFC Bournemouth for me at £70,000 and for Ian Gibson at £30,000. He said that the Board in the current circumstances could not afford to turn it down because he needed to rebuild the side. He went on to say that Bournemouth had just sold their striker Ted McDougall to Manchester United and they wanted Ian and myself in a package. I had felt for some time that it would be right to move on from Cardiff City because the bubble had burst, and Ian felt the same way. I was approaching 30 years old with a wife and two young daughters. We were living in a house which we didn't own, Gill wasn't working because she was looking after the children, and although I had enjoyed my career with its ups and downs, I hadn't made any money out of football – there wasn't much in my bank account.

So Ian and I drove down to Bournemouth and were booked into a hotel arranged by John Bond. Then we went to Dean Court, as it was then known, to meet Bond who had been a well-known full back during his playing career with West Ham United and Torquay United. He had been appointed the club's manager in 1970 and had revitalised them with new ideas on and off the pitch, one of which was to change their name from 'Bournemouth and Boscombe Athletic' to a more modern sounding 'AFC Bournemouth'. He asked me what salary I was on, saying that he knew anyway. I said it was £35 per week plus bonuses – win, draw, appearance, crowd etc. He said that he would double my salary to £70 per week plus bonuses and he also told me that because the fee for me was £70,000, I would be entitled under League rules to five per cent of that sum – £3,500. I asked about club houses to rent, but he said that it was not the club's policy to have them, that I would have to buy my own property which would be a good investment for the family and myself, and that I needed to get on the property ladder.

So I signed, as did Ian Gibson, and in financial terms for my career it was a very good move, the best I had made money-wise. I used the £3,500 as part payment on a £10,000 four bedroom detached house in Ferndown near Bournemouth not far from Fred Davies. It was certainly a good investment – I wish I'd kept it when we moved back to Cardiff in the mid-1970s because it would have been worth a great deal more than I paid for it. But at least we now had our own house and we were on the property ladder as John Bond had suggested.

When Ian and I first went down to see John, we were in a hotel for about ten days before we came back to Cardiff to sort out our domestic arrangements. In the evenings, I went to bed but Ian went out to the local casino and returned in the early hours – Bournemouth certainly suited him! Fortunately we weren't sharing a room, but he was a great lad and we had a lot of laughs together over the seasons that we played in the same team together.

Of course I was sorry to leave Cardiff City where I had some very good times, and sorry to leave the many friends that Gill and I had made – but it was right for me to move at that stage of my career. Ian Gibson was also sorry to leave Ninian Park, but he took the same view as me as regards our future careers. Cardiff City had signed me for £10,000 and sold me for £70,000, I scored over 100 League and Cup goals for the club, so I certainly didn't feel that I was letting anyone down by moving on.

We didn't get our new house for several months, having several to look at before we decided, and we were put into a Boscombe hotel by the club. In the meantime, our furniture from Cardiff had to be put into store as we had to vacate the Rhiwbina house quickly as it was now required for another player. John Bond could not have looked after us better, and we were in that hotel for a month before the club leased a house for us in Sandbanks not far from Bournemouth. It was a holiday home owned by one of the club's directors and was not used by him during the winter months. That area is now the most expensive for property in the whole of the country and is where my then teammate Harry Redknapp now lives.

I trained in the mornings, and while it was not easy living in a hotel for several weeks with two small daughters, it was a lovely place to be at, with the seaside nearby and nice walks along the front that were great for the children. I thought at the time 'I'm down here at one of the nicest resorts in the country, and getting paid well for what I like doing most'.

I don't know what Jimmy Scoular's real thoughts were about me going – I suppose he was glad in a way because he now had funds to spend on his squad. He never said much to me about it when I left. It was not, however, the last that we would see of each other, and we would be together again in the game several years in the future.

But when you're gone, you're gone, as I found out a fortnight later after my departure when John Bond, his assistant Ken Brown, Fred Davies, Ian Gibson and myself all came up by car to watch a game at Ninian Park. We went to the main entrance for our tickets – there were two for the Grandstand for John and Ken, there were three tickets for the Canton Stand behind the goal for Fred, Ian and myself. After the game the three of us wanted to go up into the Grandstand Club where we had gone on numerous occasions during our time with the club, but the attitude was 'No pass, no entry!' That upset me a little, especially after many supporters in the Canton Stand and outside had said to me that they were sorry that I had gone and that they appreciated all my efforts for the club on the pitch over the previous seasons.

The training at Bournemouth was very much different from Cardiff under Jimmy Scoular where the emphasis was on fitness. But John Bond was a great coach, although I did get to dislike him as a person during my time at Dean Court. His training methods were brilliant, the club was high profile for a Division Three outfit with very good crowds. There were some good players in the team with Harry Redknapp, who had come from West Ham in the summer of 1972, on the right wing and Alan Groves on the left. There was also Phil Boyer, who later went to Norwich, and Micky Cave both of whom played up front.

The town and its surrounding area was in a way too nice a place to live for a professional footballer. After daily training near Hurn Airport just outside Bournemouth, there were so many enjoyable places to take the family – parks, cliff top walks, the sea front. In fact Gill and I still go back to Bournemouth every year to do the walks around the places that we liked so much. As for Ian Gibson, he quickly became big mates with Harry Redknapp, especially with their shared interest betting on the horses. Although they now live at opposite ends of the country and have very different life styles, they still keep in touch. I met Harry for the first time in some twenty years during the 2004/05 season when he came to Ninian Park as manager of Portsmouth for a Carling Cup match. He was very pleased to see me, and then he asked for Ian's telephone number which he had lost.

My debut for AFC Bournemouth was against Tranmere Rovers at Dean Court on 7 October 1972 and there was a 12,769 crowd. John Bond turned up at the ground wearing a white suit, black shirt, white tie and white shoes! I thought that he might have been going on somewhere afterwards, but this was his regular gear for matches – he liked to present an extrovert image. This was one of the reasons that we didn't eventually like each other – I was more of a quiet person in the way I dressed, and I suppose that I didn't fit in with his idea of a leading player in his team. He liked flair players and I was just a hard-working bread-and-butter player, though I could get goals. Perhaps he wanted to mould me into the kind of player that he wanted, but I was maybe too old in footballing terms to change my ways. He wanted to present a First Division image of his club, and though the ground was Third Division, he managed to do that, including changing the colours from red shirts and white shorts to red and black stripes with black shorts.

In my first match Fred Davies was in goal, and Jimmy Gabriel was in the team – the former Everton and Southampton midfield player who had been a colleague of Brian Harris at Everton where they had played together in the 1966 FA Cup Final. One of the first things that Jimmy wanted to know when I met him at Dean Court was how Brian was getting on. Hooky was then player/coach at Newport County.

I had a good reception from the Bournemouth fans although I didn't score in that 1-1 draw against Tranmere. I had been brought in to replace their idol Ted McDougall who had gone to Manchester United five days before my arrival. He had scored 46 League and Cup goals for Bournemouth the previous season, including nine in their 11-0 FA Cup First Round win over Margate. How could I hope to replace him? But three days after my debut, we went to Rotherham and won 7-2 with four goals from me – something that I had never before done in a League match! I in fact scored against three different keepers because in getting the first I collided with their keeper Jim McDonagh and he had to go off. There was only one substitute in those days, he came on and one of the outfield players went in goal. I netted one against him, and at half-time Rotherham put another outfield player in goal – I scored two against him in the second half. Four days later, on the following Saturday, I scored in our 2-0 win at Notts County – five in my first three games, and it was very much like the time when I had come to Cardiff City from Huddersfield Town and had a new lease of life. The Bournemouth fans must have thought that here was the new McDougall! I can still remember that goal at Notts County in what was a very good game against a side that won promotion at the end of that season. The ball was knocked in from the right by Harry Redknapp, and as I headed it in, their goalkeeper Roy Brown caught me in the stomach with his knee – I was completely winded, could hardly breathe, and it took a few minutes of treatment for me to recover. But those are the kind of knocks that you take as a striker, and you have to accept them.

The next few weeks were quite busy, dealing with domestic arrangements, and as I was back and forth to Cardiff and the family, as was Ian Gibson, we were allowed by Cardiff City on a couple of occasions to train at Ninian Park. We changed in the referee's dressing room and worked out on our own. But it all settled down, and eventually Gill, the children and I were installed in the house at Sandbanks.

During the course of the season, John Bond took us to Guernsey for a few days on a 'positive thinking' course in which a lecturer attempted to instil various ideas into us to improve our performance on the pitch. At the back of the lecture room sat Harry Redknapp and Ian Gibson engrossed in the *Racing Post* – listening to lectures about positive thinking did not form part of their scheme of things! It was not, however, all lectures in a class room because some of us played golf while others tried horse riding.

In my first twenty League and Cup games for Bournemouth that season I scored 15 goals, which was a reasonable return. Mid-January 1973 was a time that I still remember well. On 13 January we lost 2-0 at Newcastle United in an FA Cup Third Round tie. We took sixteen players, four of whom were there to make up the squad. Before the match, John Bond brought sixteen square boards into the dressing room, each one displaying a letter of the alphabet. Bond said that we would have to carry them into the middle of the pitch at the start, and line up so that boards read 'WE AIM TO ENTERTAIN'. Alan Groves and Micky Cave said that they wouldn't do it, and that we would look stupid. But Bond told them that if they didn't comply, they wouldn't play for Bournemouth or anyone else in the League ever again. So out we went and lined up facing the main stand with these boards spelling out the words. We then had to turn round and face the other side of the ground. But instead of turning around in a long line, we all did an about turn on the spot. The message now read 'NIATRETNE OT MIA EW'! The crowd howled with laughter, the Newcastle players fell about, we felt absolute fools, and John Bond went spare on the touchline, waving his arms wildly to try and get us in the right order – we entertained them all right! It was all over the national sports pages the next day, and we never tried that again.

The following week I scored my fifteenth and last goal of the season in a 1-1 draw at Scunthorpe United's Old Show Ground. It was a freezing cold day and the temperature was dropping throughout the afternoon. We had travelled up by coach the day before, and it was starting to snow as the game finished. We were quickly showered and changed, and were on the coach for the long journey home some thirty minutes after the end of the match. The roads were white and slippery so the driver wasn't rushing, and we headed towards Doncaster to pick up the A1 going South. As we came round a bend not far out of Scunthorpe, there was a car in the middle of the road that had been attempting turn right, but had skidded. Between the car and the terraced houses on the left of the road was a gap that the coach could not get through, but as our driver applied his brakes, the coach slid onto the pavement and into the porch of one of the houses. Several of the players were shaken and bruised, I was sitting towards the front with Ian Gibson and we were all right. But the front nearside of the coach had taken the impact and had been forced inwards, trapping John Bond's assistant Ken Brown who had been standing in the well by the door. We tried to release him but couldn't, and he told us to get out of the coach quickly and leave him. We escaped through the rear windows which had dropped out in the impact, and soon the Police, Fire Brigade and ambulances were on the scene. We all went across the road to a pub where the landlord got us some hot soup and looked after us while another coach was ordered. Ken was cut free from the coach and taken to hospital with a broken thigh bone from which he eventually made a good recovery.

The incident had been reported to BBC Radio, and it was announced on *Sports Report* that the AFC Bournemouth team coach had been involved in a road accident between Scunthorpe and Doncaster, and that there had been casualties. A number of our wives heard that news, and it was not very pleasant for them. Fred Davies managed to ring his wife to tell her that, apart from Ken, we were all safe, and she telephoned Gill to say that I was all right. It was a worrying journey home in the conditions, but we arrived back safely in Bournemouth.

I played in thirteen matches during the remainder of the season and failed to score in any of them, having previously obtained 12 League goals and 3 in the FA Cup. The club's Reserve and Youth Coach Trevor Hartley had taken over from the unavailable Ken Brown. Hartley was a former West Ham and Bournemouth winger who had been forced to retire through injury at the end of the previous season. I had got on well with Ken who was my sort of person in his approach to the game, but I did not get on too well with Hartley who was John Bond's kind of person. In the end I was dropped for the final four matches of the season in which we finished seventh, seven points off the two promotion positions. I was a far post player who liked to get on the end of crosses, Bond always wanted me to come to the near post and that wasn't my game. I lost my place to Paul Aimson who had been signed in early March from York City.

It was during that season with AFC Bournemouth that I went on a four-day sales representative course in Southampton sponsored by the Professional Footballers' Association. On that course were several other players who, like me, were not far off the end of their full time League careers. It was a worthwhile exercise as far as I was concerned, and it was to prove valuable a few years later.

I had been wondering for a few months where I stood in the scheme of things at Bournemouth regarding my future, and in the last week of the season John Bond put up a list on the dressing room notice board of the squad that was to go on the club's close season tour to Persia, Australia, New Zealand and Tahiti. I was included, so too was little John Parsons who had joined us from Cardiff City the previous February. So it was a case of going home and telling the other half that once again I was off on a summer tour – not only Australia and New Zealand, but this time also Persia and Tahiti. And once again it went down very well, or rather not too well! It was an eleven game tour, leaving on 21 May from Heathrow and arriving back on 23 June. As for John Parsons, he was due to get married back in Cardiff during that time, and he asked John Bond if he could be let off the tour. Bond asked him which was more important – his football career or getting married? What could he say to the manager who had only signed him a few months earlier? He was in a difficult position, so he had to postpone his wedding and come on the tour, and that caused John a few domestic problems! But I'm sure that he was glad that he came with us because those kind of trips don't come round very often, especially in the lower divisions. From my point of view, I thought that with my career in League football not far off its close, it would probably be my last overseas tour.

I have to say that while it was a memorable trip, it wasn't as enjoyable as those that I had been on with Cardiff City. It was a more rigid tour, we did not have as much fun as I'd had previously, and that was probably because the Bournemouth squad, although a good one, was not as close as the Cardiff City one of which I had been part.

We won ten of the eleven games, our only defeat being in the opening match in Tehran, and I played in the first eight games, scoring seven goals before I was injured. For the final nine days of the tour we were in Tahiti where we had a great time, snorkelling, sunbathing and generally enjoying ourselves. I was snorkelling over a coral reef when Fred Davies swam up behind me. I didn't see him and he grabbed me round the ankle shouting 'Shark' as a joke. It frightened the life out of me and I scraped my knee on the coral as I tried to swim away. It was sharp and I had a bad gash, but that was the sort of daft thing that Fred would do.

9

DOWN THE OLD KENT ROAD

We were well settled as a family in Ferndown. I lived near Fred Davies and our wives got on well, which was great because they would get together whenever the team was away. It was a lovely hot summer in Bournemouth in 1973 following our return from the tour. Pre-season training went well, but it was a disappointing start because we lost 3-0 at home to Bristol Rovers on the opening day, two of their goals being scored by my former Cardiff City teammate Alan Warboys. It was the first of two home games against them in four days because they then returned for a League Cup First Round tie, although I was dropped for that one. I had in fact played my last game for the club because Bond had called me into his office following the opening game and said that the Millwall manager Benny Fenton had offered £40,000 for my transfer. I didn't have to go, said Bond, but money was a bit tight at Dean Court and it would help if I did go.

I thought that I wouldn't stay there if I wasn't really wanted, and I did not particularly like John Bond, so I was pleased with the thought of moving on. The next day I travelled by train from Bournemouth to London's Waterloo Station where I met Benny Fenton who drove me down the Old Kent Road to The Den in Cold Blow Lane where they then played. I'd been there several times before as an opposing player, but now it was to be my base. The Den was a homely pokey ground and Benny's office was more or less a cubby hole! Benny was a former wing half with West Ham, Millwall, Charlton and Colchester, and he was a genuine easy-going person who wasn't really hard enough with the players to be an effective manager. I had been used to hard men such as Fred Ford, Tom Johnston and Jimmy Scoular, while John Bond been highly professional in his approach to the game. I liked Benny though, and he made me very welcome, explaining that he wanted me to play up front with Alfie Wood, a useful goalscorer who had come from Shrewsbury Town a year earlier.

Benny and I talked about the move – I was now 30 and the prospect of playing again in Division Two as well as getting a five per cent cut of the transfer fee looked appealing. The only thing that I didn't fancy was living in London. Benny said that if I travelled back up by train the next day, then he would show me the areas in which the players lived. But I thought that it had taken me just one hour and forty minutes on the train from Bournemouth to Waterloo, while the players at Millwall lived at least forty-five minutes away from the ground on the outskirts of London. I could easily get a bus or tube from Waterloo to New Cross which was a short walk from The Den.

It would save the club legal and relocation expenses if I continued to live in Ferndown, so Benny agreed that Millwall would supply me with a railway season ticket, and I became a regular commuter on the Southern Region of British Rail. Gill was quite happy about that because we liked where we lived and did not want to uproot the children. As I had not asked for a transfer, I had £2,000 as my five per cent of the fee, and I used that towards paying off our house, while my weekly terms were an increase on what I had been getting at Bournemouth, so it was another good move for me.

I used to catch the 7.30 am Bournemouth-Waterloo train that called at Southampton and Winchester where the bowler hat City brigade would get on, spending the journey doing *The Times* crossword, while I was reading *Goal* and other football magazines as well as the sports pages of the papers. It was an easy daily journey, and I found that I could comfortably get to The Den by about 9.30 am in time to report for training at 10.00 am. Training was usually over by mid day, so after a bath and a cup of tea, I would be looking for a lift off one of the lads back to Waterloo, and I could get the 1.00 pm or 1.30 pm train back to Bournemouth, getting there by mid afternoon. The only problem arose when there were midweek evening games. After home matches I could get the last train back, but away games in midweek were a bit of a nightmare, especially up North. I remember on one occasion in March 1974 playing at Middlesbrough in a midweek match. I scored in our 2-1 defeat, my former Cardiff City colleague Alan Foggon playing for them. We arrived back in London and I was dropped off the team coach near Waterloo at about 3.00 am. I then had to get the newspaper train that stopped at every station along the way, arriving at Bournemouth at about 6.30-7.00 am. Fortunately Middlesbrough won the Second Division Championship under Jack Charlton that season so it didn't happen again, but that was one aspect of playing for Millwall that I didn't particularly enjoy. It was my choice, though, and I could have no real complaints about it.

I knew quite a few of the Millwall lads from having played against them when I was with Cardiff City. If the players at Ninian Park were a great bunch of guys, Millwall were not far behind with their Cockney wit and good humour. They were nearly all seasoned professionals – Harry Cripps, Bryan King, Barry Kitchener and others – while they had a 19-year-old left winger named Gordon Hill who had joined them the previous January from non-league Southall. He was to get a regular place in that 1973/74 season and had a great left foot, but the players didn't like him because they thought that he was too full of himself. They used to make fun of him and play tricks on him – so with me being a new member of the squad, I became his 'minder'! He lived to the west of London and also came in by train to Waterloo, arriving just after me, so we would meet up and travel to the ground together. Occasionally he would drive across London from his home and pick me up at the Elephant and Castle. He later went on to play for Manchester United and England, and we still remain very friendly to this day even though he now lives in the United States. But he comes back once a year to do some coaching in West Wales and we always meet up.

Millwall was then a club run more or less by the players for the players! We would come in some days and Benny Fenton would ask what we fancied doing that morning – if the lads wanted to play five-a-side on the astro-turf down at Deptford, then that's where we would go. It was a homely friendly club, and I have very fond memories of my two seasons with them. Last season I was at the New Den doing commentary summarising on Cardiff City's internet service, and there were several people at the club who still remembered me and were pleased to see me.

In those days when I was a player, clubs did not pay wages into your bank account. On Fridays you would go to the Club Secretary's office to pick up your pay packet. Early on in my Millwall career, I came out of the office on a Friday and Frankie Saul, the former Tottenham player who had played against me in reserve team football for them early in my Bristol City career, told me to come and have a look in the boot of his car. He had an array of watches, rings and cutlery, all at very competitive prices – Frankie, who regularly had a car load of gear, obviously had some good contacts in South London! I had some nice cutlery off him, and we still have it at our home in Cardiff as well as a watch that I bought off him.

One of the Millwall legends, with whom I played in that team, was left back Harry Cripps, sadly now no longer with us. He had been with them for twelve years when I joined the club, and he made over 400 appearances for them after coming from West Ham where he had been a junior. He was Millwall through and through, not a great player but one of the most reliable defenders that you would ever come across. He was very strong, would give you 110 per cent, and had a great affinity with the Millwall crowd. They were great supporters who accepted me well, and it was different to Bournemouth where they wanted skill and flair. But as long you gave your all for Millwall and were brave, then they were with you all the way.

I didn't miss a game in that 1973/74 season after I joined them, and I scored 13 League and Cup goals which wasn't too bad considering that I was coming towards the end of my League career.

I don't suppose that it was the best preparation on match days coming by train from Bournemouth, but at least I wasn't driving and I could relax on the journey. One Wednesday morning I was on the train from Bournemouth and the steward, whom I knew well from my regular journeys, told me that when I arrived at Waterloo I should head straight home again as there was to be a twenty-four hour main line rail drivers' strike at mid-day. But I went to the ground, and when I made my way back to Waterloo after training, there was chaos! The station was shut, so I went by Underground to Victoria Coach Station with the aim of getting back to Bournemouth by coach. No chance, everyone was queuing for coaches, so I tried to hire a car but none were available. But then I saw a coach going to Heathrow Airport so I took that with the intention of hiring a car when I got there. I sat next to an American who told me that he was going back to New York, and he asked me to which part of the world I was heading – 'Bournemouth!' I replied. I successfully hired a car, and arrived home safely – it was one of the occasional problems that I had in commuting from Bournemouth.

There was one occasion when we played at home to Fulham. It was on Sunday, 20 January 1974 and it was the time of the power crisis and the 'three day week'. No floodlights could be used so a number of clubs played earlier on the Saturday. I should really have driven up on the Saturday and stayed overnight at Gordon Hill's home for an 11.00 am kick-off on the Sunday. So I left home at 7.00 am on the Sunday – no problems driving to London, but as I was going over Chelsea Bridge, the car's engine cut out. It was about 8.30 am and I was in the middle of the road. The car behind stopped, and out got four lads who said that they would push me into a parking spot. They had black and white scarves on, and they were Fulham supporters on their way to The Den for the game. They recognised me and said that they would drive me near to the ground. I was very grateful and arrived there in good time. I offered to get them tickets, but they already had them for the Fulham end, and they said that they would meet me after the match and give me a lift back to my car.

I didn't think that they would be there, especially after I scored the only goal of the game after eleven minutes – the first ever Football League goal to be scored on a Sunday – but sure enough they were waiting for me. I kept in touch with those supporters while I was at Millwall, and if there was an attractive match at The Den, I would get them tickets if they were not travelling away with Fulham.

I scored the following week in our 3-0 win at Oxford United, but in the remaining fifteen League matches I managed only three goals. Perhaps all the travelling was beginning to catch up with me, and the season seemed to go on and on. We finished in mid-table, but while my goal scoring tailed off in the last few months of 1973/74, Alf Wood was knocking them in regularly – he finished with twenty-four goals and I ended with thirteen. Gordon Hill had now established himself in our line-up and he had eight goals that season, not bad for an orthodox winger. There was one occasion that season when we were away from home. We were in a hotel lounge waiting to go in for our pre-match meal. There was an announcement from the reception desk saying that there was a telephone call for Gordon. He took the call which was from a 'newspaper reporter'. It was in fact one of the lads setting him up! They talked about Gordon's progress and the 'reporter' asked about his tennis. Gordon was quite a good tennis player and the 'reporter' said that if he sent a photographer to the Den during the following week, could they have a picture of Gordon in his tennis kit holding a racket? There would be a fee involved, said the 'reporter' and Gordon agreed to do it.

A few days later, we got into the dressing room for training and there was Gordon in his tennis kit with his racket. As we got changed, Gordon sat there with his racket and none of the lads could keep a straight face. Eventually Benny Fenton asked him if he was going to play tennis or coming training with us. Everyone fell about laughing and Gordon realised what had happened. He asked me if I knew about it and why hadn't I told him. I was in a difficult position – if I had let on what was happening, I might have fallen out with the other lads. So I told him that I hadn't been in on it. If it had been a serious trick, then I probably would have told him, but this was harmless enough.

In mid-March 1974, we were at Ninian Park to play Cardiff City who were in danger of going down. At least I didn't have to travel to London and join up with the squad for the journey to South Wales. Gill, the girls and I drove to Mum and Dad's house in Horfield on the Friday, and Dad and I drove to Cardiff the next day. It was like old times, and yet it wasn't. The Jimmy Scoular era had finished, and Jimmy Andrews was now in charge, with the side including quite a few new faces. Don Murray was still there and tried hard against me – I had a few kicks off him as I would have expected. But we had the better of things that day and I scored in our 3-1 win. So too did Harry Cripps who had just returned to the side after being out for five months. I had a good reception from the crowd, and there were a number of my friends from the area at the game. But the crowd was only 7,662, and that clearly showed that the good times had gone from Ninian Park. I was pleased with our win, but a little sad that our victory had put Cardiff deeper in trouble, though they did escape the drop by getting a point in their very last match against Crystal Palace who themselves went down. It was a reasonable season for me with Alfie Wood and myself getting thirty-seven League and Cup goals between us, but I was now 31 and my legs weren't quite doing what I wanted them to on the pitch. I was never the quickest of players at my peak, and now I was slower. I was glad to see the end of the season, and the regular rail journeys back and forth to London. The family and I didn't need to go on holiday that summer, not with the sunshine and the beaches in Bournemouth.

The time passed all too quickly on the South Coast, and in mid-July 1974 I was back on the daily 7.30 am train to Waterloo for pre-season training at Millwall. The thought was crossing my mind as to how long I would be able to continue playing in the higher divisions of League football – I would soon be thirty-two, and with a wife and two young daughters to be looked after, I would have to address the future, but not quite yet. There were always the lower divisions in which I could do a job, and that would happen sooner than I thought!

In July and August of 1974, we would report to The Den each morning during that pre-season period, get changed, and go in a coach to the training ground near Crystal Palace. We would get there about 10.30 am, training would start at 11.00 am and finish at 1.00 pm in time for lunch. There would be another session in the afternoon, and by the time that I caught the late afternoon train from Waterloo, crowded with home going commuters, I would not get into Bournemouth until after 7.00 pm – they were long days to the start of the new season.

1974/75 did not start too well – we were beaten 4-1 at home by Sunderland on the opening day. The 10,573 fans who saw the game certainly let us know what they thought – if things were going well on the pitch, they would be fully behind you, but when you were getting well beaten, they would make their feelings known with typical Cockney invective! Substitute for Millwall on that opening day was my former Cardiff City teammate Billy Kellock who had been signed on trial after a season with Norwich City, but he did not stay with us for very long. We redressed the balance two days later with a 3-0 home win over Nottingham Forest, and on the following Saturday came one of the big highlights of my career – playing against Manchester United at Old Trafford. It's hard to imagine these days United being outside top level football, but they had just been relegated from the original Division One at the end of 1973/74 and were now playing in the Second Division under manager Tommy Docherty.

I was very excited about the fixture, as were we all, and I travelled to London on the Friday. We trained in the morning and I spent the rest of the day with Gordon Hill, staying at his home before we met up with the team at Euston on the Saturday morning to catch the Manchester-bound train. I had played at most Football League grounds since I had become a professional, but I had never before been to Old Trafford. Alex Stepney was in goal for them, Jim Holton and Martin Buchan were in defence, and Stuart Pearson was in attack. There were just short of 42,000 for the game in which they were far too strong for us, winning 4-0. But it was a great experience for me to play there, and I never realised until then how wide the Old Trafford playing area was.

It was soon clear early in the season that we were going to struggle, especially after we had lost six of our first eleven Second Division matches and were not far off the relegation zone. By then Benny Fenton had left me out as I hadn't scored in any of the seven League and Cup appearances that I had made up to that time. Once again it was one of those spells that all forwards go through – lack of confidence, maybe, not many scoring opportunities, and snatching unsuccessfully at those rare ones that did come along. But I was not the only one failing to score because Alfie Wood was also struggling.

In early October 1974, Benny Fenton resigned as manager. He had been under pressure since the start of the season and it was no real surprise. The lads were sorry to see him go partly for selfish reasons because they had been able to manipulate him so that they could have an easy life in training. I was sorry to see him leave because he was a nice person and he had looked after me when I had joined the club. His trainer/coach – the former Scotland and West Ham keeper Lawrie Leslie – had tried to instill a professional approach to our training, but without a great deal of success as the lads were unresponsive to his ideas, and it was becoming more and more frustrating for Lawrie. It was not that we were unfit, but everyone wanted to do things their way – five-a-sides, for instance, when they didn't feel like doing anything more strenuous. But now they were worried about who might be brought in by the directors, and how things might change.

The new man was former Charlton defender Gordon Jago who had resigned a few weeks earlier from Queen's Park Rangers after being in charge at Loftus Road for the previous three years. By the time that Jago arrived in mid-October, caretaker-boss Lawrie Leslie had reinstated me in the first team, and I scored my first two goals of the season in our 4-0 home win over Southampton. It was certainly all change as soon as the new manager took over. Within days he had transferred long-serving Harry Cripps to Charlton, and a month later Alfie Wood went to Hull City for £75,000. Harry's departure left me with the feeling that there were going to be plenty more changes. Like John Atyeo at Bristol City and Brian Harris at Cardiff City, Harry, whose final appearance for Millwall had been in that opening day home defeat by Sunderland, epitomised the club. He was part of the furniture, and it was never the same at The Den after his departure.

One thing that Gordon Jago was unhappy about was my travelling arrangments, but there was nothing that he could do about it, as it was in my contract that I could live in Bournemouth. He told me that when my contract was up at the end of the season, we would talk about the situation. I had the feeling that at the end of that season I would no longer be making that daily rail journey from Bournemouth to Waterloo.

We continued to struggle throughout that season and were always in or near the relegation zone. In fact we went down along with Cardiff City and Sheffield Wednesday, despite us bringing in ten new signings – loans and transfers. One of the newcomers was Cardiff-born full back Jon Moore from Bristol Rovers for £10,000 in early December. I got on very well with Jon as he had Cardiff and Bristol connections, and we knew the same people in the game. His brother Terry was until last summer, on Cardiff City's Academy staff. Another signing was England Amateur International forward Chris Kelly who arrived in late January, having been outstanding in Leatherhead's FA Cup run to the Fourth Round that season. His press quotes had been outstanding as well, and earned him the nickname of the 'Leatherhead Lip'.

That '74/75 season saw me obtain just six goals in thirty-four League and Cup games, one of which was at Ashton Gate when we lost 2-1 against Bristol City in mid-March. It was the 200th League goal of my career, but it was the first time that I had ever played in a relegation side. We didn't win any of our final six matches, and we played Bristol Rovers at home in the final game. They were two points ahead of us, and if we had beaten them, then we would have stayed up on goal average at their expense. But we could only draw 1-1, and we were down. It was a terrible feeling in what had been a very disappointing season, both for the team and myself – I was glad to see the end of it.

In May 1975, Gordon Jago offered me the position of reserve team player/coach and youth coach, provided that I came to live in London. He felt that I still had something to contribute, but not necessarily at first team level. I declined the offer as I had no intention of moving the family from Bournemouth to London where house prices were much higher. Two years of rail commuting had been enough for me, while AFC Bournemouth had been sounding me out about returning to them especially now that John Bond was no longer manager, but nothing definite came out of that. So Millwall gave me a free transfer, and my name was circulated to clubs on the annual PFA end-of-season list.

10

RETURN TO SOUTH WALES

I did not think that I would be short of offers, even if they were in the lower divisions. I did not want to retire, especially as I knew no other way of life – my job was scoring goals as a professional footballer, and I felt that I could still do that.

I had telephone calls from Bristol City, Oxford United, Swansea City and Newport County. Plymouth Argyle sounded interested, and I had a telegram from Harry Parsons at Cardiff City – 'Brian, contact me at Ninian Park as soon as possible.'

Bristol City had asked me to come on a pre-season trial basis, but I felt that even though they were a Second Division club, it would not have been a good move for me at 32 years of age. As it turned out, they went up to the old Division One for the first time in sixty-five years at the end of the 1975/76 season, so if I had gone back to Ashton Gate and been reasonably successful, I might even have achieved an ambition of playing in top-class League football. I also had an offer from my former AFC Bournemouth teammate Dave Chadwick who was coaching a South African side, but I wasn't quite brave enough to accept and take the family there for a year. I wish now that I had done that – it would have been a great experience for us.

So I followed up the telegram from Harry Parsons who had sent it on behalf of Cardiff's manager Jimmy Andrews because I knew Harry very well and had remained friends with him after I had left Ninian Park in 1972. Jimmy made me an offer and I signed at the start of July 1975 after talking it over with Gill. Why did I return to Ninian Park? Our two girls had both been born in Cardiff, I had enjoyed my previous spell on and off the pitch with City, and our friends were still there, especially our baby sitting circle which was still operational. If I was going to retire in the not-too-distant future and seek a career outside the game, Gill and I wanted it to be in Cardiff where we knew a lot of people, while it was only forty-five minutes away from Mum and Dad in Bristol and they would be able to see their grandchildren regularly, while I would be near enough to sort out any problems for them as they got older.

I said at the time in reply to reporters' questions that it was good to be back and that things had not changed a great deal at Ninian Park. But, of course, they had – the club had been relegated, there was new management from when I had previously been there, while a new consortium under local hotel owner Stefan Terleski had taken control of Cardiff City. Ninian Park was completely different in terms of personnel apart from a few of the senior professionals, although Harry Parsons was still very much part of the scene, while some of the younger players who had been there in my previous spell had now broken into the first team.

The move meant a change of domestic arrangements. We had to sell our house in Ferndown, and we had some difficulty in finding a suitable property in Cardiff. It took us three months to find the house which we still occupy thirty years later. But while we were looking, Gill and the girls went down to Cornwall to stay with her family. I stayed in Bristol with Mum and Dad, travelling over the Severn Bridge each day. But then we all wanted to be together, so Gill, the girls and I lived at a hotel in Cardiff's Cathedral Road for a month while the purchase of our new house was being arranged. Also in that hotel was midfield player Doug Livermore whom Cardiff City had signed from Norwich City just after the start of the new season.

I had a great reception from the fans in our pre-season matches, but I was concerned about whether or not I could still do it on the pitch and what sort of impact I could make now that I was 32. My concerns were justified because I scored just one goal in the opening fifteen Third Division and League Cup matches – I felt that my sell-by date had passed! One of the reasons was that I was devoting a fair amount of time to getting our new house sorted out as a great deal of work was needed on it. So I was not really focused enough on my football, and while I was still giving one hundred per cent in training and on the pitch, I was not really contributing enough and was not sharp enough. I was playing up front with Tony Evans who had come from Blackpool on a free transfer that summer and who eventually looked very useful in front of goal, while another good signing was our skipper Mike England. The former Tottenham and Wales defender had returned from playing in the USA that summer and was intending to retire. But Jimmy Andrews, who had been his coach at Tottenham, persuaded Mike to give it one last season with Cardiff City, and he proved inspirational at the back. Our former Manchester United and Aston Villa winger Willie Anderson returned to the club from the USA at the end of September, and the side was starting to come together. But it took time, and towards the end of October 1975 we were in the lower half of the table, having scored only fifteen goals in thirteen League games. If we were to make a promotion challenge and return to Division Two at the first attempt, then we needed more goals.

On 29 October, Jimmy Andrews signed Adrian Alston from Luton Town for £25,000. Adrian was a Preston lad who had emigrated to Australia and had been outstanding in Australia's participation in the 1974 World Cup Finals, which had resulted in Luton signing him. His arrival at Ninian Park signified the end of my regular first team involvement because he scored twice on his debut in our 4-3 home win over Chesterfield. He went on to score 20 League and Cup goals that season which saw Tony Evans finish with 29 in all competitions. Those two formed a great goal scoring partnership, and I was then out of the side until early March 1976. So I could have no argument about being left out, and I had to be satisfied with reserve team activity in the Football Combination until I was eventually recalled. Although I was playing regular games, I was not really enjoying it – I would have rather have been in the first team. But the side was doing well, Alston and Evans were scoring regularly, Doug Livermore was outstanding in midfield, so I could only be patient and hope that my chance would come again. In the meantime, I was making what I thought was a useful contribution by coaching the club's young players on Tuesday and Thursday evenings, and I was hoping that it might lead to something more permanent at the club. But I should have done my coaching qualifications during that time, and not doing so was something that I was to regret.

Jimmy Andrews, who was an excellent coach, but, like Benny Fenton, perhaps too nice to be a really strong manager, had asked me to try my hand at looking after the youngsters, and I was enjoying it. There should have been a coaching job for Mike England who was held in high regard by the players, but Jimmy didn't offer him anything, and he left the club after the final League match of the season, when we had won promotion, to return to the USA. Maybe Jimmy might have felt apprehensive about Mike being involved.

In the first month of that '75/76 season, Tony Villars had been a regular on the right wing. He had joined the club from Panteg in the summer of 1972 when I had been in my first spell at Ninian Park. He was a player of immense talent who could have gone right to the top, but he did not have the ambition to push himself and just drifted along in and out of the side. It was frustrating for me to see a player of his ability not making the most of it, and I had the feeling that playing professional football to a high level was something that did not really interest him. I might have been wrong, but that was the impression that he created. After spending the following season with Newport County, he went into non-league football, becoming a milkman in his local Panteg area and playing golf which he liked doing. I saw him a couple of years ago, and that is what he is still doing. I always compared a player like him to myself – he had the type of ability and pace which I would have liked, but did not have, and I always had to work hard in order to succeed in the game, right from the day when I began to do well with Bristol Schools.

From early March 1976 I had a ten-match League and Welsh Cup run in the side, scoring a couple of goals. Willie Anderson was out through injury, and we played three strikers during that time – Evans, Alston and myself. Things were going well at Ninian Park and we were just two points behind the three promotion positions with seven matches left. Alan Campbell, the Birmingham City midfield player, had been signed for £20,000 in early March, and his inclusion helped in the final push for promotion.

I was dropped by Jimmy Andrews in early April, when Willie Anderson returned after injury, and I was on the bench for the occasional game. But I was not in the twelve for the mid-April Wednesday night home match against the eventual title winners Hereford United. I watched from the stand and there was a massive crowd at Ninian Park to see us win 2-0 with second half goals from Doug Livermore and Alan Campbell. The previous Saturday the lads had been 1-0 winners at fellow promotion contenders Crystal Palace in front of a 25,603 attendance. After the game, their manager Malcolm Allison had apparently said that we were not in the same league as them for crowds, and that we would be lucky to get 25,000 for the Hereford match. There were 35,549 at Ninian Park for the game and it indicated to me that, if the club could continue to make progress, the support was there to carry the club to the top level.

We clinched promotion, along with Hereford United and my former club Millwall, at Bury in the final League game on 14 May 1976 when Adrian Alston scored in our 1-0 win. I was not in the squad for the game, and did not travel to Gigg Lane. I was delighted for the lads and the club that we had gone up, but was very disappointed that I had not played a bigger part in our success. I had played twenty-one League and seven Cup matches, but had scored just four goals! My final two matches for Cardiff City were against Hereford United in our two-leg Welsh Senior Cup Final in mid-May 1976 when we drew 3-3 at Edgar Street and beat them 3-2 in the return at Ninian Park. I scored our second goal, and there were just 2,648 at the game. I did not know it at the time, but that was my very last match and goal for Cardiff City. So I had helped the club once again secure a place in the European Cup Winners' Cup, I had added to my collection of Welsh Cup winners' tankards, but I was no longer to be part of the club's future. They did take me on their end-of-season week-long celebration holiday to Majorca, but I already knew that I was being given a free transfer. Jimmy Andrews had called me in, thanked me for my services, and told me that he did not think that I would be up to the standard of Second Division football for the following season.

I thought to myself that, because of my performances in that '75/76 season, he was right. I knew that I was coming towards the end of my career, but I did not want to give up just yet. Maybe part-time football was the answer with a new career outside the game?

11

REJOINING JIMMY SCOULAR

As regards my remaining football career, I had a call soon after the end of 1975/76 from my former Cardiff City boss Jimmy Scoular who had been in charge at struggling Newport County since February 1976 after a few years out of management. He did not have a great financial deal to offer me, but it was a club just twelve miles along the road and he was willing to let me play as a part-timer. It was a situation for Jimmy that was far different from anything that he had been used to during his career as player and manager. Newport had little or no money, a ground that was below the usual standards of League football, and their prospects of success in Division Four did not look promising. There would certainly be no overnight trips for away games and there would be no European excitement! It looked to me as if Jimmy did not want to let go of the game, nor for that matter did I.

My Mum had often asked me what I would do when I gave up playing, as I did not know anything else. But at the time that I joined Newport County in early July 1976, I had been offered a trial position as a sales representative with Protect-U Ltd, a Cardiff firm that distributed industrial safety wear used by various factories, firms and local authorities. Their managing director was Colin Dudderidge who was a season ticket holder at Cardiff City. I knew him from meeting him on various sporting occasions, and he felt that, with my name and achievements in football, I could be useful to his business.

Jimmy Scoular was quite happy for me to train with Newport on Tuesday and Thursday mornings, and I would work for Protect-U Ltd for the remainder of the week, getting time off for any mid-week fixtures. The arrangement suited me because I was away from the problems of Newport County for most of the time – and they certainly had problems! I joined Protect-U Ltd on a two-month trial, learning about their products in the warehouse and going out on the road with their two South Wales representatives – Clive Humphries and Keith Pearson, both of whom had been in the industrial safety wear world for a long time – they both taught me a great deal. The company wanted me as a third rep covering the Cardiff and Barry area where I was best known. I was not the kind of person to trade on my name and reputation, but it certainly helped when I called on firms asking to see their buyers. More often than not they would know my name and be prepared to see me. We would start off by talking football before getting down to business, but football alone would not get me orders – I had to have good quality products to sell to them, and be knowledgeable regarding what they needed. I was to be in the industrial safety wear business as a sales rep. for twenty-seven years, travelling throughout South and West Wales, so I had found a secure future outside of football, making many friends and acquaintances over those years, especially people involved in other sports. One of them was Swansea and Wales Rugby Union full back or centre Roger Blyth who won six caps for his country between 1974 and 1980. Roger was in fact one of Protect-U Ltd's business rivals as he was managing director of his family firm that also sold industrial safety wear. A number of years later, when Protect-U Ltd ceased trading, Roger offered me the opportunity of working for him, and I was with his firm until the day I retired in 2003.

But in that summer of 1976, my involvement in football was not yet at an end. I was now really looking forward to the season ahead and playing for Newport County in what was becoming a paid hobby. My dual life of football and work fitted nicely around family life. But as I became more and more involved in my sales representative career, my territory began to increase. I had more business appointments and could no longer train in the mornings, so Jimmy Scoular agreed that I could come over to Somerton Park on Tuesday and Thursday evenings to train with the club's other part-timers.

But I had joined a club that could not maintain the kind of

standards that I was used to. Newport County lived from hand to mouth on very small attendances, and it would often be the case that when I went in to collect my wages from their long-serving Club Secretary Keith Saunders, a great character who was an expert at 'keeping the wolves from the door', he would tell me that there was no money to pay me, and that I would have to wait until next week when I would have two wage packets. I used to leave the ground wondering what on earth I was doing there!

Signing for Newport meant that I linked up again with a number of former Cardiff City colleagues – Jimmy Scoular, of course, Gary Bell who had been there for a few seasons as had John Parsons, Peter Morgan, brother of Richie Morgan, who had arrived the previous season, Steve Derrett who had come from Rotherham United, Tony Villars who had now left Cardiff City, and Ronnie Bird who had given up his hair dressing salon in Cardiff to join Jimmy as his trainer/coach that summer. And in mid-October, Don Murray joined us after a spell with Edinburgh club, Hearts. Ronnie, who had been with Jimmy off and on for many years, was the peacemaker in the dressing room when Jimmy blew his top – and he did that quite often at Newport!

County had finished in the bottom four of the Fourth Division and had sought re-election to the Football League at the end of the previous season, so they were desperate to finish outside of the bottom four in 1976/77. But we won only two of our first twenty-six League matches and it was beginning to look a hopeless cause. Jimmy had not endeared himself to the fans because he had changed the club's colours that summer to blue-and-white stripes. County had always played in amber, and then tangerine, and the supporters felt that he was trying to create a new 'Cardiff City'. If we had been successful, they probably would not have minded, but the way things were, it was looking as if the club would not get back in if they had to seek votes once again.

Jimmy Scoular was battling on, and although he never confided in me, I knew what he was thinking about the kind of standard that he and I and his former Cardiff City players were now in. But it was a very friendly club and, despite all the problems, there was a good spirit amongst all the lads. I have to say, though, that during the first half of the season, I was not really enjoying my football because of our situation.

In our second Fourth Division match of the new season we were at Darlington on a Monday night in mid-August 1976. We left Newport by coach at 9.00 am, and took about seven hours to reach Darlington with a stop at the motorway services for a pre-match 'meal'. There was no hotel stop for us when we got there. We found a park, had a walk to stretch our legs and had some fresh air. After losing 1-0, Jimmy gave our captain a fiver, telling him to go off and get fish and chips for everyone because once we were on the coach, we would not be stopping. We faced a marathon journey home, setting off about forty-five minutes after the final whistle. It was about 3.00 am when we were coming down the long Wye Valley hill towards Monmouth and nearly everyone was asleep. I felt the coach sway, and thought there might be something wrong, so I made my way forward to see what was up. Our driver was a great lad called Tony Thomas, a Gwent Valleys boy who had played rugby for Abertillery. He was later nicknamed 'Fittipaldi' after the South American racing driver, because Tony could handle his coach superbly and drive at speed through the tightest of gaps!

So I asked Tony what was wrong, and he told me that he was starting to struggle to keep awake at the wheel. He did not have a relief driver with him, and it had been a long day. I stayed alongside him in the well of the coach, continuing to chat to him about sport, and about anything. When we reached Somerton Park, he thanked me for doing that because he admitted that he wouldn't have made it otherwise. Tony became very much part of the squad, and later on would join in our training sessions when we did travel overnight. He loved being with us, and when the good times did return, he enjoyed it as much as anyone. So we arrived home safely, and I was at work at 8.30 am that morning – such was life at Newport County.

I missed only five of County's fifty-two League and Cup matches that season, scoring eight goals, and I well remember us going to my former club AFC Bournemouth on a wet Tuesday night in early November. Don Murray was sent off in the first half for thumping their defender Stuart Morgan who had been kicking lumps out of me, so Donald 'sorted' him! Don didn't go to the dressing room, but sat next to Jimmy Scoular on the bench. Jimmy was getting more and more angry about decisions going against us, and Donald had to try and calm him down. Then Gary Bell was sent off before half-time for kicking their winger Peter Johnson, and Jimmy went absolutely berserk! He thought that the whole world was against him, and the referee told Donald to make sure that Jimmy stayed in his seat. But it didn't stop Jimmy from giving the referee's dressing room door a mighty kick as he went past it at half-time. It was in that match that I was booked for the only time in my career. I felt that the referee had lost control of the game after the two dismissals and I queried a decision that he had made. He cautioned me, and the Press in their reports of the game were indignant that I had been booked. Thirty years on, I am still angry and hurt when I think about it. We lost the game 1-0, but a few weeks later were back there for an FA Cup First Round tie. This time we drew 0-0 and beat them 3-0 at home in the replay in what was a rare success.

That season there were no fewer than eight home postponements for Newport County because of heavy rain, snow or ice, but in the end those postponements were to save us from oblivion. Before that, however, things went from bad to worse and there was financial crisis in late November as we struggled near the foot of the Division Four. Things were so bad that the club was threatened with closure! Our goalkeeper was Gary Plumley, now a successful Newport estate agent, and his father was Eddie Plumley, then Secretary/Chief Executive of First Division Coventry City. Eddie, who was obviously concerned about his son's future in view of Newport's worsening financial problems, arranged for Coventry to come and play us in a fund-raising friendly, but the game had to be called off as the Somerton Park pitch was waterlogged. So Coventry came the following night to play us in front of nearly 3,000 fans – we lost 7-1 and I scored our goal – but their actions showed that there was a great deal of goodwill throughout the football world towards Newport County.

In mid-January 1977, we were at the bottom of the table, and

Jimmy Scoular decided to resign. He and the new Board, who had taken over in December and were led by local businessman Richard Ford, felt that he could not take the club any further, and that was the end of his career in management. His final game in charge was a Welsh Cup Fourth Round tie against Swansea City at the Vetch Field on 18 January 1977, and he decided to play with five at the back. We were 4-0 down in twenty minutes, but he didn't change things, argued with the referee and linesmen, and we eventually lost 4-1. After the game he bought us all drinks in the bar, and we were there for about an hour. Meanwhile 'Fittipaldi' had been running the engine of the coach outside the ground to keep the heaters going so that it would be warm for us when we got on. But we were taking so long that he eventually switched off. When we did emerge on what was a freezing cold January night, he couldn't start it again – the battery was flat. Just down the road from the Vetch was the local bus garage, and a fitter coming off shift stopped to see what was wrong. When 'Fittipaldi' explained the problem, the fitter had a look at the battery but said that he couldn't assist as he did not have any tools with him. Jimmy, who'd had a few drinks, stuck his oar in, saying to everyone around – 'Calls himself a ✳✳✳✳✳✳ fitter and he's got no ✳✳✳✳✳✳ tools!' It was typical Jimmy, and the fitter threatened to lay him out! With that, Jimmy got underneath the open side panel to see what he could do, and the heavy panel came down and hit him a mighty blow on the shoulder, leaving thick grease marks over his light grey quality suit. None of us dared to laugh, but it was a somewhat hilarious end to Jimmy's time as manager. It was a sad end also, because in his day Jimmy had been a great player and a very good manager. Although he was hard, all his players respected him, and when he died in 1998 at the age of 73, many of his former players attended his funeral.

12

THE GREAT ESCAPE

Jimmy Scoular's successor at Newport had been watching that game at Swansea from the Vetch Field terraces, and left well before the end. It was Colin Addison, the former Hereford United manager who had taken them from the Southern League into the Football League, winning promotion at the first attempt. He was back in this country after a spell in South Africa as manager of Durban City, and he was brought into Newport County by Mike Lewis who had been appointed the club's Commercial Manager a couple of months earlier. Mike was an experienced professional fund-raiser with various charity organisations and he knew what he was doing. He and Colin Addison were to change the club's fortunes, along with the new directors who were businessmen and professional men from the Newport area.

The arrival of Colin was like a breath of fresh air sweeping through the club. I knew of him by reputation, and I had played against him for Cardiff City when he was at Sheffield United in the late 1960s. When he came to Newport, he faced a massive task because we were firmly entrenched in the bottom four, and if we finished there, it was well known that we would be out of the League. He took over a squad of honest professionals who were not top quality players, and one of the first things that he did was to arrange for us to meet up before home games at The New Inn, Langstone, on the Newport-Chepstow road. We would have egg on toast, tea, and a chat about the game ahead. Our preparations would be carried out as professionally as the club's financial situation would allow. And if we had a long away trip, then if possible we would travel overnight. It was on those trips that Colin nicknamed our driver Tony Thomas, calling him 'Fittipaldi'.

Under Colin, a bright bubbly character full of enthusiasm, things gradually began to change on the pitch, but not immediately – we took only one point from the first six games under him! We then started picking up a win every two or three matches, and in early April we defeated Cambridge United 4-2 at Somerton Park. Their Manager was Ron Atkinson, and I well remember the game because I scored a hat-trick for only the third time in League football – I still have the match ball amongst my memorabilia. It was a vital win because we were still in the bottom four of the entire Football League! John Relish scored our other goal against Cambridge – he was a very hard-working professional and a very pleasant lad. He has now worked for the PFA for many years, and at the time of writing was still directly involved with the game as manager of Bath City.

Colin was able to get the best out of his players, especially part-timer Roddy Jones who had been with County for a number of seasons as a striker, but was now playing at the back. Roddy, a tough player, was good enough to have made a decent living from the game in the lower divisions, but he had a secure job as a maintenance fitter at the Alcan steelworks in Rogerstone near Newport. He would organise his shifts in order to play in midweek matches, and if we arrived home in the early hours of the morning, he would go straight off to work on his return! There was also Eddie Woods who played up front with me, and John 'Ivor' Emanuel in midfield, both of them former Bristol City players.

At the end of April 1977 and with five matches to go in the League we were twenty-second, but if we could win them all we would be safe. It looked unlikely because we had not won two successive matches since the previous September! Because of the home postponements over the season, four of those final five matches were at Somerton Park. We beat Watford (home 3-0), Crewe (home 2-1), Southend United (home 3-0) and it was beginning to look as if we might achieve a miracle! Two players who had a major input at that time were early March signings Tony Byrne from Hereford United and Brian Preece, also from Hereford. Tony provided a steadying influence in midfield, Brian was quick and enthusiastic in a wide attacking role, scoring some useful goals.

Our final two matches were both against bottom club Workington who had no chance of escaping from the re-election zone. We were to meet them on the Saturday up there, and then at Somerton Park on the following Tuesday in a re-arranged match because the original fixture had been postponed on several occasions.

Colin persuaded the Board to let us travel to Workington on the Friday and stay overnight. We left early in the morning and 'Fittipaldi' was looking forward to driving us there because we were playing golf at Whitehaven on the Cumbria coast that afternoon. We had to win at Workington, and we did so with a Brian Preece goal before Don Murray was sent off for one of his usual tackles that the referee did not approve of! But we hung on, and if we could beat them again on the Tuesday night, we would be safe. Our attendances had crept up to 3,500 in those closing stages of the season, but on that Tuesday, 17 May 1977, against Workington there were long queues at the Somerton Park turnstiles, and an attendance of 8,313 was there for the game.

It was a brilliant atmosphere, the place was alive, everyone was behind us, and Workington did not really stand a chance. There was an air of anticipation in the dressing room before the game, Colin was encouraging us, and he was the right man at the right time. His team talk inspired us, he was banging the table to get us going, and we responded. But it was a tense scrappy game, and we were all very edgy. It was decided by an Eddie Woods goal that gave us a 1-0 victory to end the season in nineteenth place, two points clear of the bottom four. The fans invaded the pitch at the final whistle, and the players were carried off shoulder high – it was as though we had won promotion and the Cup Final! The celebrations went on long into the night, and that period was one of the most memorable spells of my career because of the way that things had turned out. It was the players who had done it on the pitch, but it was Colin Addison who had masterminded what became known as 'The Great Escape'. He was a great motivator, and together with Ronnie Bird, transformed the dressing room, making ordinary players feel ten feet tall. Nearly thirty years on I still see Colin regularly at Cardiff City matches when he is working for BBC Radio Wales – he is in his mid-60s now but looking almost as young as he was during that memorable spell at Newport, and is still the same enthusiastic outgoing character.

The effect of that achievement at Newport was quite clear to me in my business dealings over the next few weeks. Whenever I called to see a customer, they wanted to talk about our escape, and it was obvious that Newport County were a very popular organisation in Welsh sporting life. They were the long-standing underdogs in football, and people wanted them to do well. No one in Welsh football wanted to see them go out of the League, and now the future, under Colin Addison, was bright – I was really looking forward to the following season.

13

MY FOOTBALL LEAGUE FINALE

Things were starting to take off at Somerton Park and I genuinely felt that, under Colin Addison, Newport County could do something. He was pleased to have me there, even as a part-timer, because my experience was useful on the pitch as well as in the twice-a-week evening training sessions with the other part-timers. We were to end the 1977/78 season sixteenth in Division Four, comfortably clear of the re-election zone, but without ever looking as if we could maintain a promotion challenge. Nevertheless it was progress and I had a good season for my age, playing in 42 League and Cup matches, and scoring 11 goals. One new player who came in that season was former AFC Bournemouth striker Howard Goddard whom Colin signed from Swindon in mid-August 1977. Howard and I played up front together for most of that season, and though he was a very talented forward, he tended to get into trouble off the pitch, which was a worry to Colin. When Howard arrived at Newport, he came on from the bench for his first few games, one of which was a Tuesday night home match against York City in early September '77. The previous Saturday, Howard had come on for me during a 1-0 defeat at Barnsley, and on the day of this York game I'd had a frustrating day at work. I rushed over to the team meeting at The New Inn, got there a little late, had my egg on toast, and then went off with the lads to the ground. I did not have a good first half against York, and at the interval Colin Addison made a change – I was off, and Howard Goddard was on. My pride was hurt, I had a bath, got dressed and drove away from the ground not long after half-time to go home. I had been taken off several times before during my career, but I had never previously reacted like that! Gill was surprised when I arrived home before the time that the game was due to finish. I wanted to say that the game had been abandoned, but I told her the truth. As it happened, County won the game 2-1.

Colin rang me the following day and said that he would have a chat with me in training the following evening. He said that he thought I might react in that way because my pride had been hurt, but he said that he had to do it because I looked what I was – a 34-year-old part-timer. In the old days, I used to have a rest in the afternoon before a midweek match, but now I could not do that because of my business commitments. I accepted what Colin had said, and I was going to have to live with the fact that my career outside the game was now far more important than my playing commitments. But I was back in the starting line-up the following Saturday, and although there were spells when I was on the bench, I played in most of the remaining matches that season. I had one final purple patch in terms of goal scoring – from mid-November 1977 to early January 1978 I scored seven goals in nine League and FA Cup matches. I was really playing well and it was just like the old days at Bristol City and Cardiff City.

I had always kept in touch with my former Millwall colleague Gordon Hill who was by now a well-established member of the Manchester United line-up. He had won an FA Cup Winners medal with them the previous May, and was a regular England International. Gordon had given me an open invitation to come up and stay with him in Manchester, and attend a home game at Old Trafford. My chance came in mid-December 1977 when Newport County had a blank weekend, having been knocked out of the FA Cup in the First Round. United were at home to Brian Clough's Nottingham Forest, so Gill and I drove up early on the Saturday to stay with Gordon and his wife at their home near Wilmslow. We arrived there at about 11.30am, Gill remained with Gordon's wife and we headed off to Old Trafford in his sports car. After he had signed numerous autographs, we went to the players' lounge for some tea and toast before he went to the dressing room. I had a great seat amongst the 54,000 crowd, but it was not a good day for Gordon and his team – they lost 4-0! After the match I met up with Gordon in the players' lounge where there was a subdued atmosphere after that result. Gordon decided that we would leave immediately, and we headed off in a different direction from the way we had come. He said that he had an appointment with someone, and while it had been a home game for Gordon, I suspected that he was 'playing away'. I didn't ask any questions, and we drove about a mile to a Manchester University students' accommodation block in Salford where he said that he had to see someone. He said that he would not be more than half an hour, so he told me to wait across the road in a pub where I had a drink and read the match programme. He eventually came back and we drove off to his home to meet our wives. Months later he rang me for a chat, and said that he and his wife were getting divorced. He also told me that his wife's father had hired a private investigator to have him checked out, and that we had been followed on that occasion when we drove to Salford. According to the investigator's report '....*Mr Hill and a tall fair haired man drove to Salford. Mr Hill went into a students' accommodation block where Mr Hill spent just over half an hour. The tall man who had accompanied him waited in a nearby pub. The two then met up again and drove to Mr Hill's home.*' It was the only time in my life, that I know of, that I have been followed by a private detective and been part of a divorce case!

Back in South Wales I was really having a busy life – the job was going well, I was enjoying the games, as well as the training sessions where I helped with the coaching together with David Williams who was connected with Newport County for years as player and coach, even manager for a short spell. Also helping was youth team coach Jimmy Jenkins, a local coal merchant who was a really nice guy, and who sadly died a few years later from cancer. It was hard to fit everything into my domestic life, but Gill and I knew that I was near to the end of playing career, so we accepted the situation. I was taking that much longer to recover from matches, especially as I was only training two evenings a week, so I knew that it would not be long before I finished.

I thought about retiring at the end of 1977/78, especially as Colin Addison resigned from Newport County in May '78 to become assistant to Ron Atkinson at West Bromwich Albion. The Newport fans were devastated – there had been a strong possibility of him going to Swansea City earlier that season but he had been persuaded to stay. He had to go, however, because he was an up and coming manager who needed to be tested at a higher level, and the potential at Newport County, lovely club that it was, had to be limited because of their financial situation and general lack of regular support. I had been enjoying my football under Colin, but I was wary about who might replace him at Somerton Park – would his successor want a part-timer like me who was now 35 years of age?

I didn't have to wait long to find out who was Colin's replacement. In early June 1978, Newport appointed the ex-Sunderland full back Len Ashurst who had been manager at Hartlepool, Gillingham and Sheffield Wednesday. I knew Len by reputation and had once played against him when Bristol City lost to Sunderland in an FA Cup match at Roker Park just over fourteen years earlier. Len soon asked to see me and wanted me to be his reserve team manager in the Welsh League as well as being available for first team duties when required. Len began to bring in some good players such as defender Grant Davies from Preston, midfielder Trevor Thompson from West Bromwich, full back Richard Walden of Sheffield Wednesday, midfielder Neil Bailey of Burnley, defender Keith Oakes from Peterborough, defender Dave Bruton and winger Kevin Moore, both of Swansea City. And later on that season Len signed forwards Tommy Tynan from Lincoln City and John Aldridge from South Liverpool. It was clear that the days of Newport County being a last resting place for ex-Cardiff City players were over, and Newport intended going places.

But while I began the season looking after the reserves, it was not a good start for Len with six defeats in the opening seven Fourth Division games. However, the side began to recover and in those first couple of months of 1978/79, he included me as substitute on a few occasions – I even came on to score in a mid-September 3-1 home defeat by Wimbledon. It was the very last goal of my Football League career. There was, however, some tension behind the scenes in the first half of that season because Len didn't get on particularly well with Ronnie Bird who was still trainer/coach after being under Jimmy Scoular and Colin Addison. Things came to a head in mid-January 1979 when Ronnie's contract was terminated, and thirteen days later Jimmy Goodfellow was appointed in his place. Jimmy and Len had been long standing friends from Len's time at Sunderland and they had always kept in touch.

In late September 1978, Len wanted me to play in a reserve Cup match on a Wednesday afternoon at Somerton Park against Swansea University. He had a number of young players in the side and wanted to use my experience to help them. I didn't really want to play because I had a number of business appointments that day, but I re-arranged them and told Len that I would be there. We won the game 7-1 but I never finished the ninety minutes. In out jumping their central defender, I smashed my cheekbone on the back of his head. It was a depressed fracture, and I was taken by ambulance to the Royal Gwent Hospital in Newport. They said that I would need a fairly immediate operation to repair the damage, so the following morning I went into St Lawrence Hospital in Chepstow where they specialised in my kind of case. The specialist had a look at me and carried out the operation two days later – I was in there for a total of four days, which rather upset my business arrangements. Protect-U were great about the situation, and there were hardly any problems over my appointments.

I recovered well enough, or so I thought, and in mid-December '78 was back in reserve team playing action. On Saturday 16 December, I had been away with the reserves while the first team battled out a 0-0 home draw against Worcester City in the FA Cup Second Round. The Draw for the Third Round was made after the game, and if Newport County could beat Worcester in their replay at St George's Lane, it would be a home tie against West Ham United. It was important for County that they got through the replay successfully, mainly for financial reasons in addition to not wanting to go out to a non-league side. That replay was to take place on the following Monday night, and on the Sunday morning Len Ashurst rang me at home telling me that I was in the side for the replay as Eddie Woods was out through injury. There was a 10,233 crowd at Worcester that night, and they were very confident of beating us. In fact, they were 1-0 up until just before the end of the ninety minutes when Howard Goddard equalised. So it went to extra time, and just after the start of the first period, Howard scored again. The course of the game was completely changed and we held on comfortably for a 2-1 victory and a Third

Round home tie against West Ham. It worked well with Howard and myself up front, and Len kept me in for the League visit to Hereford United on the following Saturday when we were to win 3-0 – it was three days before Christmas. We had a corner, I went up for the ball, collided with their central defender, and my cheekbone was fractured again! It had still been weak from the previous fracture, and if I had known that, then I certainly would not have played in those reserve and first team matches. After the first fracture, my Mum didn't speak to me for a week because she felt that, at my age, with a wife and two young daughters to look after, and with a good career outside the game, I shouldn't be playing professional football. So I promised her that I wouldn't play again. I didn't tell her that I was back playing again and when she found out what had happened, she was very angry. Gill, however, was very understanding about it.

The following day I was back at St Lawrence Hospital, the specialist took one look at me and said 'What, you again – what have you been up to this time?' He said that I could have Christmas Day and Boxing Day at home but I would have to be in the hospital on 27 December for another operation that took place on 29 December. I was due out on New Year's Eve, but there was heavy snow and neither the hospital staff nor I could get home. We all had a great time considering our predicament, but I was sorry that Gill and the girls had to celebrate the New Year without me. The specialist had asked me how old I was and I told him that I would be 36 a fortnight later. He said that now was the time that I had to finish playing, and he signed a letter to that effect so that I could claim an insurance pay out from the Football League. I never kicked a ball in League football again, but I did take part in a few reserve games over the next two seasons, while in future years I occasionally played in charity matches.

I was very sad that my League career ended in the way that it did. I would liked to have finished it by scoring a hat-trick and then deciding that it was all over. But then again, I might have been struggling to reach the standard that I once enjoyed, and people might have been thinking that I had gone on too long – in retrospect, I should have called it a day after the first fracture. Gill was pleased for me that I had now finished playing in League football – as a nurse, she knew what could have happened as a result of those two cheek injuries with the possibility of my sight being affected. As it was, I had lost all feeling down the left side of my face, but gradually it came back though it must have been about six months before I was fully recovered.

I'd had a great League career lasting almost nineteen years as a professional, I had travelled over most of the world and, despite the inevitable ups and downs, I had enjoyed it. But my involvement in the game was far from over – Len Ashurst wanted me to continue in charge of Newport County's reserves for the remainder of the season. I really liked doing that since the travelling was not too difficult, and I was still doing the coaching on Tuesday and Thursday evenings, passing on the benefit of my experience over those nineteen years. I felt a little envious when I watched Newport County defeat West Ham United 2-1 at Somerton Park during early January in the Third Round of the FA Cup, but my time had now gone.

In late April 1979, Len Ashurst signed a little known twenty-year-old forward named John Aldridge from non-league South Liverpool FC. John had been recommended by Len's brother Robin who worked with John at British Leyland in Speke near Liverpool. On Saturday 28 April, the reserves were to play at Llanelli, always a difficult place to get a good result. As usual, Len rang me the night before to talk about the game and who would be playing. He told me that he had this new lad who had been on trial, training all week and who had signed a contract that day. Len wanted him to play at Llanelli and I queried it because I knew how hard it could be down there. But Len said to play him, and I sat next to John Aldridge on the coach journey to West Wales, finding out all about his background and at what kind of standard he had played. It was not a good start for John – he struggled throughout the first half with the pace of the game and the strength of opposition defenders. We were losing the game at half-time and in the dressing room I said to him that I was taking him off as he looked very tired, and I did not want to make things more difficult for him in his very first game for the club. John agreed with me and said that he was absolutely shattered after training morning and afternoon over four days that week! It was his first experience of training as a full-timer. John went on to be a goalscoring success with Newport, Oxford United, Liverpool, Real Sociedad and the Republic of Ireland over the next twelve years before becoming manager of Tranmere Rovers – and I took him off at half-time in his very first match as a full professional. If somebody had said to me at half-time in that game at Llanelli that John would achieve great heights in football, I would not have believed them. In later years I met up with John occasionally at football functions and we would remind each other of that day at Llanelli.

Newport County finished eighth in Division Four that season and in mid-May 1979 I had a nice letter from Len Ashurst '...*Dear Brian, Just a note to thank you for your work during the course of last season. The season was quite successful all round and the contribution you made to the club and the help you have given me was a big factor in our successful season. When things have settled down I would like us to have a chat with regard to the coming season and hope that you will be continuing in your present role.*'

So my coaching career had started and I just wished that, over the previous five years, I had combined playing with getting some coaching qualifications and done the necessary courses. Even so, I was happy with the way things were going because I was enjoying my business career based in Cardiff where we were settled, and I was enjoying my involvement with Newport County.

The 1979/80 season was one of the most successful in Newport County's history. The club won promotion from Division Four and the Welsh Cup, my reserve side won the Championship of the Welsh League Premier Division, while the youngsters won the Gwent Sunday Youth League. We had a number of promising youngsters in the reserves, including Mike Bruton, brother of first team player Dave. Mike scored thirty-two League and Cup goals for me, and though John Aldridge was mainly in the first team that season, he began '79/80 in my Welsh League side, scoring twenty-one goals in thirteen League and Cup appearances. Len Ashurst and Jimmy Goodfellow had really got the club going and the younger players benefited from the experience of the good signings they had brought in. I had a lot of help from Assistant Trainer/Coach David Williams and Youth Team Coach Jimmy

Jenkins, and in my travels around the Welsh League clubs I made a number of useful contacts that were to help me over the next few years.

Newport reached the Quarter-Finals of the European Cup Winners' Cup the following season (1980/81), and although I was not directly involved, it was good to be at the club and share the excitement of that European run.

I stayed with Newport County until just after the start of the 1982/83 season, by which time Len Ashurst had gone, losing his job in February 1982 and immediately being replaced by Colin Addison who returned to the club for a second spell in charge. In early July 1982, Colin brought in Bobby Smith who was his assistant, having come from a similar role at Blackpool. I did not like the way that Bobby Smith spoke to the reserve and youth players from the touch line and in the dressing room. I felt his language was disgraceful and abusive towards young players and I did not want to work in that kind of atmosphere. During my nineteen years as a professional, I had of course heard 'industrial language' during matches and in dressing rooms, but that was from senior players, and you accepted it. But I was not prepared to accept it as a coach involved with youngsters as I felt that you could gain respect from young players without using that kind of language. Bobby Smith may have been a good coach but I did not like his methods. I told Colin that I was finishing as reserve team coach because my work commitments were steadily increasing and I wanted to spend more time at home with the family. I left the club on good terms, and twenty-four years on, I am still very friendly with Colin whom I see quite often at matches and various football social occasions.

I was not out of the game for long because, shortly after leaving Newport County, I was offered the manager's job at Maesteg Park who played in the Welsh League. In fact they wanted me to be player/manager/coach, but I told them that my playing days were now over and I would join them as manager/coach. It was a part-time position, and training took place on Wednesday nights. The club was run by some very nice people, including the Chairman Ron Clair, who appointed me, and the Secretary/Treasurer David Griffiths. It was a very good set-up at Maesteg with a good Social

Club that was well attended each night, and which brought in good money through the fruit machines. That allowed the Committee to allocate me a budget which enabled me to bring in good players at that level and pay them proper travelling expenses as quite a few of them were from outside the area. It was a big mining area and the main colliery was St John's where several of my players worked. Because many of the people in Maesteg worked in and around the collieries, they would use the Social Club regularly even if they were not regular supporters of the football club. I signed several players from Welsh League football in and around the Cardiff area and we had a useful team. The players respected me and it was a happy club. The travelling was not too difficult, the furthest journeys that we had were to West Wales. We were reasonably successful though we could not challenge Barry Town who were funded by Neil O' Halloran and his wife Paula, and could pay good money to get the best players. But we enjoyed our football at Maesteg Park and we often had good social get-togethers, especially at Christmas. The weather, however, was often a problem on Wednesday training nights in mid-winter. I would collect three or four players in Cardiff, and if it was raining there, by the time we got into the Llynfi Valley up to Maesteg, it was usually sleeting. So we would switch on the floodlights, do our training, have some refreshment in the Social Club, and slide back down the Valley to the M4.

As the players regarded the game as a paid hobby and were working during the week, I had to impress on them that if they wanted a few beers, have them after the game on Saturdays and not on a Friday night! On a few occasions players would turn up for a game smelling of alcohol after being at some function on a Friday night, and then I would leave them out – they soon got the message, because if they didn't play then they didn't get paid. I had an enjoyable two seasons at Maesteg Park, but in 1984 came the Miners' Strike with the closure of St John's Colliery as with many other pits throughout the country. It severely affected the Maesteg community and our Social Club suffered financially since people did not have the money to spend. The fruit machines were somewhat idle and my budget had to suffer. I could not maintain the quality of players such as Alan Couch and Peter Morgan, who had been with me at Cardiff City, and goalkeeper Trevor Knott, ex-Barry Town – so they all left the club. Another player who left was someone that I spotted one Sunday morning when I was taking my two daughters for a walk at Caedelyn sports fields in Whitchurch. I watched one of the games taking place and saw this tall forward run through the opposing defence and score three goals. I made some enquiries with someone on the touch-line whom I knew and found out that the player in question was Chris Pike whose team was Park Lawn. He had been to various clubs, including Bristol City, on trial but nothing had come of it. I obtained his telephone number and invited him to come to Maesteg Park for training sessions which he agreed to do, provided that he could bring his friend Gareth Joslin, a very good left back whose father Phil was Cardiff City's goalkeeper in the late 1940s and early 1950s. Chris was a very talented player, a good runner and a good golfer. He played for me for a season and scored many goals, before going on to play for Fulham and Cardiff City.

At the end of 1983/84 I decided to leave Maesteg Park mainly because the funds were no longer available to enable me to put together the kind of team that I wanted. We parted on very good terms and I still to this day see several of the club officials and players of that time. It was a good two years for me at Maesteg and I have very fond memories of the club. But it was still not the end of my involvement in the game. I went to AFC Cardiff who were then playing in the South Wales Amateur League, but they were then accepted into the Welsh League. Their home ground was at Cwrt-yr-Ala near Culverhouse Cross and I coached them on a completely voluntary basis. It wasn't far from home and training was on Tuesday and Thursday nights under floodlights at Maindy sports stadium. They ran five sides and I looked after the first team.

The first match for them in the Welsh League was at Aberystwyth and the season was something of a struggle for them financially, especially with the cost of the journeys. The players all had jobs and quite often at training there was not a full turn-out. But it was a great little club and the committee members were all very enthusiastic, marking the pitch, cutting the grass etc. The club had several changes of name while I was there – they had started off as Lake United, then AFC Cardiff, then Inter-Cardiff, then

Inter-Cable-Tel when they amalgamated with Sully AFC.

So I was very much into local football in the mid-1980s, while I was saddened to see Cardiff City go down in successive seasons from the original Second Division to the Fourth Division with very low crowds. That was one of the reasons why, at that time, I lost interest in them because of the poor standard in which they were now playing compared to my good years at Ninian Park. I spent eighteen months with AFC Cardiff during which time results weren't good, and I wasn't really enjoying it, though I got on very well with the people who ran the club. There were a few arguments with players who were not prepared to accept my standards – their social life was more important to them than playing, so I left.

It was in 1986 that I joined up again with Ronnie Bird who was running the Social Club at Bridgend Town FC as well as looking after the team. He was very popular there and it was great to be with him again. I was officially his assistant, but we both worked equally well together. We were as successful as we could be in the Welsh League where Barry Town were the dominant side, and we had a great atmosphere at Bridgend. I really enjoyed it with them, especially working with Ronnie. At home matches we would make full use of the social facilities after the game, while the away trips, especially the long ones, were happy whether we won or lost. One of our players was a Cardiff lad named Mark Bloom, a centre forward who, as a young boy, worked on his father's milk round and delivered my pints in Whitchurch. These days, Mark is one of the *South Wales Echo's* football reporters and I regularly see him at Ninian Park – he still thinks that Ronnie and I should have picked him more often!

I stayed at Bridgend for a couple of seasons until Ronnie left. We were on a run of nine consecutive Welsh League wins but Ronnie had fallen out with the club's Chairman because Ronnie would not select the Chairman's son who was not as good as the forwards that we then had in the side. Ronnie told the Chairman what he could do with the job, and left the club – I went as well because I agreed with Ronnie. One success that we did have was to beat Barry Town in the Final of the SA Brain Cup at Ton Pentre in May 1988. We knew that Barry were stronger than us and were firm favourites to win, so Ronnie and I decided to treat the game in the most professional way that we could. We booked into a Ton Pentre hotel for a pre-match meal, had a team talk and a rest, and we won the game 1-0. I had been involved in bigger occasions during my career in the game, but this victory was one of the most satisfying in my managerial and coaching career. Our players were brilliant on the night, they performed above themselves and Ronnie and I were so pleased for them.

During my time at Maesteg Park, I had become involved with the Boys Clubs of Wales team as manager/coach, a role that I occupied for fourteen years. It had started through one of my customers who managed their Under-18 side. I became in charge of the Under-14 squad and it involved a couple of matches each season, the squad being selected from numerous boys from all over South Wales. I really liked helping and coaching these youngsters, and going with them to Scotland where they played their corresponding Scottish rivals. Two of my youngsters went on to become full Welsh Internationals – John Hartson and Robert Page. They both played in my side that beat Scotland 5-0 at Dundee. John Hartson broke his wrist early in that match – as a fourteen year-old he was just five feet tall, nothing like the big lad that he now is. At a reception the night before, their manager told me that he thought they had a good side and they were confident of beating us. I knew him quite well because we played Scotland once each season – away one year, and home the next. Assisting me with that Under-14 squad was my neighbour Paul Morgan who still lives opposite me in Whitchurch. I first met him when I linked up with AFC Cardiff where Paul looked after the fifth team. He was very enthusiastic, had done his coaching badges, and when I left AFC Cardiff, I asked Paul if he would assist me with the Boys' Clubs of Wales side. For ten years he assisted me, and without his help I would have found the job difficult – I cannot thank him enough.

After I finished with Bridgend Town, I still carried on with the Boys Clubs of Wales, but that was now my only connection with the game. I wasn't sorry to be out of the senior game, but players' attitudes in non-league local football generally had begun to disappoint me, though not at Bridgend, but I did not want to go anywhere else after that. With the Boys Clubs, I could put something back into the game and the youngsters appreciated my input.

I had always been reasonably interested in rugby. My Dad had been a good player in his teenage days before joining Bristol City, and we used occasionally to watch Bristol Rugby Club that was just down the road from our house in Horfield. And when I was with Cardiff City, I would watch Cardiff RFC matches in midweek if we were not playing. After my coaching career, I became a season ticket holder at the Arms Park in the latter part of the 1980s through being friendly with several of my customers who were also season ticket holders. It was also a social thing because, apart from enjoying the game, I would go into the Athletic Club after matches and meet people, which would lead to useful business contacts. Although I did not go to Cardiff City matches, I still followed their results as they moved up and down the lower divisions without showing any real signs of making progress, apart from the early 1990s under Rick Wright, but that progress was not maintained. In addition to my coaching on Sundays with the Boys Clubs, I would follow Cardiff RFC over South Wales and I enjoyed my trips to places like Llanelli. On Saturday evenings as we travelled home, we would often stop in a pub and I would watch the League results come up on television. But Cardiff City's results did not mean as much to me then as they had done in the past. It was a period in my life when I had become very disillusioned with professional football.

I would still, however, see former teammates at various functions. I still attended Bristol City ex-players' reunions, and I would come across my old Cardiff City colleagues on similar occasions, but my days of going to watch League football now looked as if they were over. I ended my connections with the Boys Clubs of Wales in the latter part of the 1990s – I was in my mid-fifties and coaching the boys was more of a younger man's job. It was becoming hard work, the regulations set by the South Wales FA were increasing as regards the running of the teams, added to which there were occasions when members of my squad would not turn up for training sessions. Once again I wasn't able to maintain the standards that I required, and I stopped enjoying it. One of the incidents that led to me finishing with the Boys' Clubs of Wales concerned a proposed trip to Merseyside. Two of my squad had signed associate schoolboy forms for Liverpool. The club's Youth Development Officer Steve Heighway, a former player with them, contacted me to ask if I would bring my squad up to play their schoolboys at the Liverpool training ground. It was to be on a Sunday afternoon and Liverpool would pay all expenses as well as taking us on a tour of Anfield after the game. Our players were very excited about going, and their parents were coming as well. The idea of the match was just for them to see the kind of standard at which we played and it promised to be a great day out for all concerned. A few days before the game was to take place, I had a call from a woman at the FA of Wales who asked if I was in charge of the team. I told her that was correct and she said that if the game went ahead, then we would be breaking the rules of the South Wales FA concerning matches being played against 'overseas' teams. I thought that while the River Mersey was quite wide, it was hardly an ocean voyage to get across it! She said that we did not have permission for the game, and if it went ahead, all of us would be banned from any involvement in amateur football for a considerable time. I asked on whose authority she was telling me this, and she said that it was a man called Langley who was some official of the South Wales FA. So I asked for permission but she said that a form would have to be filled in. I offered to go straight to her office and get a form filled in, but she said that we would not be allowed to travel – Langley apparently would not allow it. So we had to cancel what would have been a harmless enough game and I had to stop all the arrangements, much to the disappointments of all concerned. I wonder if Langley ever thought how those boys felt – such was the petty officialdom that we had to put up with. I had had fourteen years with the Boys Clubs of Wales, they were mainly good years and I had no regrets over my involvement with the organisation. It has always been my policy that, whatever I was involved in, once I stopped enjoying it then I got out. That was the case at Bristol City when I left, that was the situation at Huddersfield as well as my two spells with Cardiff City, and at Newport County.

14

BACK TO NINIAN PARK

In the late 1990s, Ronnie Bird was landlord of the Romilly Arms in Canton, having previously been at The Golden Cross in Custom House Street. I used to call in on him at the Romilly Arms and he began to look after the bar arrangements at Ninian Park on a part-time basis. He also took on a match-day sponsors' hospitality-host role in which he would encourage former well-known players to join him and mix with the sponsors. At that time in the late 1990s Cardiff City were winning promotion from Division Three under Frank Burrows, it was the time of the club's Centenary (1899-1999) and the Board were enthusiastic. Ronnie would say to me that I should be helping the club on the hospitality side and not going off to watch rugby on Saturday afternoons. So I started going to the occasional home game when Ronnie asked me, and I have to say that I enjoyed going back – I had a good reception, and supporters liked talking to me about my time at the club especially the match against Real Madrid. In addition, the quality of the football began to improve, and although Cardiff City went down again in 1999/2000, a year after going up, there was a good atmosphere about the place.

One evening in the summer of 2000, Ronnie invited me to accompany him to the Quality Hotel near Tongwynlais where the former Wimbledon owner Sam Hammam was addressing the supporters of Cardiff City following his acquisition of The Bluebirds, and setting out his view of the club's future. I listened to what Sam had to say, and thought that he might find it difficult to achieve everything that he wanted for the club which included promotion to the higher divisions and a new stadium. Six years on, he has achieved much of what he wanted, it looks as if the new stadium will go ahead this year, and while the Premiership may be some years away, it is achievable.

Ronnie had by now given up the Romilly Arms and was full time at Cardiff City. I was pleased for him because he loved his involvement with the club, and through him I felt a close connection with Cardiff City. One of his roles was as commentary-summariser for away matches on *Cardiff City World*, the club's internet station. I too became involved in that, usually at home games after my hospitality work with Ronnie. It is something that I still do regularly, and it continues my involvement in the game. The other summariser at home games is my former City teammate Gary Bell, and we both enjoy our coverage of the matches with commentator Richard Shepherd. I hope that our listeners don't get fed up with the reminiscences of Gary and myself. But we take our commentary duties seriously, do our preparation before the games, and enjoy watching Cardiff City play at the level at which Gary and I used to play for the club. I even go to a few away matches – the relatively near ones such as Reading, Plymouth or Southampton where my old AFC Bournemouth colleague Harry Redknapp was manager. He is one of several acquaintances from my past football life that I come across in covering matches. I go to watch every Wales home game, thanks to my good friend Paul Doubler who works in freelance sponsorship and public relations for Coors Brewers and other organisations. Paul was, and still is, a keen supporter of Cardiff City when I played for them in the late '60s and early '70s, and always enjoys meeting the players of that period in a social atmosphere. He gets us tickets for the Internationals and invites us to the annual FA of Wales Awards Dinner. He also organised a twenty-fifth anniversary reunion of our side that played Real Madrid, and did the same on the thirty-fifth anniversary in March 2006.

The results that I always look for first, are those of Bristol City and Cardiff City if I have not been at a Bluebirds match, and then I look for Huddersfield, AFC Bournemouth and Millwall. Although it is many years since I played for them all, I still have that affinity with them, the first two perhaps more than the other three.

Working with the Press and Media at Ninian Park has meant

that I am asked to comment occasionally in Radio, TV and newspaper interviews on the state of play at Cardiff City, and I am pleased to offer my opinion for what it is worth. I always got on well with the journalists who covered my various clubs. There were three regular reporters covering Bristol City – Peter Godsiff (*Evening Post*), David Foot (*Evening World*) and Herbie Gillam (*Western Daily Press*). Peter, David and Herbie used to travel with us on our team coach and when we went by train, as did Peter Jackson (*South Wales Echo*) and Clive Phillips (*Western Mail*) when I was with Cardiff City. There was an unwritten rule that whatever was said on our journeys by the players or management, it would not be reported. Quite often, with Bristol City or Cardiff City on away trips, the respective managers – Fred Ford or Jimmy Scoular – were not too happy at having to wait after a game until the journalists covering us had finished their interviews and reports. Fred or Jimmy were always threatening to leave them behind!

I enjoy my current involvement covering the matches, and when I park my car in Canton and walk to Ninian Park for matches, it is nice to have a chat with the fans, some of whom remember me playing while others know of me from reading about the Jimmy Scoular days.

I retired from my Sales Executive position in 2003 at the age of 60, while Gill also officially retired around the same time. I could have stayed on with Roger Blyth's company in Swansea for a few more years, but he sold his controlling interest in the firm to another organisation. There were obviously going to be changes, and as I had been very happy working for Roger for eleven years after Protect-U ceased their business, I thought that it was the right time for me to finish. Along the way our two daughters, now in their mid-to-late thirties, have made successful careers for themselves. Alison, our eldest, lives with her partner and his children in Marshfield near Newport. She has a senior management position in the hotel industry in Cardiff, while Jacqueline, our youngest, is married, living in Thornhill, Cardiff, with her husband, and she manages a children's day nursery. They have a two year-old daughter Emily and a recent addition in Lauren who was born in June 2006.

As for my parents, Dad retired from his Transport Manager's job at the British Aircraft Corporation in Filton in 1982 when he was 65. He and Mum sold their home in Horfield and moved to a bungalow near Paignton in South Devon where they were a few hundred yards from my sister and her husband. They were very happy there but then Mum started to show signs of loss of memory that began to grow gradually worse. It was the onset of Alzheimer's Disease, and her condition became such that Dad was unable to look after her. On one occasion she disappeared from the bungalow while Dad was mowing the lawn, and she was discovered walking along the road to Newton Abbott by the Police. It was a challenge that our family had to deal with, and in 1998 Mum and Dad left Paignton to come to Cardiff where Dad lived with us and Mum went into a Residential Home – Burges House in Roath where she still is at present. Dad was happy with us and would visit Mum every day, but then he started showing symptoms of loss of memory and eventually could not be left at home on his own. So after six years with us he moved into Burges House and the two of them are there together, being well looked after by the staff. Whenever I go to Bristol City, people still ask me about him. We all visit them regularly, and I act as their Receiver under the Court of Protection, looking after their financial affairs. We as a family are coping with the situation and I feel that we are doing the best that we can for Mum and Dad.

Gill and I are very happy in our retirement. We are able to go out and about together in our own time, and we have our various interests to pursue. I play golf regularly with friends and acquaintances, I enjoy my regular involvement watching football, and continue to take a keen interest in the game. Gill likes me to watch matches – she feels that it is good for me, and she doesn't mind me travelling for the occasional away game.

In my life I have done the things that I wanted to, been to some wonderful places in the world, thanks to football, and I have had a very happy home life and marriage. Gill and I will have been married forty years in June 2007 and she has been a wonderful support to me in everything that I have done. Our two daughters have been a credit to us and we are very proud of them. There were the inevitable ups and downs in my football career, but I look back on my time in the game – from schoolboy football, through my senior playing days to my coaching and managerial spells – and realise how lucky I was to be able to do what I did. I would like to have played at top level, I would like to have played in an FA Cup Final at Wembley, and I would like to have represented my Country at any level. But bearing in mind my limitations as a player, I cannot complain at what I achieved as a professional footballer. What would I like for the future as far as my interest in football is concerned? – A Premiership rivalry between Bristol City and Cardiff City is something that I would really love to see. Who would I want to win? – Well, I have so many happy memories of both clubs that I would settle for draws at Ashton Gate and Ninian Park, and perhaps wish that I could still be out there alongside Big John or Tosh.

APPENDIX

Brian Clark's record with his Football League clubs
N/A = Not Applicable – his club was not in the competition

Bristol City - Appearances   Goals

Season	League	League Cup	FA Cup	Welsh Cup	ECW Cup	League	League Cup	FA Cup	Welsh Cup	ECW Cup
60/61	1	0	0	N/A	N/A	0	0	0	N/A	N/A
61/62	8	0	0	0	N/A	2	0	0	0	N/A
62/63	42	1	4	N/A	N/A	23	0	2	N/A	N/A
63/64	46	1	5	N/A	N/A	19	0	2	N/A	N/A
64/65	46	1	4	N/A	N/A	24	0	1	N/A	N/A
65/66	42	1	1	N/A	N/A	15	0	0	N/A	N/A
66/67	10	2	0	N/A	N/A	1	0	0	N/A	N/A

Huddersfield Town - Appearances   Goals

Season	League	League Cup	FA Cup	Welsh Cup	ECW Cup	League	League Cup	FA Cup	Welsh Cup	ECW Cup
66/67	20	1	0	N/A	N/A	8	0	0	N/A	N/A
67/68	8	2	0	N/A	N/A	3	0	0	N/A	N/A

Cardiff City - Appearances   Goals

Season	League	League Cup	FA Cup	Welsh Cup	ECW Cup	League	League Cup	FA Cup	Welsh Cup	ECW Cup
67/68	14	0	0	1	0	6	0	0	0	0
68/69	39	1	2	5	2	17	0	0	2	0
69/70	42	1	3	6	4	18	0	0	8	2
70/71	35	1	2	6	6	15	0	0	3	4
71/72	42	2	5	5	2	21	1	2	2	1
72/73	11	2	0	0	N/A	1	1	0	0	N/A

continued over

AFC Bournemouth - Appearances / Goals

Season	League	League Cup	FA Cup	Welsh Cup	ECW Cup	League	League Cup	FA Cup	Welsh Cup	ECW Cup
72/73	29	0	4	N/A	N/A	12	0	3	N/A	N/A
73/74	1	0	0	N/A	N/A	0	0	0	N/A	N/A

Millwall - Appearances / Goals

Season	League	League Cup	FA Cup	Welsh Cup	ECW Cup	League	League Cup	FA Cup	Welsh Cup	ECW Cup
73/74	41	6	2	N/A	N/A	10	3	0	N/A	N/A
74/75	30	1	3	N/A	N/A	6	0	0	N/A	N/A

Cardiff City - Appearances / Goals

Season	League	League Cup	FA Cup	Welsh Cup	ECW Cup	League	League Cup	FA Cup	Welsh Cup	ECW Cup
75/76	21	2	0	5	N/A	1	1	0	2	N/A

Newport County - Appearances / Goals

Season	League	League Cup	FA Cup	Welsh Cup	ECW Cup	League	League Cup	FA Cup	Welsh Cup	ECW Cup
76/77	41	2	3	1	N/A	8	0	0	0	N/A
77/78	35	2	2	3	N/A	9	1	1	0	N/A
78/79	4	0	1	0	N/A	1	0	0	0	N/A
Totals	608	29	41	32	14	220	7	11	17	7

Summary

215 first-team appearances for Bristol City - 89 goals.

31 first-team appearances for Huddersfield Town, - 11goals.

267 first-team appearances for Cardiff City in two spells - 108 goals.

34 first-team appearances for AFC Bournemouth - 15 goals.

83 first-team appearances for Millwall - 19 goals.

94 first-team appearances for Newport County - 20 goals.

Total - 724 first-team career appearances, 262 goals